Britain and the United States in Greece

Britain and the United States in Greece

Anglo-American Relations and the Origins of the Cold War

Spero Simeon Zachary Paravantes

BLOOMSBURY ACADEMIC
LONDON • NEW YORK • OXFORD • NEW DELHI • SYDNEY

BLOOMSBURY ACADEMIC
Bloomsbury Publishing Plc
50 Bedford Square, London, WC1B 3DP, UK
1385 Broadway, New York, NY 10018, USA
29 Earlsfort Terrace, Dublin 2, Ireland

BLOOMSBURY, BLOOMSBURY ACADEMIC and the Diana logo
are trademarks of Bloomsbury Publishing Plc

First published in Great Britain 2021
This paperback edition published in 2022

Copyright © Spero Simeon Zachary Paravantes, 2021

Spero Simeon Zachary Paravantes has asserted his right under the Copyright, Designs and Patents Act, 1988, to be identified as Author of this work.

Cover image: Side by Side – Britannia! used during World War I to show the joining of Britain and the USA in the fight against Germany and its allies. Uncle Sam (with the eagle of the USA) is marching side by side with Britannia (with the lion of the UK). (© Susan E. Meyer / Alamy Stock Photo)

All rights reserved. No part of this publication may be reproduced or transmitted in any form or by any means, electronic or mechanical, including photocopying, recording, or any information storage or retrieval system, without prior permission in writing from the publishers.

Bloomsbury Publishing Plc does not have any control over, or responsibility for, any third-party websites referred to or in this book. All internet addresses given in this book were correct at the time of going to press. The author and publisher regret any inconvenience caused if addresses have changed or sites have ceased to exist, but can accept no responsibility for any such changes.

A catalogue record for this book is available from the British Library.

Library of Congress Cataloging-in-Publication Data
Names: Paravantes, Spero Simeon Zachary, author.
Title: Britain and the United States in Greece : Anglo-American relations and the origins of the Cold War / Spero Simeon Zachary Paravantes.
Other titles: Anglo-American relations and the origins of the Cold War
Description: London; New York: Bloomsbury Academic, [2020] | Includes bibliographical references and index.
Identifiers: LCCN 2020025547 (print) | LCCN 2020025548 (ebook) | ISBN 9781788310413 (hardback) | ISBN 9781350142015 (ebook) | ISBN 9781350142022 (epub)
Subjects: LCSH: Great Britain–Foreign relations–Greece. | Greece–Foreign relations–Great Britain. | Greece–Foreign relations–United States. | United States–Foreign relations–Greece. | Great Britain–Foreign relations–United States. | United States–Foreign relations–Great Britain. | Greece–History–20th century. | Cold War.
Classification: LCC DA47.9.G7 P37 2020 (print) | LCC DA47.9.G7 (ebook) | DDC 327.49504109/044–dc23
LC record available at https://lccn.loc.gov/2020025547
LC ebook record available at https://lccn.loc.gov/2020025548

ISBN:		
	HB:	978-1-7883-1041-3
	PB:	978-1-3502-1553-5
	ePDF:	978-1-3501-4201-5
	eBook:	978-1-3501-4202-2

Typeset by Integra Software Services Pvt. Ltd.

To find out more about our authors and books visit www.bloomsbury.com and sign up for our newsletters.

To Mum and Dad

Contents

List of Tables	viii
Acknowledgments	ix
Note on the Text	xv
List of Acronyms	xvi
Introduction	1
1 Historical Background: British Relations with Greece and the United States until June 1945	17
2 The Aftermath of Varkiza and Inter-Allied Confrontations	51
3 A New Era of American Intervention: The Truman Doctrine, the Marshall Plan and the Beginning of the Cold War	89
4 "Paved with Good Intentions": British Influence and American Intervention in Greece	119
5 The Tide Turns: The End of the Greek Civil War and the Supremacy of the United States	153
6 Détente and the Revelation of the New World Order	177
Conclusion	201
Epilogue	213
Appendix: Chronology	215
Bibliography	218
Index	231

Tables

1 British and American policy changes towards Greece   203

Acknowledgments

My journey into Greek history began at home. Ancient Greek myths and legends ignited my imagination, and the history of Ancient Greece and Rome interested me even more. The stories of the city-states, Alexander the Great, the Roman Empire, and the Punic Wars fed an eager young mind and brought these times to life in my home in western Canada. I also grew up with different stories, stories about the Greek Civil War.

My father and uncle lived through the occupation and talked about the *andartes* coming to their village when they were boys; my father was four and my uncle eleven years old. I kept the two histories of Greece separate; Classical Greece remained the history of my books, school projects and Halloween costumes, while the Civil War was a more private family history.

The Second World War also fascinated me, even from a young age. Coming home from school, I would watch *The World at War*, the epic BBC series. Even now, I remember the opening theme music, and the first episode beginning with a tour of the remains of *Oradour-sur-Glane*. It was an early awakening to the legacy of the deadliest conflict in human history, and it has stayed with me for almost thirty years.

It was only as an undergraduate, however, that I began to read what historians had written about the Greek Civil War. Professors John Belshaw and Michael Gorman at Thompson Rivers University were the first people to encourage me to take family heritage and turn it into history, and then to show me how to do it. From there, it was a long but inexorable journey to this book.

As a postgraduate student, I received guidance and training as a historian of modern Greek history from André Gerolymatos, Director of the Stavros Niarchos Foundation Centre for Hellenic Studies at Simon Fraser University. He was a wonderful mentor and role model, but sadly he passed away before I could finish this manuscript. To him, and to my many friends and colleagues from Simon Fraser University, I give a heartfelt thank you.

After Simon Fraser, the question of where to continue my research into this period of Greek, American, and British history led me to Greece, where I was incredibly fortunate to work with Professors Eirini Lagani and Nikos Marantzidis.

Both welcomed me into the Department of Balkan, Slavic, and Oriental Studies at the University of Macedonia, in Thessaloniki, and guided me through my PhD. I remain indebted to them both—especially as their help did not cease with my graduation. Since then they have been constant sources of support, remaining available for discussions about this manuscript. They have read numerous draft chapters and offered invaluable feedback, which was critical for the completion of this book. I must also thank Professor Eftichios Sartzetakis of the Department of Accounting and Finance at PaMak, who welcomed me when I arrived in Thessaloniki, whose door was always open, and who helped me feel at home.

I would also like to express my thanks to Professor James Pettifer of the University of Oxford, who has become a great friend and mentor over the past years. Not only did he teach me a great deal about writing international and British history, but his comments on this manuscript also greatly helped me refine my research scope and arguments prior to its publication.

As a member of the University of Luxembourg in the Faculty of Language and Literature, Humanities, Arts and Education, I can also begin the happy duty of thanking the individuals who had a direct positive impact on the completion of this book. First and foremost, my former supervisor, friend, and mentor René Leboutte, who took me under his wing when I arrived. The incorporation of analyses from the perspective of economic and social history came from working under his tutelage. From him I also learned much in terms of lecturing, how to care for students, and how to present the material I was teaching them. Countless letters of reference, constant support, and precious conversations helped me begin to feel at home, after almost ten years away from my family. Though I cannot hope to repay him, I hope that I can help other young researchers the way he helped me.

The Dean of the Faculty, Georg Mein, always kept his door open for me. I cannot thank him enough for the advice and support he offered me as a researcher as I "learned the ropes" of academia. The importance of having someone like this who believes in you cannot be measured, nor can it be repaid. To David Howarth and Robert Harmsen of the Institute for Political Science and the Robert Schuman Initiative for European Affairs I also extend a heartfelt thank you. We have collaborated numerous times over the years on courses, seminars, and conferences. Having such collegial and supportive senior colleagues helped me learn and grow. Also, welcoming a historian into the RSI and Institute of Political Science, combined with their warmth, support and inclusion made me feel truly at home.

I must also thank Professors Frank Hofmann and Lukas Sosoe of the Institute of Philosophy at "UniLu" for their thoughtful revision and comments on key chapters. Their perspectives greatly aided me in the reframing of some of my key arguments and reinforced the importance and benefits of interdisciplinary cooperation. Finally, I would like to thank Professor Johan van der Walt of the University of Luxembourg Faculty of Law, for inviting me to help found the philosophy of law reading group, for reading early chapter drafts, and for countless meetings, letters, and statements of support. Thank you so much for everything.

If "thank you" has not yet become an over-used term, then I fear it will be in the lines that follow, since finishing a full draft of this book occurred during my stay as a visiting scholar at the University of California, Berkeley, in 2017–2018. I am very fortunate to be able to thank my colleagues at UC Berkeley. At the Institute of European Studies (IES), Director Jeroen Dewulf welcomed me and invited me to participate in institute events, and I consider him one of my best friends and colleagues. The environment Jeroen has created at the IES inspired me, and directly contributed to the completion of this work.

John Connelly in the Department of History at Cal also welcomed me right away, and we had many excellent conversations. His thoughtful comments about German historiography helped me round out the analysis of the occupation years, while his expertise on the Habsburgs and pertinent questions about the Slavic Macedonians gave me the framework through which I could reformulate key parts of chapters 4 and 5.

I am also very grateful to Daniel Sargent, a fellow international historian, who invited me to numerous conferences, events, and round-table discussions during my time as a visiting scholar and in my role as a senior fellow at the IES. Conversations with him about the field in general and recent works in international history helped me form a clearer idea of the place this book fills in the historiography, and allowed me to formalize my thoughts on what the book was trying to do, beyond just telling a story.

Numerous colleagues in the "Mario Romani" Department of Economic and Social History and Geographical Sciences at the Catholic University of the Sacred Heart (*Cattolica*) in Milan also deserve a heartfelt thank you. Being a part of this department helped me develop if not a secondary specialization, then a secondary interest in economic history and the principles and methods it advocates. These too made their way into the manuscript. Professor Andrea Locatelli, my friend, colleague, and mentor, welcomed me into the department, offered me access to the university's resources and gave excellent feedback on this project. Professors Gianpiero Fumi and Claudio Besana also deserve a heartfelt thank you. As many reading these lines will know, having encouragement from colleagues to keep going is as important for finishing a book as direct contributions of material, methods, and revisions.

Francesca Fauri at the University of Bologna has encouraged and guided me over the past five years as a consultant on the research project that also supported this book. She remained a constant source of advice on how to frame questions of European security in the early Cold War period and then how to integrate them into this book. She also helped greatly as I have struggled to balance work, research, service, and family while completing this manuscript.

I also owe a debt of gratitude to Giles Scott-Smith at Leiden University and the Roosevelt Institute of American Studies, who over the past two years has hosted me in the Netherlands numerous times to help me complete my research. I must thank Steffen Rimner (UC Dublin) for reading a final draft of this book and offering very helpful comments and suggestions for re-writes of a few key passages. I also gratefully acknowledge the help of my research assistants Branimir Stanimirov and Dr Stylianos Sotiriou, who read numerous drafts and re-drafts, helping me to catch numerous mistakes, typos, missing or incomplete sentences, and more, which otherwise would have survived much further into the editing process. However, no one helped me more in the final stages of preparing the manuscript for publication than Sarah Cooper of the Translation Centre at the University of Luxembourg. She proofread every one of the almost 85,000 words that make up this book, each time finding the perfect way to rephrase, reformulate, or correct the text to make it more readable. Thank you so very much! Thank you also to the three anonymous reviewers of this book. Your time, comments and suggestions, revisions, and criticisms were immeasurably helpful for me in finishing this work.

I also extend a heartfelt thank you to my team assembled by Bloomsbury, editor Laura Reeves, project manager Rebecca Willford, and copy editor Sophie Gillespie. Their patience, support, and guidance were critical in getting this book into print, and did not go unnoticed or unappreciated. I must also acknowledge the generous support of the Luxembourg National Research Fund, whose financial support of my research over the past five years allowed me to complete this book in parallel with my research into European security during the early Cold War.

Acknowledgments

To my brother Nic Paravantes and his family, Semana, Ben, and Luke, you have all supported me and helped make this book a reality. It has been very hard to be away and to miss so many moments over the years. I love and miss you all. To Peter, Mayumi, Branden and Natasha, Dean, Jennifer and Nina, and Aunt Mavis, it's so great to catch up when we have the chances, and I am looking forward to the next visit, whenever and wherever it may be. To Eleftherios and Kali, getting to know you has enriched my life, and helped me reconnect with a past that I had known only through stories. To Josh, Sam and Aunty Jenny, the other half of my family lies half a world away, but you are always in my heart.

Στον Σάκη και τη Βίκυ, σας ευχαριστώ πολύ για την στήριξη, τη βοήθεια και τη φιλία σας όλα αυτά τα χρόνια. Χωρίς εσάς, που υποδεχθήκατε με αγάπη αυτόν τον «ξένο» στην οικογένειά σας και στη συνέχεια φροντίζετε την Κορίνα μας σαν να ήταν η δική σας κόρη, η ολοκλήρωση αυτού του βιβλίου, αν θα μπορούσε καν να ευοδωθεί, θα είχε σίγουρα διαρκέσει πολυ περισσότερο. Νιώθω πολύ ευλογημένος που μπορώ να σας θεωρώ οικογένεια μου και φίλους. Θα ήθελα επίσης να ευχαριστήσω όλους τους ανθρώπους στην Κατερίνη και τη Θεσσαλονίκη που με έκαναν να αισθάνομαι σαν στο σπίτι μου όλα αυτά τα χρόνια, και που είστε πάρα πολλοί για να σας αναφέρω εδώ. Χωρίς τη συντροφιά σας, τη ζεστασιά, το χιούμορ και τη φιλοξενία, η ζωή μου θα ήταν πολύ διαφορετική. Σας ευχαριστώ όλους!¹[1]

To the rest of my extended family and friends, from whom I have spent too much time away over the past ten years, you too deserve a thank you, though I fear the words are too weak to express how deeply I appreciate your support, enquiries, notes, and conversations. You have all helped me immeasurably over the course of the past decade, and I would not have been able to do it without you. To quote *The Matrix*, "I am here, not because of the path that lies before me, but because of the path that lies behind me." This is not to say that you are the path, but rather the signposts along the road, the rest stops, and the refuges.

There are also two people no longer with me who I must also thank. To my Uncle Ted, I miss you very much, and I miss our conversations. Thank you for everything.

---

[1] "To Sakis and Vicky, thank you so much for your support, help and friendship these last years. Without you, accepting and welcoming this 'foreigner' into your family, and then looking after our Korina like she was your own daughter, this book, if possible at all, would certainly have taken even longer to finish. I feel very blessed to be able to call you family and friends. To everyone in Katerini and Thessaloniki who has also made me feel at home over the years, of whom you are too many to name here, I would also like to thank you. Without your company, warmth, humor, and hospitality, life for me would have been very different. Thank you all!"

To my Mum. I miss you every day. The more I go through life, the more I realize how important were the moments that we had. It is too easy to be caught up in the details of *la vie quotidienne,* and I try to remember how important it is to focus on that which I have directly in front of me.

My greatest thanks, however, are reserved for three people.

To my father, the first historian I ever knew, who brought the past alive through reading and through stories. The wisest and kindest person I have ever known. Every time we speak, I learn something new.

To my wife, my best friend, confidante, and partner. The one who keeps me honest and grounded. The person I trust and treasure above all others.

To my daughter. My darling Corinne. Every day you teach me something. It is truly an honor, privilege, and blessing to watch you grow and learn. My life is infinitely better because of you.

This work has meaning to me, as I have you all to share it with.

Note on the Text

When translating Greek names into English, there are often several ways to transcribe names of people and places. Zachariadis may also be written Zachariades, Vafiadis as Vafiades, etc. I have used the former, with "i," in most cases.

The same holds for places. Litoxoro may also be written Litochoro, Xalikidiki as Chalkidiki, etc. I have used the common English spelling here, replacing "x" with "ch".

As for abbreviations/acronyms, the text is full of them. There is a list of acronyms. In terms of the abbreviations for Greek organizations such as KKE and DSE, I have simply used Latin letters to represent their Greek equivalents. This is the way much of the literature in English does it, and I am not going to offer a replacement to that system here.

Format of the footnotes

Generally, the notes have been shortened to only the author(s)'s last name and page number. The full references can be found in the Bibliography. However, in the case where more than one work from the same author is used, then a short form of the title is added, in order to more clearly distinguish the works. I find this is more clear than adding just the date, considering that sometimes the dates may be the same. In cases where a work is referenced only to support supplemental / contextual information in a footnote, then the full bibliographic reference is used.

Acronyms

AMAG	American Mission for Aid to Greece
AMFOGE	Allied Mission to Observe the Greek Elections
AMM	American Military Mission
BEM	British Economic Mission
BIS	British Information Service
BLO	British Liaison Officer
BMM	British Military Mission
BPM	British Police Mission
BSC	British Security Co-ordination
DSE	*Dimokratikos Stratos Ellados* Democratic Army of Greece
EA	*Ethniki Allilegyi* National Solidarity
EAM	*Ethniko Apeleftherotiko Metopo* National Liberation Front
ECA	Economic Cooperation Administration
EDES	*Ethnikos Dimokratikos Ellinikos Syndesmos* National Republican Greek League
ELAS	*Ethnikos Laikos Apeleftherotikos Stratos* National People's Liberation Army
ERP	European Recovery Program
FARA	Foreign Agents Registration Act
FO	Foreign Office (British)

GNU	Government of National Unity (Greece)
KKE	*Kommounistiko Komma Ellados* Communist Party of Greece
SB	Security Battalion
SOE	Special Operations Executive
UNSCOB	(I and II) United Nations Special Committee on the Balkans

Acronyms for document collections

BDFA – British Documents on Foreign Affairs

BDPO – British Documents on Policy Overseas

FRUS – Foreign Relations of the United States

Note: Documents cited without these abbreviations are unpublished and were found in the archives in Kew, Chapel Hill, and the Truman Library.

Introduction

There is a small chapel built over a cliff face in a village close to the town of Litochoro in Macedonia. The cliff descends into a ravine some four to five hundred feet below. If you walk through the chapel, you can go behind the altar and out onto a ledge overlooking the ravine. When I visited the church in August 2012, I overheard the conversation of two women behind me who were taking in the view. "It was here that the communists threw people off the cliff," the older one said to the younger. I said nothing and waited for them to leave, but no sooner had they done so than another couple of women came out onto the ledge, and one said to the other, "This is where the police threw the *andartes* (i.e. the Greek communists) off the cliff."

Oral historians, who deal with similar situations regularly in the course of their work, state that the importance of such a story lies not in whether or not it conveys "truth" about a specific event, but rather what it reveals about the importance of that event. This place clearly held significance for people in their collective memory of the Greek Civil War. For a Canadian of Greek descent, born and raised in British Columbia, this was a direct encounter with a past that I had only heard about in stories from my father and uncle. The diverging accounts made me think about the ways in which history is remembered and spread across generations and the role that perception plays in memory. What was also clear to me, chillingly, was that on the very spot where I was standing, human beings had thrown other human beings, quite likely from the same city or neighborhood, to their deaths. This book is the culmination of that feeling, or rather of my attempts to explain the chill triggered by that feeling. How did Greeks get to the point of throwing each other off a cliff, and how could institutions be formed that allowed such things to take place? What is it about those years that has prevented healing?

The devastation of Greece after the occupation and Civil War can be summed up in statistics. By December 1949, 800,000 people had died and there were still a million internal refugees. The occupation and Civil War had wiped a thousand villages off the map. Ninety percent of the merchant navy had been sunk, and 90 percent of the railways had been destroyed. Seventy percent of the livestock was gone and it was not until 1952 that Greece was able to return to its 1939 economic levels. These are sobering statistics, but to me they were not enough to explain why Greek society was still so polarized. What was it about those years that kept diverging narratives alive in popular discourse, and why are Greek institutions, even today, so associated with these divisions?

Perhaps I could look at this period of Greek history from the perspective of foreigners, i.e., the British and the Americans, to find an answer. I wanted to understand what these countries were actually trying to accomplish in Greece, and if a link between their efforts and ongoing divisions in Greek society could be uncovered. What the United Kingdom and the United States sought to accomplish in Greece after the Second World War, and how their experience in and expectations for Greece affected their relations with each other, are the questions that form the basis of the work that follows.

My experience of living in Greece through the financial crisis also had a profound impact on the progression of this book. Greece was once again making the international headlines. In the late 1940s, Greece was the first battleground of the Cold War. Recently it became another battleground for the struggle over how the Eurozone should function. Just as contemporary economic and political ideologies were struggling to gain influence over Greek decision-making today, in the years immediately following the Second World War Greece was on the front line of the clash between communism and capitalism. It was believed (or at least stated to be believed) that the outcome in Greece would dictate outcomes for the rest of Europe. Then, as now, the question was what did Greece mean to, and for, the West?

This book, therefore, argues that the British intended to use Greece, first to maintain their influence in post-war decisions, and second to tie the US into guaranteeing security in Western Europe, the Mediterranean, and the Middle East. In this context, Greece mattered not only for its strategic value but also for what it represented in the struggle to contain communist expansion in Europe. Greek institutions, specifically the army and the executive, rebuilt by the British and Americans, were also shaped with these priorities in mind: they were to be democratic, capitalistic, and resistant to communist influence and infiltration. The effects on Greece would be felt for decades to come. The experiment of institution-building in a country ravaged by occupation and civil war yielded results that kept Greece in a permanent state of crisis, even though it remained in the Western sphere of influence. In order to fully understand the nature of the Anglo-American relationship with regard to Greece in this period, and to clarify the strategic considerations that shaped Anglo-American policy over two governments in each country, this book examines the considerations, assumptions, fears, perceptions, and objectives that affected their strategic decisions, as found in numerous archival sources.

The book draws on an analysis of complete archival series, published and unpublished, in which prime ministers, presidents, foreign secretaries and secretaries of state read, wrote, and annotated diplomatic exchanges between embassies, memoranda of meetings with government officials, foreign leaders and communist diplomats, and weekly and monthly reports on both foreign and domestic policy. While it focuses predominantly on the policy- and decision-makers of the period, it also looks at key thinkers, diplomats such as Orme Sergent and George Kennan, who influenced the strategic thinking of Britain and the United States.

This is not to say that the Greek policy-makers are ignored. Their views, concerns, priorities, and actions are also included in order to better illustrate how they perceived and reacted to Anglo-American policy. It is also important to bear in mind the significance of diplomatic papers and correspondence. Though some may initially be dismissed as being only of ephemeral interest or not being binding policy statements of lasting significance, they nonetheless fill in the picture of a state's culture of diplomacy; the ebb and flow of ideas and perspectives that makes up and reflects a country's foreign policy. Furthermore, though relying heavily on the established literature on the post-war Anglo-American relationship to frame the analysis, the work uses primary sources, extensively in some cases, to recreate the London–Washington relationship vis-à-vis Greece, as contained and revealed within the diplomatic record.

Finally, this book seeks to clarify how the "special relationship" between the UK and the US affected the Greek experience of the Cold War, and to examine the role played by Greece in shaping this relationship. In particular, it sets out to explain how the US assumption of Britain's role as the superpower of the West, coupled with Anglo-American intervention in Greece after the Second World War, did not lead to reconstruction and reconciliation in Greece (as was the case in Western Europe) but may have actually inhibited Greece's economic, social, and political reconstruction.

Theoretical Issues, Historicism and this Book

This book focuses on British and American decision-makers in the aftermath of the Second World War: Winston Churchill, Franklin Roosevelt, Harry Truman, and Clement Attlee. It also focuses on the Foreign Secretaries/Secretaries of State Anthony Eden, John Foster Dulles, Ernest Bevin, and George Marshall. To quote Daniel J. Sargent, in *A Superpower Transformed*:

> This tight focus serves an analytical purpose, Presidents (*and Prime Ministers*) and those who advise them deal (or try to deal) with world politics in a holistic fashion. Lowlier Bureaucrats are often more knowledgeable about particular issues and regions, and it is they who generate the options among which the top decision-makers choose. In this sense, the bureaucracy makes foreign policy, the myriad of actions and choices, of decisions and nondecisions that mediate relations with other international actors. It is nonetheless, at the very highest levels that policies cohere and overarching strategic purposes emerge.[1]

The making and pursuit of strategic objectives are, almost by their very nature, beset with difficulty, since the environment within which these objectives are created is constantly shifting. This pursuit also necessitates a triage of sorts when responding to events, which in turn results in oversights, distortions and omissions. British and American decision-makers after the Second World War, though allies, had diverging views in numerous areas, particularly in regard to the post-war world, where both saw the rise of communism as a threat, but it was the British who first described the relationship between capitalism and communism in terms approaching a "clash of civilisations." The Greek case is important because it clearly illustrates the nature of Anglo-American intervention and the unpredictability of outcomes, regardless of the planning and investments made in order to secure a desired result.

From 1946 to 1949, it was in Greece that the British and Americans saw the communists making their first advance into Western territory. While both the US and the UK intended for Greece to remain in the West, they struggled to agree on the steps they should take to secure that future. Examining how Roosevelt and Churchill initially formed and implemented policy for Greece and analyzing the effects of that policy can both clarify our understanding of that period of modern Greek history and help explain the post-Second World War order that emerged. It was in Greece first that the disagreements over

---

[1] Sargent, pp. 7–8. (Text in *Italics* in parentheses added)

the post-war world that so frequently divided President Roosevelt and Prime Minister Churchill revealed themselves most clearly. These divisions would continue into the Truman-Attlee era.

British and American involvement in and disagreements over Greece reveal these deep divisions, but also an earnest desire to make things better. The picture captured in this "snapshot" of post-Second World War history revealed a new image of how the special relationship came into being. While it can be tempting to rely on hindsight to explain what British and American policy-makers and reporters were writing, planning, and doing in Greece after the Second World War, this book attempts to place these decisions "in real time." In so doing, it provides the context for the period during which the documents were produced in order to really understand what they mean and represent.

It is vital to historicize British and American sources, since students of the human past may often be tempted to explain their observations and analyses simply in terms of a theory or rule, or sometimes just as a good story. The narrative surrounding the special relationship in Greece is no different. The way in which the US and the UK collaborated during the Second World War was unprecedented in world history. However, that does not mean that the relationship was as open and congenial, as Churchill described it after the war. The special relationship was undeniable, but as many authors have pointed out, it was very complex. While Britain and the United States were indeed very close allies, they did not always agree on policy during the war and in the early post-war years; there were also disagreements and friction, especially in the case of Greece. Repeatedly from 1946 to 1952, just when it appeared that conditions were improving in Greece, there would be a reversal. The invariable frustration and angst this caused the British and Americans was recorded in the diplomatic records. This book is therefore also a cautionary tale about the dangers of foreign intervention and institution-building, since by 1948—despite massive amounts of military aid and over 300,000 active duty personnel—the Greek army had been unable to make the gains that were expected of it. The massive military investments also came at the cost of economic and social reconstruction; the long-term effects of these delays is well known as Greece has limped along economically, socially, and politically since the end of the Civil War.

An important tool in the interaction between the United States and Britain was the collection and dissemination of information, including intelligence and secret information, and even misinformation in the scope of their interactions in, policies toward and involvement in Greece. Prior to the Japanese attack on Pearl Harbor the United States had no foreign intelligence service and therefore relied heavily on the British for war- and security-related information. When General William Donovan became Roosevelt's chief of intelligence/espionage, being a staunch Anglophile, he unsurprisingly looked to the British for guidance in establishing his organization. When the United States declared war on Germany and Japan, even closer Anglo-American cooperation in confronting the Axis was of paramount importance to both countries—and this included sharing vital intelligence. The British and Americans shared information of every kind, generally for the benefit of both countries but also as a way for the information provider to influence the decision-making of the information receiver. This state of affairs was clearly demonstrated in Anglo-American policies in Greece.

While overtly offering assistance in its formation, the British worked to prevent "Wild Bill" Donovan's Office of Strategic Services from outperforming the Special Operations Executive in the field, especially in the Balkans. Until 1946-7, although American officials—including Roosevelt until his death in 1945—saw Greece as a country under British authority and had plenty of information (of varying accuracy) on Greece from their own sources, they nonetheless relied on the British to inform them of the realities and developments on the ground, and they deferred to British policy there. This changed in 1947. The Truman administration decided to take the lead in supporting and shaping the Greek army and executive branch of the government from Britain. This decision was based partly on the United States' own information and perceptions, but it was also a result of British influence, information, and persuasion. The book fills in the picture of UK–US relations in the early Cold War and again highlights why Greece is relevant beyond its own borders.

So, while this work is indeed about Greece and the memory of the war years, the method and theories summarized above mean that it is also about the special relationship. It is about the unavoidable fact that historical investigations reveal multiple levels of "truths" that may be simultaneously true or false. Students of history must therefore be able to hold conflicting truths in mind while reconstructing these lost worlds that make up the human past. The special relationship was both open/honest and closed/manipulative. It was beneficial to both parties but also carried a high cost. In terms of Greece and its government, examining Greek policy-makers trying to balance the need to rebuild their shattered homeland while fighting a civil war revealed its own set of contradictions. Some cared about their people deeply, but some were also content to divert reconstruction loans into their own pockets or businesses. They wanted to build a large and effective military to defend the country against foreign enemies, while also relying heavily on the British and Americans to build the country up as a means of winning the internal conflict. Therefore, while recreating in part Greece during the Cold War, this book can also serve those researching civil wars, and the role played by external forces in such conflicts. How civil wars are fueled by these forces, regardless of their intentions, is clearly of paramount concern to researchers, and the case of Greece is an important case study as a result.

In light of these contradictions, reading such a span of diplomatic records is a humbling experience, for while it reveals human frailty, weakness, and selfishness, at times on a very broad scale, it also demonstrates earnest efforts to discern the right course of action in a chaotic and rapidly changing world. It is far too easy to be cynical about politics and diplomacy. That cynicism can blind the researcher into discarding nuance, detail, and contradiction in favor of supporting the underlying belief that all politics boils down to selfish acts of self-interested states and individuals. This is simply not true, or perhaps too simplistic to be fully true. Those reporting on events or prescribing courses of action, though guided by national priorities, *were not guided solely* by those priorities, and this realization was perhaps the most rewarding, if unanticipated, effect of this work. The people examined in the pages that follow were just that: people. Real, feeling, flawed, thinking people, dealing with great strain during a time of immense chaos and uncertainty. They were constantly pulled in numerous directions by the force of events beyond the embassy, state department and foreign office doors, and this chaos was not diminished by the end of the Second World War.

The emerging Cold War increased the levels of chaos and uncertainly felt by those reporting on events and those prescribing courses of action. Fostering a certain level of empathy with the people living and working at this time will help the reader to keep conflicting facts and truths in mind and to embrace these contradictions as an inescapable facet of human existence and history. If one truly wishes to understand the past and how it laid the foundations for the present, one must not explain the lives and experiences of these people as being generated solely by virtue of their role as agents of their state. They were that, but they were also individuals: burdened, flawed, thinking, and striving individuals. If we can come to terms with this fact, then understanding the present may become a bit easier after all.

Theoretically speaking then, though this work may at times appear to be a narrow diplomatic history thesis tracing Anglo-American relations through archival material, it also seeks to do something broader. In the Anglo-American relationship presented here, the intervening variable is the Greek Civil War. This helps to show the importance of British involvement in Greece and how Britain used the numerous crises there from 1946 to 1952 to influence US foreign policy. Not enough scholarly attention has been paid to the international implications of the Greek Civil War in its Cold War setting or in Anglo-American relations, and how these implications can explain foreign intervention and dominance in the Cold War.

Historiography and Contribution

While diplomatic historians see the Anglo-American relationship in Greece during the early Cold War as an arena through which competing plans for the post-war world order were tested, this book sits perhaps more comfortably in the field of international history. It sees the Greek Civil War as an intervening variable in Anglo-American relations after the Second World War. The book highlights the influence that the British had over American foreign policy, as Winston Churchill and Anthony Eden (British Prime Minister and Foreign Secretary, respectively, during the war) sought to solidify the wartime arrangement whereby Britain and the United States, and even the Soviet Union, could meet and decide things in consultation with one another. Roosevelt had something else in mind, a new world order, articulated by the formation of the United Nations, in which international markets were opened up and colonial and Commonwealth preferences were diminished and/or eliminated, reflecting the United States' desire for open and liberalized international trade post-Second World War. With the death of Roosevelt and his replacement by Truman, and with Labour's Clement Attlee replacing Conservative premier Churchill, what might have been an expected pro-left shift in British policy did not occur. Foreign Secretary Bevin, acting almost like the prime minister at times, was determined to maintain a British presence in Greece, and described the restoration of British power in much the same way as had Churchill. In the second part of the book, the exchanges between Bevin and Marshall are almost as important as those between Attlee and Truman, if not more so.

The continuity of British policy contrasts with a change in US policy, however. Where the Roosevelt administration had sought to liberalize markets and increase international cooperation, the Truman administration, influenced by thinkers such as George Kennan but also pushed and prodded by the British, sought to cut the communist world off from the West. Former enemies Germany and Japan soon became indispensable allies in these new containment efforts. The Truman administration, facing the perceived threat of communist revolutions in numerous countries, rushed through the approval of the Marshall Plan and supported the formation of the Western Union and the North Atlantic Treaty Organization (NATO), both of which, from a legal and philosophical perspective, represent the antithesis of the United Nations. The relationship and policies established between the United States and Great Britain by Churchill, Roosevelt, Attlee/Bevin, Truman, Marshall, and the others listed above in these years shaped their interactions with each other and other states for at least the next two decades of the Cold War, and arguably beyond. Moreover, as well as the connections between the three states at the highest levels, there were also a few "lower-level" connections between the countries, which directly influenced if not the course of events then certainly the way in which these events were recorded and transmitted.

One of the most surprising links I found between Greece, Britain, and the United States is in the person of noted children's author Roald Dahl. As a pilot in the RAF, he not only served in Greece but he subsequently also became a key figure in the British wartime spy network in the United States. There he played a crucial role in conveying information unofficially between Britain and the US. Another example of links between the three countries is C. M. Woodhouse, the Oxford-educated scholar who served during the war as a British liaison officer in Greece, coordinating resistance activities against the Axis occupying forces and relaying intelligence to the British government. After the war he published *Apple of Discord*, one of the first academic works about the Greek Civil War, and in the early 1950s he served at the British Embassy in Tehran, coordinating the coup that toppled Mohammad Mosaddegh with the CIA and one of its founders, Kermit Roosevelt Jr.

Canadian W. H. McNeill, who served in the US Army in Greece from November 1944 to June 1946, was also one of the pioneers in the historiography of the Greek Civil War. His first book, *The Greek Dilemma: War and Aftermath*, examines Anglo-American-Greek relations; it was published while the Greek Civil War was still under way. *The Greek Dilemma: War and Aftermath* and *Apple of Discord* were published at roughly the same time, the latter under the strict supervision of the British Foreign Office, and both present a survey of "current" events in Greece from British and American perspectives. While both works comment on Anglo-American relations in Greece at the time, McNeill writes in one part of his book that the Greeks preferred the Americans to the British.[2]

---

[2] McNeill, *The Greek Dilemma*. pp. 256–8.

McNeill also hints at an interest in the geography and demographics of Greece as they influenced Greek society, foreshadowing his later work *The Metamorphosis of Greece*, published in 1978.[3] Both men enlarged the historiography in the 1970s, with their later works *The Struggle for Greece* (Woodhouse, 1976) and *The Metamorphosis of Greece* (McNeill, 1978). These works are more comprehensive than their predecessors, relying upon a much greater level of published and archival material to complete their analyses.

Bruce Kuniholm's *The Origins of the Cold War in the Near East* (1980) places importance on the agency of the states making up the northern tier against communism (Iran, Turkey, and Greece) in their attempts to "push back" where they could against the "Great Powers" that were intervening in their affairs. Kuniholm also set the stage for British influence in Greece, highlighting Churchill's conversation with Stalin in Moscow in October 1944. He points out that from the date of the first proposal on October 9, 1944 to the final agreement on October 11, 1944, only in Greece and Yugoslavia did the British secure the influence they had sought in the beginning.[4] According to Kuniholm, the impact of Britain's commitment in Greece was to unify British and American policy for the Eastern Mediterranean and make the two "inseparable" by 1947.[5]

All of the works summarized above contributed to establishing and maintaining a historiography on post-Second World War Greece and its relations with and place in the West. However, they do not fully clarify how and why the British used Greece in pursuit of grand strategic objectives, and neither do they show the importance of Greece for Britain's efforts to restore its pre-war status, and the shift that occurred in 1946 and 1947. They also tend to view developments in Greece from a traditional perspective, suggesting that it was simply the first battleground of the Cold War, where Great Power politics were played out and where Anglo-American policy, if even described as such, was more or less coordinated. This book will show that the reality was more complicated. Yes, Greece was a battleground of the Cold War, but it was much more than that. By 1947, Anglo-American policy toward Greece was diverging far more than has thus far been explained in the historiography, and the Soviets were not the principal actors supporting the Communist Party of Greece. As

---

[3] McNeill, *The Metamorphosis of Greece*, p. 272.
[4] Kuniholm, pp. 109–15.
[5] Kuniholm, p. 431. It must be noted however, that anti-communism was not enough to bind together Anglo-American policy in the Middle East indefinitely, as the 1956 Suez crisis would reveal.

revealed by Peter Stavrakis in *Moscow and Greek Communism*, that role was played by Tito and the Yugoslavians.

In terms of the Churchill–Roosevelt relationship, dealt with in the early parts of this book, the edited volume by John Kimball, *Churchill and Roosevelt: The Complete Correspondence*, was indispensable. It particularly depicts the prevailing tension between the two men, who, despite having a close personal relationship, were also at odds over numerous issues in Greece. Disagreements over the Dodecanese Campaign, the support of the Greek monarchy, and most significantly the "percentages" agreement (described in detail in Kimball's work and also traceable through the diplomatic records of the time) show how the machinery of diplomacy in both the US and Britain reflected the will of the president and prime minister. David Stafford's *Churchill and Roosevelt, Men of Secrets* and Joseph Persico's *Roosevelt's Secret War* were also of vital importance in establishing the role that intelligence played in shaping US and British policy and the two countries' relationship. Stafford also highlights how both men used their intelligence services not only to wage war but also to exercise personal power.[6]

Persico's work clearly establishes the precedent of the British in using false intelligence (regarding Nazi activities in South America, for example) to lure the US into the war. Persico also highlights that, notwithstanding their differences of opinion and objectives, their half-truths and manipulations, Churchill and Roosevelt were united in their passionate anti-fascism.[7] Stafford's work also helps base the analysis in the present book on an Anglo-American alliance rooted not only in shared values and the friendship of Churchill and Roosevelt, but also in tough negotiations, misinformation, manipulation, and pressure. Following on from Stafford's analysis, this work highlights the role that affairs in Greece played in establishing the Anglo-American relationship post-Second World War. It clarifies how this relationship, forged by anti-fascism, evolved, and how, because of developments in Greece, it came to be based on anti-communism. This is why Greece was important for the British as they attempted to restore their pre-war strength and influence. If they could firstly show the US that the way they were dealing with communism in Greece was effective, then convince the US that they were going to have to withdraw from Greece, this meant that US involvement, while not a certainty, could be relied on.

---

[6] Stafford, p. xix.
[7] Persico, pp. 177–85.

For works examining the leaders of the Big Three (the United States, Britain, and the Soviet Union), three biographies stand out: Andrew Roberts' book *Churchill: Walking With Destiny*, David Kennedy's *Freedom from Fear: The American People in Depression and War, 1929–1945*, and Stephen Kotkin's first and second volumes of his planned three-volume biography of Stalin.

Roberts explains Churchill's guiding principle as primarily the survival of the United Kingdom but also, if possible, the survival of the empire and of British influence. Kennedy, quoting Woodrow Wilson, outlines Roosevelt's primary guiding principle as "making the world safe for democracy." Kotkin's *Paradoxes of Power* and *Waiting for Hitler* greatly clarify Soviet intentions, policy, and actions. In a lecture and debate by Kotkin regarding the projected third volume of his biography, *Stalin at War*, he put the USSR's grand strategic post-war visions in focus as well, while also further explaining the nature of the Soviet state and the way in which power was exercised.[8] Stalin, like Churchill, was initially concerned only with survival, but as the war turned in the USSR's favor, he too began looking beyond its borders. For Britain and the United States, even after Roosevelt's death and Churchill's election defeat, both the administration of Harry Truman and the government of Clement Attlee would to a large degree follow the objectives of their predecessors. While conditions in Greece were not the cause of this, they were perhaps at least indicators that could help explain why, after the Second World War, all of these competing priorities came into contact, albeit at times indirectly.

The interplay between collective and individual interpretations of the events and conflicts in Greece at the time is also a crucial component of this book. Prior to the German occupation, the country had been unified in opposition to the Italian invasion. Political differences were set aside as the war in Albania unified the country. But this unity would not last. Triggered by the harsh conditions of the occupation and continuing as various factions tried to secure post-war control and influence, Greek society splintered and descended into violence. As chronicled by scholars such as Stathis Kalyvas and Mark Mazower,[9] often the victims and the perpetrators of violence knew each other. As a result of this line of enquiry, the book *Violence and the Sacred* by Rene Girard was also a great help in formalizing my thoughts about the link between conflicting values and the widespread violence that tears societies apart. Greece matters even more in this context. Outside forces played a significant role in defining the values

---

[8] Stephen Kotkin, "Stalin at War." Lecture, available online at: www.ias.edu/ideas/s-t-lee-lecture-stalin-war

[9] See the various essays in *After the War was Over*, edited by Mark Mazower.

over which conflicts would arise regarding how Greek society should organize itself, and state institutions are key objects of analysis when trying to explain the state's underlying values.

The book is also among the first interpretations of Anglo-American policy in Greece to be based on the dual-track archival source approach described in the next section, but the pages that follow provide more than just new evidence. They provide a new perspective on the late 1940s—a time when Anglo-American decision-makers were attempting to deal with the domestic and international concerns heaped on them by the cataclysm of the Second World War, a new post-war international order was emerging, and the United States was replacing Great Britain as the world's pre-eminent superpower. By re-examining their relationship at this time, the book also links scholarship on the "special relationship," the early Cold War, post-war alliance- and institution-building, and foreign intervention, clarifying how the United States and Britain would respond to threats to this new international order. Re-examining this relationship and period also provides new insights into the ideologies and objectives of the dramatis personae of this book, and why Greece mattered to them at this time. The book argues that for the British, Greece provided a way for them to hold on to and act upon their "Great Power" status and maintain a semblance of their pre-war influence—for long enough, it was hoped, to rebuild their strength, guide American policy into greater alignment with their own, and give them a hand in shaping the post-war international order.

Primary Sources

To support the preliminary observations made above and to fill the gap identified in the historiography, numerous archival sources were consulted for this book. The main obstacle, however, was not access to documents, but rather the sheer volume of material that was available. Tens of thousands of dispatches are available in archives, in print and online, in addition to the numerous diaries and memoirs of the individuals who participated in the events this book analyses. In order to come to terms with the volume of material, I had to find a way to summarize it in a way that was readable and accessible, but also true to the original sources. To do so I narrowed the investigation and tracked conversations and exchanges between the British, the Americans, and the Greeks relating to the issues that occupied the bulk of their attention at the time. In alphabetical order, these were the army, the Civil War (often referred to as a Bandit War and

Internal Instability), the economy, the government (including elections and the plebiscite), the northern frontier and the Soviet Union. I then looked at British and American sources relating to these issues and followed conversations about them between governments, embassies, and consulates from 1946 to 1952.

In addition to the British, American, and Greek archives discussed above, records from United Nations agencies—the United Nations Relief and Rehabilitation Association and the United Nations Special Committee on the Balkans I and II—as well as other organizations such as the World Bank and the Red Cross, were consulted. These sources provided a more detailed image of the period in which these decision-makers lived and worked. The results of this research are both elucidating and confusing, for while the US and the UK designed and pursued their strategic interests, conditions on the ground changed so fast that improvisation was necessary in order to deal with the changes.

It was then necessary to cross-reference records from British and American embassies elsewhere (for example London, Washington, Athens, Moscow, Sofia, and Belgrade), from both British and American sources, so as to be able to create a more complete picture of their relationship and their Greek policy from 1946 to 1952.

Structure

The chapters that follow present the analysis in six parts, structured chronologically. Chapter 1 examines the wartime relationship between Great Britain and the United States in Greece and their plans for the country after the war. It highlights the conflicting views held by decision-makers in the two countries and examines the ways in which US and UK policies in Greece reflect these views. The divergences between British and American policies and positions in Greece, particularly with regard to the Greek monarchy, were significant, and the chapter examines them in the context of a more evident Soviet threat. The Roosevelt–Churchill relationship vis-à-vis Greece is examined, not only with respect to clashes between the two over Greece and views of the post-war order but also to establish a contrast with the Truman–Attlee relationship which would follow. The chapter analyses the role that British intelligence played in the gradual shift of US policy toward Greece, coinciding with the increasingly tense US–USSR relationship. Chapters 2 and 3 deal with the early Cold War period and the shifts in Anglo-American policy toward Greece that came with the change of leadership in both countries. These chapters show how the British attempted to use Greece as a way to tie the US to Europe, gain its support for British objectives in the Eastern Mediterranean and secure a return to their pre-war dominance afforded by the empire.

The focus of Chapter 2 is how the British managed to draw the US into greater levels of involvement in Greece, emphasizing the picture painted by British diplomats that the critical situation in Greece would lead to the second round of the Civil War. It also highlights the surprising continuity of Labour government policy toward Greece, following the same lines as the policy of Churchill and Eden (support of the Greek monarchy, restoring the British Empire, and maintaining influence in India, Palestine, and Cyprus).

Chapter 3 looks at the impact on affairs in Greece and the relationship with the US as a result of the change of government in Britain. Examining the lead-up to the Truman Doctrine, the chapter investigates this change, while placing developments in Greece within the international context of the time. The chapter also shows how influential events in Greece, or rather, British reporting of events in Greece, affected the state department and the formulation of the Truman Doctrine. The underlying motivation of British policy was to have the US assume the bulk of the financial and military responsibility for Greece, while maintaining some level of influence over both Greece and the US in the hope of delaying, mitigating, or even reversing Britain's post-war decline.

Chapter 4 examines how these hopes were finally proved to be unrealistic; it describes a shift in British strategy, coinciding with the determination of the United States to contain any further communist expansion. Greece was used again in this shift, and the British sought to "rebrand" themselves as the United States' closest and most valuable ally in the struggle against communism, a struggle that was playing itself out on the ground in Greece. Though the British rejected being cast as an obsolete power, the realities of the Cold War showed them that they could not compete on an equal footing with the United States or the Soviet Union. By the autumn of 1948, the effects of this shift in power were being felt in Greece. The Greek Army had increased in size and was well equipped, but it was consistently underperforming. This failure was exacerbated by the continuing economic and social crises gripping the country. Solving them consistently took a "back seat" to the military struggle. Compounding the crises in 1948 was a Greek political and social elite that was either unable or unwilling—or both—to improve its country. The year 1948 was crucial, however, since—notwithstanding domestic grievances—Greece had become an important if frustrating symbol for the US, and with the British having urged them on since 1945, they had simply invested too much in the country to leave.

Chapter 5 shows how the British accepted their diminished role but still sought to influence US policy, particularly in Greece during the final phases of the Civil War. The improvisations, disillusionment, fears, and assumptions made by both governments about the role of the Soviets in Greece through the final phase of the Civil War are highlighted throughout the preceding chapters, and notions and perceptions of power—much like those of strategy, with its shifts and redefinitions—are central to this book. Anglo-American relations are a key focus, but a detailed consideration of the Greek Civil War's final phase, along with the roles of Greece's neighboring countries (Yugoslavia, Bulgaria, and Albania), places the fate of the country in the context of Great Power politics. The two United Nations Special Committees on the Balkans, set up to investigate Greece's northern borders, failed to solve the issue and served mainly to reiterate the positions of the British, the US, and the USSR. The Soviets argued that Greek domestic conditions and continued British and American involvement in Greece were keeping the conflict going. The British and Americans stated that it was continued communist assistance to the Greek communists that was to blame.

Chapter 6 draws these analyses together, showing how, as the US and USSR were clearly revealed as the world's superpowers, second-tier powers like Great Britain sought to redefine themselves—in part through their role in Greece. Placed in the context of the profound change wrought by the Second World War and its aftermath, the transformation of the Anglo-American relationship played itself out in Greece, with grave consequences not only for the Greeks themselves but for the entire world. The contrast between US policy toward Greece in 1946–9 and then in 1950–2 is shown in order to illustrate just how much the country shifted toward and then beyond British objectives for the Greek government and for Greece itself.

In the Conclusion, the book shows how the methods of and justification for intervention and institution-building in Greece were used as models for future interventions elsewhere, and the perceived mistakes made in Greece from 1946 to 1952 were used to shape subsequent policy for a new generation of policy-makers. The effects of this transformation, brought about by a reassessment of the effectiveness of the methods of intervention and cohesion used in Greece, led to a shift in interactions between the UK and US governments and a change in practice that lasted throughout the twentieth century.

1

Historical Background: British Relations with Greece and the United States until June 1945

Like any regional power or superpower, the British have a long and well-documented history of intervening in the domestic affairs of foreign nations in pursuit of their national interest. Although the depth and breadth of that involvement has varied, the predisposition of the British to intervene in the affairs of other states has not. Their intervention has ranged from economic subversion and trade wars to coups (as in Iran in the 1970s) and the installation of rulers, as in Greece in the early nineteenth century with the installation of King Otto in 1821.

Relations between Great Britain and the United States also have a long and unique history and have been as diverse as the countries in which these nations have become involved. The last time that Great Britain and the United States came into direct military conflict was in 1812. One hundred and thirty years later, the Second World War forever altered not only the way(s) in which the United States and Britain related to each other but also, perhaps more significantly, the way in which they intervened in the affairs of foreign states. For the first time in history, two world powers switched positions of supremacy without coming into military conflict—but this shift was not without problems. It allowed the British to believe that they could regain their pre-war status and made the Americans more trusting of British intentions, information, and policies. These elements were extremely influential, not only to the British and American people but also to the people of Europe, who became pawns in the British and American "chess match" against the Soviet Union and its real or perceived intentions for world domination.

In terms of United States policy toward Greece, the end of the First World War saw the Americans, disillusioned with post-war European politics, withdraw into isolationism. By December 1940, after almost two years of war in Europe, the only commitment the US could make was to be the "arsenal of democracy" to provide the supplies needed by the British to fight the Germans.[1] It was not until the Japanese attacked the US on December 7, 1941 that isolationism was at least officially abandoned, and the United States embarked on an unprecedented and long-lasting period of direct intervention in European affairs.

Between 1922 and 1939, British policy toward Greece was not overly concerned with Greece's strategic value because the possibility of war in the Mediterranean was not taken seriously. For their part, Greek politicians were content to maintain the current level of good relations with Britain because of British military power in the Mediterranean. However, the traditionally close Anglo-Greek economic links of the nineteenth and early twentieth century were beginning to wane, and by 1935, Greece enjoyed closer economic ties with Nazi Germany than with Britain because of favorable trading terms.

In the period between the Asia Minor catastrophe and the start of the Second World War, US interest in Greece also dwindled. It was not until after the end of the war that the dramatic reversal of Anglo-American positions and the perceived threat represented by the USSR and its satellites led to a change in the United States' position.

The Special Operations Executive: The Impact of British Spies in Greece

In early 1941, the Special Operations Executive (SOE) performed many duties in Greece, since it acted as a liaison between the Foreign Office and the beginnings of what would become the Greek resistance groups, in addition to its duties of equipping and training saboteurs.[2] The SOE's activities in Greece were kept secret because post-occupation planning may have implied that the defeat of Greece was inevitable and thereby undermined the will of the Greek military.[3] The SOE was also tasked with coordinating action against the expected German occupation forces and relaying intelligence to the British government about the Germans and the Greek resistance should an occupation occur.[4]

---

[1] Franklin Delano Roosevelt, *Radio Broadcast*, 29 December 1940.
[2] Hammond, p. 13.
[3] Clogg, "The Special Operations Executive in Greece," p. 111.
[4] MacKenzie, p. 450.

When Hitler invaded the USSR in May 1941, he turned Stalin into Churchill's most significant ally. Although the Nazi-Soviet peace had lasted for nearly three years, the USSR was under-equipped and unprepared to meet the German offensive. The rapid seizure of most of the Soviet Union's European territory by the Germans reinforced Britain's belief in the utter incompetence of the Soviet military, thereby reducing the importance placed by the British on the USSR as an ally.[5] This reductive attitude was in turn furthered by Churchill's outspoken anti-communism; however, his position did not sway the USA, which extended lend-lease to the USSR.[6]

Once the United States entered the war, it was initially able to agree with Great Britain only that the defeat of Germany and Japan should be the primary objective. Two main aspects of Britain's efforts to influence US policy are truly remarkable. The first is their level of success, which was unexpectedly high, and the second is the degree to which the Americans would follow the British example after the Second World War was over.[7]

The fact that Churchill needed to establish an organization tasked not only with relaying information about but also shaping US policy indicates how far apart US and British policy were in the early years of the Second World War. On December 7, 1941, the Japanese attack on Pearl Harbor instantly drew the United States into the war. Despite gaining two allies (the USSR and the USA) within a period of six months, the British felt that they were in an unenviable position and still risked being the "odd man out" in the relations and planning conducted between the Big Three. The forces of isolationism, which had prevented the United States from joining the League of Nations in 1919, were still very strong and threatened to reassert themselves once the Second World War was over.[8] To counter this, in the first few months after the United States entered the war, Roosevelt put forward his idea for the post-war era, which he called the "Four Policemen." His plan was to

---

[5] The belief that the Soviet military was incompetent was further strengthened by post-war interviews with German officers, and formed the basis of this long-standing view. However, recent research in *Wehrmacht* archives shows that, notwithstanding the significant casualties inflicted on the Soviet armies, the offensive capability of the German armed forces was significantly degraded by "suicidal" Soviet counterattacks. See: Lev Lopukhovsky, *The Viaz'ma Catastrophe, 1941: The Red Army's Disastrous Stand Against Operation Typhoon* (Helion and Company; reprint edition [February 29, 2016]).

[6] On March 11, 1941 American President Franklin D. Roosevelt signed the Lend-Lease bill, which permitted the US to supply its anti-Hitler coalition allies with materiel to sustain their war efforts. Though downplayed by the Soviet Union, the program was of vital importance to the USSR's war effort, as Marshal Zhukov later admitted.

[7] Two of the most significant examples where that was not the case were the formation of Palestine, which the British opposed, and the use of nuclear weapons in Korea, which was stopped nearly at the last minute by Prime Minister Attlee's direct intervention with President Truman.

[8] Stephenson, pp. 224–5.

create an organization similar to the League of Nations, but rather than relying on consensus amongst a hundred or more members, the United States, Great Britain, the USSR, and China (which together represented more than 1 billion people) would be the main decision-makers in the post-war world.[9] It was the precursor to the United Nations Security Council and formed the basis for Roosevelt's post-war strategy. Since Greece had fallen to Germany the previous year, and because the US was mainly focusing on the Pacific theatre, it was happy to allow the British to continue to deal with the Greek government and resistance.

Politically, in the spring of 1942, the official British policy was to support King George II and the war effort, but through the actions of the SOE, in practice Britain was actually supporting groups that desired the collapse of the Greek government. SOE agents made contact with Venizelists, communists, and other Metaxas opponents as part of Churchill's plan "to set Europe ablaze." However, it seemed from the outset that British policy leading up to and during the Second World War was destined to keep Greece as divided as it had been in the 1920s. The SOE worked with republicans and communists because they were the most willing and able to operate underground. On the other hand, most of those loyal to the king and the Greek government were seen by the British as satisfied with the current political situation, and if they decided to resist the occupation at all, they did so too late and were therefore of little use to British intelligence.[10]

Though the occupying forces represented a common enemy, the forces that would rise up to oppose these occupiers had diverging political agendas. The British expected that these agendas would be set aside until the end of the war. British policies toward the war efforts of the Greek government in exile and the Greek resistance, despite appearing complementary on the surface, were in practice almost completely incompatible. They were effectively flawed from the outset, since those upon whom the British relied to support the first were also the least likely to accept or support the second. Not only did this create problems in Greece; it also created many problems between the main British agencies responsible for operations in Greece, the Foreign Office, and the SOE.

The SOE had been in Greece since 1941 training saboteurs, and the first SOE mission to support the Greek resistance in the mountains took place in October 1942. Nicholas Hammond, C. M. Woodhouse and Brigadier E. C. W. Meyers parachuted into Greece to destroy the Gorgopotamos railway bridge.[11] On March 8, 1943, British Foreign Secretary Sir Anthony Eden reiterated a policy

---

[9] Butler, pp. 4–5.
[10] Woodhouse, *The Apple of Discord*, p. 37.
[11] Hammond, pp. 15–16.

of "full support for the Greek King and his government, even at the expense of some loss of active effort against the occupying powers."[12] What Eden and the Foreign Office seemed not to be aware of was that with some 10,000–12,000 armed men, the Greek People's Liberation Army (ELAS) was the only force large enough at the time to make any headway against the occupying forces.

Churchill ordered the SOE in a different direction. He stated that unless operational necessity dictated otherwise, aid to the Greek resistance "would favor the groups willing to support the king and his government."[13] However, this statement was not binding, and beyond stating that His Majesty's government supported King George, the SOE was free to work with ELAS. The SOE continued to work with all groups that were opposed to the occupation and attempted to keep them from turning on each other. Had Churchill's recommendation been followed, it is unlikely that aid would have been provided to any Greek resistance groups throughout the German occupation; but in practice the British supplied these groups with food, clothing, weapons, and gold. Despite the conditions of the war in Europe at this time, the amount of aid that ELAS and EDES received was impressive, especially considering the logistical problems that were involved in supplying it.[14]

The American attitude toward the Greek resistance was also greatly influenced by the British. At Britain's insistence, the Americans helped repress news of the Greek military's mutiny in the Middle East to avoid further damaging the prestige of the Greek government in exile.[15] Furthermore, the British made it clear to the Americans that they desired the return of King George to power, and that while they would not use force to achieve this goal, they would attempt "to sell the King and the Tsouderos government" to the Greek people, at least in part by persuading them that the king intended to rule as a democratic constitutional monarch. The Americans agreed with the British and recognized the Greek government in exile and the king as the legitimate government of Greece.[16] However, they stressed that the Greek people should be given the opportunity

---

[12] MacKenzie, p. 461.
[13] Churchill, *World War II, Volume II*. p. 130.
[14] Papastratis, pp. 151–4.

*Table:

Oct 1943 to Jan 1944	EDES	ELAS
Food and Clothing	14 tons	34 tons
Arms and Ammunition	74 tons	22 tons
Gold Sovereigns	18,000 coins	927 coins *

* Table reproduced from: Papastratis, p. 155.

[15] Kirk to Hull (505), March 13, 1943, FRUS 1943 Vol. IV, The Near East and Africa, p. 125.
[16] Memorandum, Murray to Hull, March 16, 1943, FRUS 1943, Vol. IV, The Near East and Africa, p. 126.

to express their views against the monarch and, in keeping with their own fears of foreign manipulation (which were well founded), insisted that the Greek king should not be "promoted" by a foreign power.[17] The Americans feared that foreign intervention would re-stimulate longstanding political divisions in Greece and that Britain's belief that only a monarchy would be suitable was supported "neither by the facts of recent Greek history nor by a reasonable analysis of the present temper of the Greek people."[18] The US view was that forcibly restoring an unpopular government would raise the possibility of armed conflict amongst organized groups that were prepared to oppose the return of the king and his government. Additionally, the Americans believed that if the Greek people were not supported by the United States in their right to choose their method of government, then they would likely turn to the Soviet Union for support.[19] Therefore, although the United States followed British policy by recognizing and supporting the Greek government in exile and the king, it succeeded in its policy objectives by persuading the Greek king to declare that at the end of the war, he would "submit himself to the free expression of the will of the Greek people," although the pledge was only for the *composition* of the government, not its actual *form*.[20] In another memorandum to the United States, the Foreign Office outlined the reasons for its support of the Greek king, including the fact that the king had stood by England as a "loyal ally" during the early stages of the war; however, it also stated that it needed a strong administration in Greece to be able to use the country as a "base of operations" in the later stages of the war.[21]

In Greece, despite some limited successes in coordinating resistance activities against the Axis occupiers, the SOE continued to face the problem of reconciling short-term military objectives with long-term political ramifications. The SOE often pointed out that the policy of the Foreign Office conflicted with the job that the SOE had to do. This conflict, in turn, allowed the SOE's opponents in Britain to assert that it had a policy of its own and that it was not committed to following the policies of the British government.[22] Furthermore, Ambassador

---

[17] Memorandum, Murray to Hull, March 16, 1943, FRUS 1943, Vol. IV, The Near East and Africa, p. 127.
[18] Memorandum, Murray to Hull, March 16, 1943, FRUS 1943, Vol. IV, The Near East and Africa, p. 126.
[19] Ibid.
[20] Memorandum of Mr. Foy de Kohler, March 24, 1943, FRUS 1943, Vol. IV, The Near East and Africa, p. 130. See also: British Embassy to Department of State, April 24, 1943, FRUS 1943, Vol. IV, The Near East and Africa, pp. 131–2 and Department of State to British Embassy, July 2, 1943, pp. 133–4.
[21] British Embassy to Department of State (868.01/397), April 24, 1943, FRUS 1943, Vol. IV, The Near East and Africa, pp. 137–8.
[22] Sweet-Escott, pp. 14–16.

Reginald Leeper, based in Cairo, was given complete control over the political aspects of the SOE's work in Greece.²³ Therefore, the SOE's task was hindered even further as it was forced to comply with the often unrealistic political objectives of the Foreign Office (e.g., the return of King George). The Foreign Office expected a post-war return to the pre-war status quo in Greece, while the SOE had to deal with the reality that those who resisted did so for their own reasons and to further their own agendas.²⁴

The SOE was faced with a task that seemed increasingly unworkable: to coordinate a unified Greek resistance as tensions between the National Liberation Front (EAM) and ELAS and the rest of the resistance groups continued to increase in 1943. Furthermore, the extent to which the EAM had grown since the spring of 1943 was not fully appreciated by the British until the Cairo Conference, to which Brigadier E. C. W. Myers brought many EAM representatives. It was another situation in which political interference made the "on-the-ground" job much more difficult to perform. At this point, British policy toward Greece and the United States was divided, which was not surprising considering the status of the war, but the Cairo Conference did convince the British of the seriousness of the threat posed by the Communist Party of Greece (KKE) to their post-war plans for Greece. In terms of Anglo-American policy in 1943, divisions appeared in two main areas. The first was when the two governments were formulating policy for the liberation of Greece, and the second came with the Dodecanese campaign that began with the Italian surrender in September 1943. The British insisted that both for purely military reasons and because it would take time to accurately assess the feelings of the Greek people about their government, the Greek government in exile needed to be fully supported as soon as it returned to Greece so that it could resume its functions as quickly as possible. Furthermore, going against American wishes, the British intended to allow King George to return to Greece as the commander-in-chief of the Greek armed forces. With regard to ELAS and the National Republican Greek League (EDES), the British stated that in their opinion, these groups in no way represented the views of the majority of the Greek people, and there was no reason to expect that the occupation-period cooperation between Allied and resistance forces would continue after the occupation had ended. It was therefore in the Allies' best interests to support a side that could guarantee post-occupation support.²⁵

---

²³ MacKenzie, p. 463.
²⁴ Woodhouse, "Summer 1943," p. 117.
²⁵ British Embassy to Department of State (868.01/391), August 4, 1943, FRUS 1943, Vol. IV, The Near East and Africa, pp. 137–41.

The US refusal to comment on either the position of the king or the demands of the resistance[26] had two significant effects. The first was to fuel speculation that there was a rift between British and American policy (which in fact there was) and the second was to implicitly allow British policy to dictate the course of events leading up to the liberation of Greece and the status of the Greek monarchy.[27] The Americans also claimed that the violence between the resistance groups had begun with the return of the EAM representatives from Cairo, who, after the conference of August 1943, having failed to secure all the concessions that they desired from the Greek government, believed that only by controlling all of Greece at the liberation could they hope to force their concessions on the Greek government in exile. The Americans were of the view that the situation would be resolved only when the government in exile issued a clear statement that the king would not return to Greece until permitted to do so by a plebiscite, which would not occur until the British changed their policy of support for the monarchy.[28] However, the Foreign Office's continued support of the Greek monarchy hindered those objectives. The SOE was aware of the strength and numbers of ELAS and proposed a plan to separate EAM from ELAS by creating a Regency Council headed by Archbishop Damaskinos and the Venizelist General Plastiras.[29] However, over the next few months, fighting continued between ELAS and EDES, with the greatest number of casualties amongst the civilians who were caught up in the conflict. Agreeing on a resolution to end the civil war became even more important as the Allies planned Operation Overlord.

Greece's impact on Overlord was felt even more after the failure of the Dodecanese campaign, with the loss of almost five infantry battalions, one hundred aircraft and some warships by the end of November 1943. What exacerbated tensions between the US and Great Britain was the fact that the campaign had been planned despite the objections of the United States and the British Chiefs of Staff.[30] It was to be part of Churchill's larger strategic effort to impose pressure on the Dardanelles (perhaps he was still haunted by the memory of Gallipoli) and to have a strong British presence close to Turkey, which would offer the twofold benefit of pressuring

---

[26] Berle to Hull (868.01/390), August 31, 1943, FRUS 1943, Vol. IV, The Near East and Africa, p. 149. See also: Kirk to Hull (63), September 10, 1943, FRUS 1943, Vol. IV, The Near East and Africa, pp. 152–4.
[27] Kirk to Hull (57), September 4, 1943, FRUS 1943, Vol. IV, The Near East and Africa, p. 150. The rift was apparent in the US Congress, where the Republican Party used it to attack FDR's policy.
[28] Memorandum (868.00/1340), December 10, 1943, FRUS 1943, Vol. IV, The Near East and Africa, pp. 156–7.
[29] British Embassy to Department of State (868.01/426), December 22, 1943, FRUS 1943, Vol. IV, The Near East and Africa, pp. 160–3.
[30] Rogers, p. 49.

Turkey and controlling Soviet access to the Mediterranean. However, the US was highly skeptical of this plan, seeing it (correctly) as an operation designed to secure post-war British interests and as a distraction from the planned invasion of Sicily.[31] Without adequate Allied air support, the campaign failed, becoming one of the greatest British defeats of the war and one of the last German victories.[32] Although it did not alter the course of the war, it did affect the Italian campaign (which would drag on until 1945), and it delayed the liberation of Greece.

Anglo-American Policy Conflicts: November 1943, the Cairo and Tehran Conferences

The significance of the wartime conferences cannot be overstated, and certainly in the grand scheme of the Second World War, the issue of Greece was less important than the overall Allied strategy. It is therefore beneficial to take a brief look at these "broader" concerns, before returning to affairs in Greece. The Cairo Conference (codenamed Sextant) took place from November 22 to 26, 1943. Among other things, it addressed the Allied position against Japan during the Second World War and made decisions about post-war Europe, Asia, and Greece. Roosevelt, Churchill, and Chiang Kai-shek of the Republic of China attended, while Stalin refused to attend since he believed it could provoke the Japanese, with whom the USSR was not at war due to the five-year Soviet-Japanese Neutrality Pact of 1941.

Casablanca, Cairo, and Tehran: Conferences Looking Ahead to the Post-war World

In Casablanca, Morocco, from January 14 to 24, 1943, Churchill and Roosevelt met to further coordinate Allied strategy. Aside from declaring that they would accept only unconditional surrender from Germany, they also agreed on a Mediterranean strategy for this phase of the war. The objective was to draw off German forces from the Eastern Front. In this context, Italy and France were considered as potential locations for the Allied invasion of Europe, but Greece also began to refigure in Allied planning, particularly for the British. Ten months

---

[31] Rogers, pp. 51–2.
[32] It is possible that the failure of this campaign contributed to Churchill's post-war determination to maintain Greece as a sphere of influence.

later the Allies met again in Cairo. The Cairo Declaration was signed on 27 November 1943 (just five days after the failure of the Dodecanese campaign) and broadcast over the radio in the "Cairo Communiqué" on 1 December 1943. It stated the Allies' intention to fight until they received Japan's unconditional surrender. The Cairo Conference was organized by the British, who also wished to discuss issues surrounding their concerns relating to the USSR with the Americans on their own. However, Roosevelt refused to discuss the USSR, focusing instead on issues relating to Japan and China, and Roosevelt and Churchill agreed with Chinese leader Chiang Kai-shek that China would have a pre-eminent role in post-war Asia.

The subsequent Tehran Conference was encouraged by Roosevelt, who wanted the Big Three to meet to clarify their plans for the rest of the war and settle post-war considerations. From 28 November to 1 December 1943, Roosevelt, Stalin and Churchill met at the Soviet Embassy in Tehran to secure Soviet support for wartime Allied objectives. In return for such guarantees, the Soviets asked for post-war considerations, most notably support of the Yugoslav communists and control of the Russian-Polish border. Additionally, the Western Allies promised the USSR that they would open a second European front; however, rather than opening this front somewhere in the Mediterranean (as desired by Churchill), which would have protected British interests in the Middle East, the Allies agreed to open it in France.

Despite giving in to US desires on this occasion, the British did not abandon their objective of securing the Eastern Mediterranean. Believing that the USSR was determined to control Eastern Europe, the British determined that they had to find a way to maintain their presence in the Eastern Mediterranean.[33] As a result of divided Anglo-American policy and recent Soviet victories against the Axis, Stalin was able to secure Western acceptance of post-war Soviet influence over Eastern Europe.

At Tehran, the British were increasingly concerned with the post-war world and how the "spoils" would be divided. One of the main conflicts within the British government, particularly between Lord Beaverbrook, Lord Privy Seal, and the Chiefs of Staff, was what to do about American plans to control the

---

[33] Dilks, pp. 25–6. Churchill's advocacy for the second front to be opened in the Balkans (the "soft underbelly of Europe") was a result of both his overall strategic desires and his determination to vindicate his First World War Eastern Mediterranean policy. It is therefore not surprising that as soon as it was possible, the British returned troops to Greece in October 1944, since their presence also ensured that the British had a significant "foothold" in Europe in order to maintain a stronger bargaining position. Bevin shared this view. See also: Bearentzen, pp. 145–6.

world's airways. Using its spies and influence in the United States, the British government moved to press a joint US-British solution through which they could share equal access. The British soon became aware of the American business interests that were arrayed against them and were attempting to influence the US government. The president of Pan Am Airways, Juan Terry Trippe, successfully lobbied for low US government regulation of aviation but heavy protection through policies, pressure, and subsidies. The "free market" that the Americans said they wanted (one of the US justifications for attacking British Empire preferences) was under attack by American business.[34]

While the main concern of both the US and British governments was to end the war, they also planned for its aftermath, and it was in the area of Allied post-war planning that Greece assumed particular importance. As long as the British were "on the ground" in Greece, they could have a say internationally, and through the winter of 1943–4, with the German army retreating in Russia, the Allies refocused some of their attention on the southern Balkans.

In January 1944, in collaboration with the British and the Americans, the Soviets issued a statement supporting the Greek government's initiative to form a government of national unity that included all groups and urged the Greek resistance and people to unite and oppose the Germans together.[35] This statement coincided with British support for Tito, with whom the British believed cooperation was vital in order to divert as many German divisions as possible in Eastern Europe. To this end, against the wishes of Prime Minister Churchill, the Foreign Office was prepared to accept EAM/ELAS representatives in the new coalition Greek government. After fourteen meetings and numerous proposals and compromises, an armistice (the Plaka Agreement) was signed on February 20, 1944.[36]

At the urging of the British, by April 1944, the United States government was increasingly apprehensive of Soviet support for the left in Greece. Soviet radio and press had been issuing statements of support for the Greek left, which, while understandable, greatly concerned the British.[37] US Ambassador Lincoln MacVeagh expressed doubt, however, that the Soviet comments actually reflected

---

[34] American private enterprise, particularly the commercial air travel industry, placed heavy pressure on the US government to force concessions from the British. In addition, companies such as Standard Oil lobbied against British interests in the United States. See: Stephenson, pp. 145, 149–50.

[35] US Ambassador (USSR) to Secretary of State (19), January 4, 1944, FRUS 1944, Vol. V, The Near East, South Asia, and Africa, the Far East, p. 84.

[36] Thomopoulos, p. 133.

[37] US Ambassador (USSR) to Secretary of State (19), January 4, 1944, FRUS 1944, Vol. V, The Near East, South Asia, and Africa, the Far East, p. 85.

a Soviet desire to supplant Britain as the main power in Greece. Furthermore, the Greek Ambassador communicated to the United States representative in Cairo, Paul Alling, that the Greek government was extremely concerned about British influence over the Greek military and Soviet hostility toward the Greek government of national unity, particularly in light of another mutiny of the Greek military in the Far East, with the mutineers holding twelve of the Greek Navy's ships.[38] As a result, MacVeagh recommended to Secretary of State Hull that President Roosevelt urge Stalin and Churchill to meet directly to sort out the situation and clarify their respective positions on Greece.[39] At the same time, the US and British governments were negotiating about post-war air commerce.[40] When US Ambassador MacVeagh approached British Ambassador Leeper to ask whether the United States should intervene in the crisis, Leeper refused, stating that the British held military responsibility for Greece. Leeper went on to say that the Soviet broadcasts were exacerbating the situation and that if the Soviets so desired, they could solve the situation immediately, but they were instead deliberating over whether to provoke a confrontation between the British and Greek armed forces.[41] In the British view, the Soviet actions were a direct contravention of the "spirit of Tehran" and were "in line" with Soviet intentions toward Eastern Europe and the Mediterranean as a whole.[42] This demonstrative statement illustrated the British perception of Soviet intentions and also a US willingness to accept the British direction and interpretation of these events.

The Americans went so far as to support the British in urging King George to remove the Greek Prime Minister Venizelos and to appoint the "stronger

---

[38] The Greek government in exile was based in Cairo, hence the meetings there with US, British, and Soviet representatives. References here to Cairo are not to be confused with the previous Cairo Conference.

[39] Alling to Secretary of State, April 18, 1944, FRUS 1944, Vol. V, The Near East, South Asia and Africa, pp. 99–100. Additionally, through their British Security Coordination (BSC) networks in the United States, the British managed to achieve some compromises with some of the politicians who had been supporting Pan Am's objectives of completely liberalizing post-First World War air-traffic. See: Conant, pp. 184–9.

[40] Conant, pp. 239–40, 236. Additionally, in May 1944, Lord Halifax lodged an official complaint with the United States government over Vice President Marshall's pamphlet on what he believed US foreign policy objectives should be after the war, with priorities that included massive decolonization. The British Ambassador stated that the timing was very poor considering that the Allies were planning Operation Overlord and tried to make an illogical connection between the vice president's statements and endangering the secrecy of the planned invasion of Europe. As well as trying to influence the United States against its own vice president, the BSC surveyed American companies, particularly Pan Am Airways, to assess their objectives and prepare countermeasures.

[41] Alling to Secretary of State, April 18, 1944, FRUS 1944, Vol. V, The Near East, South Asia and Africa, p. 100.

[42] MacVeagh to Hull (120), April 19, 1944, FRUS 1944, Vol. V, The Near East, South Asia, and Africa, the Far East, pp. 100–2.

personality," George Papandreou.[43] The Americans supported and relied upon Papandreou to provide them with information about the EAM/ELAS and the disposition of the Greek people toward it. Papandreou informed them that the EAM/ELAS had ceased being a political movement and was focused only on imposing a communist dictatorship on the people of Greece, the majority of whom "hated and feared" the organization. Because he had been recommended by the British, his analysis was accepted.[44] Whether his statements were accurate is irrelevant for this book. What is relevant is the fact that on British recommendation, the Americans accepted Papandreou as prime minister and then based their policy toward Greece on the information that he provided instead of on the intelligence provided by the SOE, which had two years of on-the-ground intelligence regarding the situation in Greece.[45]

The Lebanon Conference

In contrast to the previous international conferences, where Greek issues were secondary to the grand strategy of the Allied war effort, the Lebanon Conference was held exclusively to deal with the ongoing Greek political crises. However, the seemingly irreconcilable differences that had divided not only the British government over Greece, but also the various domestic factions vying for post-war control of the country, made the prospect of finding an agreement, let alone adhering to it, daunting at best. Churchill's dislike and suspicion of the KKE was equaled by the KKE's mistrust of the British and their post-war objectives. This was highlighted on May 17, 1944, when representatives from almost every political party in Greece arrived in Lebanon for a conference that was intended to create a government of national unity for Greece. Over the four days of the conference, the Papandreou government sparred with the KKE over the roles that each would play in the new national unity government. In the end, although the KKE managed to gain a few minor ministries, the conference was a victory for Papandreou. Furthermore, one of the main articles in the Lebanon charter

---

[43] MacVeagh to Hull (120), April 19, 1944, FRUS 1944, Vol. V, The Near East, South Asia, and Africa, the Far East, pp. 100-2.
[44] MacVeagh to Hull (122), April 20, 1944, FRUS 1944, Vol. V, The Near East, South Asia, and Africa, the Far East, pp. 102-3.
[45] Cited in: Papastratis, p. 198. and Ryan, pp. 122-3. Ryan also stated, "One might note the remarkable extent to which attitudes that characterise what we call the Cold War, and particularly America and the Cold War, can be found in Britain's policy as its officials reacted to the Greek crisis."

was the unification of all resistance groups into a single armed force under the control of the government of national unity.

American support was so strongly desired by all the participants in the conference, including the EAM representatives, that Alexandros Svolos, president of the Political Committee of National Liberation (the political wing of the EAM, which had tried to form a government in Greece prior to the German withdrawal), issued a letter to President Roosevelt pledging to work within the government of national unity and imploring the US president not to allow the mutinies in the Middle East, fermented by the "mad actions of irresponsible persons," to reduce his opinion of the Greek people who had resisted the Axis in the "towns and mountains" of Greece.[46] President Roosevelt issued a response that pledged full American support of Greek unity, and on May 22, 1944, upon his return to Cairo, Papandreou was "entrusted with the formation of the Greek government."[47] The British were extremely pleased. Not only had they secured US support for the Greek government, but they had limited the KKE's influence and succeeded in appointing the man whom they wanted as prime minister.

The British also informed the United States of ongoing conflicts with the Russians over control of Romania and asked what the American position would be should the British and the Russians agree to the Soviets holding a "controlling influence" in Romania in exchange for a British "controlling influence" in Greece. Secretary of State Hull promised to give the question "serious thought," but informed the British Ambassador that it was unlikely that the United States would abandon its "broad basic declarations of policy, principles and practice."[48]

The Soviets approved of the agreement, provided that the United States also agreed to it. However, aware of President Roosevelt's distaste for the spheres of influence policy, Churchill assured FDR that the agreement regarding who would have a controlling interest in Greece and Romania "would apply only to war conditions" and that the British "do not of course wish to carve up the Balkans into Spheres of Influence." They wished only to prevent "the divergence of policy between ourselves and them in the Balkans."[49] Though not declared as such, this

---

[46] MacVeagh to Hull (154, 155), May 15, 1944, quoting the Lebanon Conference participants' letter to President Roosevelt, FRUS 1944, Vol. V, The Near East, South Asia, and Africa, the Far East, pp. 108–9.

[47] MacVeagh to Hull (168), May 23, 1944, FRUS 1944, Vol. V, The Near East, South Asia, and Africa, the Far East, p. 112.

[48] Report by Hull about meeting with Halifax (870.00/42), May 30, 1944, FRUS 1944, Vol. V, The Near East, South Asia, and Africa, the Far East, pp. 112–13.

[49] Churchill to Roosevelt (870.00/46), May 31, 1944, FRUS 1944, Vol. V, The Near East, South Asia, and Africa, the Far East, pp. 113–15.

decision was the precursor to the "percentages agreement" that would be signed in October 1944 between Stalin and Churchill; aside from deceiving the United States regarding what this May 1944 agreement actually represented, it also cemented the division of Eastern Europe. It may therefore be argued that the fate of the KKE and its armed struggle was sealed before the Second World War was over.

In June 1944, the representatives to the Lebanon Conference returned to Cairo to confer with the Greek government. The British and American Ambassadors were confronted by the fact that despite the positive statements made by the participants in the conference, implementing the results would be difficult. The British again attempted to persuade the United States to issue a statement to enforce a settlement on the Greeks, but MacVeagh, speaking for Hull, again reiterated the American policy of non-interference.[50] A few days later, Roosevelt informed Churchill that the US government could not approve the proposed British and Soviet agreement since it felt that such an agreement would go beyond military considerations and further divide Soviet and British policy in the Balkans. Furthermore, Roosevelt professed his preference for a consultative arrangement rather than a division of zones of responsibility. Churchill replied that such an arrangement would be a "mere obstruction, always overridden in any case of emergency by direct interchanges between you and me, or either of us and Stalin." In the end, Churchill suggested trying the agreement for three months so as not to "prejudice the question of establishing post-war spheres of influence."[51] The British were strongly in favor of a spheres of influence arrangement to preserve their influence and their ability to be players on the international stage after Germany had been defeated. Although he agreed to the trial period, Roosevelt continued to oppose the British initiative. The conflict even found its way into relations between the Office of Strategic Services (OSS) and SOE operatives, with the former criticizing British policy and action in Greece. American agents' criticism of the British was so severe that British Ambassador Leeper complained to US Ambassador MacVeagh, who personally asked the US Army and OSS directors to do all they could to stop "an evil highly detrimental to allied relations."[52]

However, the issue of the Anglo-Soviet agreement on the Balkans was not yet settled. US Secretary of State Cordell Hull wrote to President Roosevelt to

---

[50] Hull to MacVeagh (24), June 10, 1944, FRUS 1944, Vol. V, The Near East, South Asia, and Africa, the Far East, pp. 116–17.
[51] Roosevelt to Churchill (557) and Churchill to Roosevelt (700 and 703), June 11, 1944, FRUS 1944, Vol. V, The Near East, South Asia, and Africa, the Far East, pp. 117–18, 123.
[52] MacVeagh to Hull (190), June 13, 1944, FRUS 1944, Vol. V, The Near East, South Asia, and Africa, the Far East, pp. 121–2.

express his department's continued opposition to this "dangerous proposal." Hull reminded the president that although the British stated that their responsibility in Greece had arisen because of their sacrifices for Greece during the military campaign of 1941, nowhere did they refer to the Greeks' sacrifices for the British. Furthermore, Hull argued that the British plan was not only for Greece and Romania but also for the entire Balkan region, and that the British were using the US position in South America as an example to justify their intention to continue with the spheres of influence approach in the Balkans. Furthermore, Hull objected because the British had discussed the proposal with the Soviet Union prior to discussing it with the United States, then presented it to the United States as a "Soviet initiative" that "arose out of a chance remark" by Eden to the American Ambassador in London. Hull advised Roosevelt to confront Churchill about these inconsistencies. Roosevelt then contacted Churchill, raising all the issues that Hull had communicated to him and stating that he hoped nothing similar would occur in future.[53] Churchill responded that not only did he not feel that he had done anything wrong, but that he was simply acting in a way that had been established by practice. He reiterated that the loss of 40,000 British soldiers in Greece in 1941 gave the British rights in Greece, that the Soviets were already in a position of prominence in Romania, and that although the Americans had given the British the lead in Turkey, Churchill had continued to advise Roosevelt of his intentions and actions there. Churchill also pointed out that Roosevelt had not consulted him regarding the message Roosevelt had "quite properly" sent to Stalin about the situation of Poland. Churchill then said that he and Roosevelt were clearly both acting unilaterally but in pursuit of winning the war, and that all Churchill had been doing in Greece (and in Yugoslavia) was persuading the resistance groups and the governments (recognized by the Allies) to work together to prevent civil war, the outbreak of which would benefit only the Germans. Finally, he stated that both the British and the Americans had to come to an agreement with the Soviets to keep the latter from continuing to support the EAM. Roosevelt's reply was short, indicating an acceptance of Churchill's arguments; he simply stated that the United States and Britain "should always be in agreement in matters bearing on our Allied war effort."[54] It was an implicit

---

[53] Hull to Roosevelt (870.00/497), June 17, 1944, and Roosevelt to Churchill (565), June 22, 1944, FRUS 1944, Vol. V, The Near East, South Asia, and Africa, the Far East, pp. 124–5.

[54] Churchill to Roosevelt (712), June 23, 1944, and Roosevelt to Churchill (570), June 26, 1944, FRUS 1944, Vol. V, The Near East, South Asia, and Africa, the Far East, pp. 125–6. See also: Memorandum to Soviet Embassy (870.00/7-144), July 15, 1944, ibid., pp. 130–1.

acceptance of the British plan because although the Americans objected to it, they were not prepared to force the British to back down.

On August 17, 1944, Churchill wrote to Roosevelt seeking to clarify Anglo-American policy toward Greece once the Germans withdrew from the country. He informed Roosevelt that it seemed "very likely" that the EAM would attempt to seize control of Greece upon German withdrawal. He advised that in order to allow the Greeks the freedom to decide between "a monarchy or a republic" and to prevent civil war and the establishment of a "tyrannical communistic government," the Allies were prepared to send troops to Athens at the time of liberation. Official British thinking was also reflected in War Cabinet papers and other documents kept in the Public Record Office at Kew. On the same day (August 17, 1944), Churchill wrote a "Personal and Top Secret" memo to US President Roosevelt to say that:

> The War Cabinet and Foreign Secretary are much concerned about what will happen in Athens, and indeed Greece, when the Germans crack or when their divisions try to evacuate the country. If there is a long hiatus after German authorities have gone from the city before organized government can be set up, it seems very likely that EAM and the Communist extremists will attempt to seize the city.[55]

Roosevelt approved the plan to send Allied troops to Greece, as well as the use of such American air transport planes as were available for the operation.[56] The Americans had, for the time being, accepted British influence in Greece and British influence over Allied policy for the country.

While this decision may have been the result of American military concerns being focused on Western Europe and the Pacific, the United States was also designing the occupation of Germany and what should be done with the German population. Roosevelt ordered the Joint Chiefs of Staff to draft a plan that "drove home" to the German people that they were responsible for the "lawless conspiracy against the decencies of modern civilization." Shortly thereafter, a directive labelled "JCS 1067" was drafted and accepted under which the military government was to "take no steps looking toward the economic rehabilitation of Germany or designed to maintain or strengthen

---

[55] Churchill to Roosevelt, August 17, 1944, War Cabinet papers, Kew.
[56] Churchill to Roosevelt (755), August 17, 1944, Roosevelt to Churchill (608), FRUS 1944, Vol. V, The Near East, South Asia, and Africa, the Far East, pp. 132–4.

the German economy."[57] However, it is important to note that the directive did not come into effect until 1946.

Meanwhile, on August 19, in response to Soviet pressure, the EAM joined the national unity government, and by the beginning of September, the Greek government in exile had flown to Italy in preparation for its return to Greece. Furthermore, all resistance groups pledged to work together against the occupying forces.[58] While all of the public statements seemed positive, the overarching strategic issues would nonetheless be settled between Churchill and Stalin alone, in Moscow.

The Percentages Agreement

Although Germany was on the defensive by October 1944, Britain, the United States, and the Soviet Union were still dependent upon each other in the alliance against the Third Reich. Stalin was concerned that the KKE's actions could disrupt the alliance and force the British and Americans to take serious action in the Balkans. Unbeknownst to the British liaison officers in Greece and the KKE, Churchill and Stalin met in Moscow in October 1944 and entered into secret negotiations over their respective spheres of influence. The plan had been in development since May 1944, and after gaining the reluctant temporary approval of the United States, Churchill proposed that the USSR would have 90 percent influence in Romania, the British would have 90 percent influence in Greece, and in Yugoslavia, the influence would be shared on a 50/50 basis. Churchill wrote these figures on a piece of paper and added "Hungary 50/50, Bulgaria, Russia 75%," and Stalin put a check mark on the paper with a blue pencil.[59]

---

[57] Quoted in: Warburg, p. 279. A notable protest against the implementation of the plan came after the war was over from the Allied general most feared by the German army, George S. Patton. In June 1945, Patton was named the occupation commander of Bavaria. He was later relieved of duty after refusing to implement JCS 1067. He believed that with Hitler gone, the German armed forces could be rebuilt and used as an ally in a potential conflict with the USSR. Patton was also highly critical of the Allies' use of German prisoners for forced labor. He commented, "I'm also opposed to sending PoWs to work as slaves in foreign lands (in particular, to France) where many will be starved to death" and "It is amusing to recall that we fought the revolution in defence of the rights of man and the civil war to abolish slavery and have now gone back on both principles." See also: Dorn, pp. 481–501, and: Dietrich, p. 127.

[58] Doc 868.01/8-1944, August 19, 1944 (281), September 2, 1944 (295), September 8, 1944, FRUS 1944, Vol. V, The Near East, South Asia, and Africa, the Far East, pp. 133–5.

[59] Gilbert, Vol. 7. See also: Record of meetings at the Kremlin, Moscow, October 9 at 10 p.m.: Foreign Office papers, 800/303, folios 227–235, pp. 991–2. See also Papastratis, pp. 199–200, and Ponting, p. 662.

The American government was not enthusiastic about Churchill's agreement with Stalin, fearing that it would lead to future confrontations over spheres of influence. Roosevelt preferred a consultative arrangement through which future actions could be discussed to dispel misunderstandings and to limit the possibility of exclusive spheres. However, as a result of British and Soviet support for the "percentages agreement," the US government reluctantly agreed to it but refused to become directly involved in Greek affairs for the remainder of the war.[60] Whether or not the percentages agreement was the embodiment of the British plan to re-establish the Empire and the people of Eastern Europe were being sacrificed for the security of British communications and access to Middle Eastern oil, and whether or not Stalin was using Greece to entice Churchill into the spheres of influence agreement, guaranteeing Soviet control of Romania, this agreement was another example of the US giving in to British demands over Greece.[61] For it to be successful, Stalin had to restrain the KKE, and since this agreement was kept secret, the KKE continued to hope in vain for significant Soviet aid.

The percentages agreement caused the British to be overconfident of their position in Greece, and they made an immediate blunder after the Moscow Conference by deciding to withdraw the SOE. The work that the SOE had done in Greece during the occupation was not enough to prevent the British government from relieving it of its duties, and in October 1944, as Churchill and Stalin were meeting in Moscow, the SOE was withdrawn from Greece.

In the process, the British government deprived itself of three years' worth of experience and detailed corporate knowledge of the political, social, and militaristic conditions in the country. Just as the labors of the SOE were beginning to yield results, the British government turned all of its operations over to an inexperienced military mission, discarding the relationships and knowledge that the SOE agents had built with resistance and community leaders alike. However, Stalin had given the British a free hand in Greece, and while British intentions were demonstrated by direct action, American and Soviet intentions were demonstrated mainly by inaction.

---

[60] Jones, pp. 22–3.
[61] Richter, pp. vii–ix.

Liberation and Confrontation

By October 1944, the Red Army had pushed the Wehrmacht out of Hungary and Yugoslavia and was well positioned to enter Greece if ordered to do so. Instead, it turned west to continue the assault on Germany, a direct result of the percentages agreement.[62] It is worth noting that Stalin had never been extremely supportive of foreign communist movements. Although he was the "de facto" head of worldwide communism as leader of the USSR, his attitude toward world revolution was "essentially lukewarm."[63] Twenty years after Stalin came to power, his sentiments had changed little. He needed the Western Allies to defeat Germany, and the KKE and its requests had to be restrained to preserve the Alliance and his hold on Eastern Europe. That is why the KKE was encouraged to participate in the Greek government of national unity and the elections but not to pursue armed struggle.[64]

The war in Europe was still raging, and even though the Germans were on the defensive, they had not yet been defeated. The Soviets also needed continued British and American support against the Germans on the Western front, and they feared that any confrontation in Greece may divert the men and material needed for that effort. For their part, the British and Americans did not want to appear overly anti-communist at this time because they needed Soviet support, particularly in the Pacific. In fact, Roosevelt's main priority prior to the successful development of the atomic bomb was to secure Soviet aid in the war against Japan.[65]

With US priorities clearly focused on the Pacific and Western Europe, the British continued to work on regaining influence in the Balkans. In July 1944, Lieutenant Grigorii Popov was dispatched by the Soviets to Greece. Although the

---

[62] Iatrides, "Revolution or Self Defence?," p. 12.
[63] Ulam, pp. 264–66. His "Socialism in One Country" speech, though Marxist / Socialist / Leninist in tone, also contradicted the "traditional" communist ideals of uniting with and relying on external communist movements to spread socialism. Stalin was determined to accelerate economic development at home, but to many communists, especially Trotsky, "socialism in one country" was an abandonment of the struggle for political revolution abroad. However, Stepehn Kotkin has corrected many of the misinterpretations of this speech. On the basis of access to archives that were closed when Ulam wrote the above interpretation, Kotkin argues that Stalin was a fully committed communist but that he also believed that it was vital to ensure socialism's success at home first, rather than jeopardizing that progress for the sake of a worldwide communist revolution. See: Kotkin, "Stalin, Vol I."
[64] *Archives of the Soviet Secret Service*, cited in, Iatrides, "Revolution or Self Defence?," p. 6.
[65] Glantz, p. 250. Stalin used this to his advantage. In a way that was analogous to his vague promises to the KKE, he made vague promises of support to the Western Allies in the struggle against Japan to encourage them to use greater resources to defeat Germany, while actually committing no Soviet resources to that purpose.

EAM/ELAS received him "joyously," it was reported to have been quite surprised when it was rebuked by the second-in-command, Lieutenant-Colonel Nikolai P. Chernichev, for not accepting the Lebanon agreement.[66] This was a small but significant indication of what Stalin expected of the Greek communists. As a result of the Popov mission and the instructions that it conveyed to the KKE, the KKE allowed the British liberation forces to land in Greece, even though it had the manpower to stop them, at least temporarily. The British landed in Piraeus in early October 1944, and the first British troops arrived in Athens on the 14th. They were followed by the Greek government on the 18th. Their immediate objective was to re-form the Greek government and to disarm all the guerrilla groups, especially ELAS, since it controlled 75 percent of the country outside Athens. From April 1944 onward, the objective of British foreign policy in Greece was to create a parliamentary democracy, and the percentages agreement provided the freedom to accomplish that goal.[67]

For the time being, British intelligence agencies continued to report on affairs in Greece but advised courses of action that they believed the British should pursue in order to achieve their strategic, economic, and geopolitical objectives. At this time, the main problem that the British faced in attempting to establish a parliamentary democracy in Greece was that only the political extremes had armed forces. The British therefore had to provide military support for the moderates in the hopes that they would be able to assume power.[68]

The Greek moderates were unsuccessful, and by December, the British were fighting the KKE in Athens. In Washington, the American attitude was to allow the British to do whatever they felt they had to, especially considering that the Germans and Japanese had not yet been defeated. In London, although there was opposition to Churchill's policies, it came mostly from back-benchers in the Labour Party. Attlee and Bevin, for their part, remained consistent in their support of Churchill.[69]

Ambassador MacVeagh commented to Secretary of State Hull that in his opinion, the main issue causing civil unrest was the continued suffering of the Greek people because of the destruction of the Greek economy. He added that

---

[66] Stavrakis, *Moscow and Greek Communism*, p. 29.
[67] Alexander, p. 245.
[68] Alexander, p. 246.
[69] Saville, p. 83, and Thorpe, p. 1078. It is important to note that despite high-level Labour Party support of British policy for Greece at this time, there was significant "lower-level" Labour Party opposition to the government's actions in Greece in December 1944. See also: Thorpe, pp. 1079–83, for numerous examples and statistics.

more problems would arise should the government fail to stabilize the currency or enforce the "strict price and other financial regulations" on which Greek economic stabilization depended, and that General Scobie had thus far proved unable to control "demonstrations in the city or [to ensure] order and public safety."[70] Therefore, from the point at which Greece was liberated, the Americans were well aware of both the British plans for the country and the obstacles to the implementation of those plans.

Anglo-American Policy During the December Uprising

The tensions observed in Lebanon and blamed for its failure boiled over in Athens in December 1944. The *Dekemvriana*, or December events, regardless of their actual cause, pointed toward what lay in store for Greece after the war had ended.

The Battle for Athens took place between December 3, 1944 and January 17, 1945, and has been described as evidence of Churchill's planned counter-revolution in Greece.[71] It is worth remembering that Greece was an important political symbol for both the Labour and Conservative Parties in Britain from December 1944 to February 1945,[72] as it would be again for the Americans from December 1946 to June 1948. These two critical periods illustrate the divergence of opinion regarding what Greece represented. For the Conservatives, Greece was a symbol of the pre-war status quo that they wished to restore, but for the Labour Party it was symbolic of the war's failure to move society toward a new era of democratic socialism.[73] It was also a very important issue for the Labour Party in Britain, which viewed the conflict as an opportunity for British communists to lure "grass-roots" Labour support away from the Labour Party. From December 1944 until the end of the conflict in January, the Labour Party, apart from its members who were part of the cabinet, saw the conflict as an attack upon the post-war socialist ideals-based societies (both British and Greek) that they hoped would be established in their respective countries. They saw that Labour values were incompatible with communist values, but it was a difficult political position to maintain publicly, particularly given their support

---

[70] MacVeagh to Hull (14), November 9, 1944, FRUS 1944, Vol. V, The Near East, South Asia and Africa, the Far East, pp. 136–7.
[71] Woodhouse, *Apple of Discord*, p. 224. For counter-revolution, see: Saville, "Ernest Bevin," pp. 82–4.
[72] Thorpe, p. 1085.
[73] Thorpe, p. 1086.

from trade unions in Britain.[74] Additionally, as had happened numerous times before, events beyond Greece's borders diverted attention from events taking place in the country.

In Western Europe, on December 16, 1944, the course of the Second World War was altered by an unexpected German offensive in the Ardennes, and the British could not press their advantage in Greece. The German campaign overran thousands of Allied troops and captured or destroyed tons of military material. After the D-Day landings in June, the Allies had believed that the war would be over by Christmas, but the Battle of the Bulge extended the war for another six months. For Greece, the result was that overnight, the fighting in Athens "took a backseat" to the fighting in France, and British material and attention were diverted from Greece back to Western Europe. The fighting in Athens therefore lasted much longer than it would have done otherwise. Perhaps what is most significant about this conflict is that it made the British believe that the KKE was determined to seize power in Greece, and it proved to the KKE that it could not hope to do so without substantial amounts of foreign aid.[75]

The American assessment of the conflict, as expressed by Ambassador MacVeagh, was that the majority of the combatants with the EAM/ELAS were actually patriots who had joined out of a misguided fear that the Greek government intended to restore the king (whom they held personally responsible for the Metaxas dictatorship) and a fascist government by force. The other side feared that the EAM/ELAS would install a communist dictatorship. MacVeagh stated that the mutual suspicion was being exploited by "enemy agents and subversive propaganda" but was "too profound and too firmly sealed by the blood which has now been shed" to be solved by any "purely Greek initiative."[76] Therefore, although he had previously stated that the United States position of non-interference had benefited the US image, he seemed to be advising the State Department to support continued British intervention in virtually all aspects of Greek life. In response to MacVeagh's report, the State Department issued a declaration to be published in the communist newspaper *Rizopastis*. It stated that, in line with the United States policy to refrain from any interference in the internal affairs of other nations, the United States had "scrupulously" refrained from interfering in the affairs of nations liberated from the Germans and that

---

[74] Thorpe, pp. 1092–3.
[75] Iatrides, "Revolution or Self-Defense," p. 10. For a detailed account of this conflict see: Iatrides, "Revolt In Athens."
[76] MacVeagh to Hull (132), December 8, 1944, FRUS 1944, Vol. V, The Near East, South Asia and Africa, the Far East, p. 145.

unless the military security of the Allied struggle against Germany was at stake, the United States would continue its policy of non-interference.[77]

However, despite this strong statement, the State Department communicated with President Roosevelt regarding the proposal for a joint Anglo-American and Soviet committee to mediate a solution in Greece or for the United States to take a more active role.[78] Roosevelt responded directly to Churchill and said that although he was sympathetic with the situation in Greece, he was subject to public sentiment. That sentiment was increasingly averse to the British role in Greece and to the traditional US policy of non-interference, and it was "not possible for this government to take a stand along with you in the present course of events in Greece." The advice that Roosevelt offered was for the British to encourage King George to form a regency and for elections to be set for a fixed date so that the Greek people would know that they would have the opportunity to express themselves freely.[79]

As the fighting continued, Churchill wrote to Roosevelt, thanking him for his moral support and stating that the British would continue to fight, for if they were to leave there would no doubt be a "frightful massacre" and a left-wing dictatorship would be installed. He also informed Roosevelt that the cabinet was not prepared to withdraw British forces and that Ernest Bevin had made a speech to the Labour conference (which had been highly critical of the British government's role in the conflict) that had won "universal respect." Churchill then proposed that the best solution was to have Archbishop Damaskinos appointed as regent.[80]

Ambassador MacVeagh responded positively to this suggestion, informing the State Department that not only had the most prominent members of the Greek government endorsed it, despite the opposition of the Greek king, but Damaskinos felt that he could work with the EAM/ELAS. MacVeagh urged the State Department to support the British and Damaskinos to bring a swift end to the fighting.[81] The State Department's reply, though not overly explicit in

---

[77] Stetinius to MacVeagh (114), December 12, 1944, FRUS 1944, Vol. V, The Near East, South Asia and Africa, the Far East, pp. 147–8.

[78] Stetinius to Roosevelt (768.00/12-1344), December 13, 1944, and Stetinius to Roosevelt (868.00/12-1344), December 13, 1944, FRUS 1944, Vol. V, The Near East, South Asia and Africa, the Far East, pp. 148–50.

[79] Roosevelt to Churchill (673), December 13, 1944, FRUS 1944, Vol. V, The Near East, South Asia and Africa, the Far East, pp. 150–1.

[80] Churchill to Roosevelt (851), December 15, 1944, FRUS 1944, Vol. V, The Near East, South Asia and Africa, the Far East, pp. 155–6.

[81] MacVeagh to Stettinius (150), December 15, 1944, FRUS 1944, Vol. V, The Near East, South Asia and Africa, the Far East, p. 156. Damaskinos promised a general amnesty, a re-formed and fully representational government, and no retaliation from the British should ELAS lay down its weapons.

its approval, described the proposal as "most promising" and in close parallel with the State Department's plans that had already been "communicated to the British."[82] The State Department also recommended United States participation in the supervision of elections in Greece should the British and Soviets also be involved.[83]

On 26 December, the KKE's leaders attended preliminary peace talks. However, after two days of discussion, Archbishop Damaskinos was nominated as regent, and the EAM representative, General Siantos, said that the EAS would accept the appointment of "generally respected but non-political personalities," such as General Plastiras.[84] Churchill spoke with MacVeagh and asked him to convey to Roosevelt that the British wanted nothing from Greece but "a fair share of her trade" and that neither Greek airfields nor ports were desired since "we've got Cyprus anyhow." Churchill ended by saying that the British wanted no more than to "get out of this damned place."[85] This statement was contradicted by future British actions. The Americans also contradicted their policy of non-interference.

On 28 December 1944, Roosevelt wrote to King George and urged him to accept the proposal to nominate Archbishop Damaskinos (who had been personally recommended by Churchill) as regent and to affirm that elections would be held on a fixed date.[86] On December 29, Churchill returned to England in an attempt to convince the Greek king to accept the creation of a regency, which he succeeded in doing after threatening to recognize the new Greek government instead of King George. Churchill thanked Roosevelt for his support and asked for the president's continued support for the Damaskinos government.[87]

By 17 January, most of the fighting had subsided, and the British attempted to stabilize the shattered Greek economy and infrastructure. Throughout the initial stages of the British clash with ELAS, the press in the USA and

---

[82] Stettinius to MacVeagh (124), December 16, 1944, FRUS 1944, Vol. V, The Near East, South Asia and Africa, the Far East, p. 158.
[83] Lot 122, Secretary's Staff Committee Documents 1–45, December 22, 1944, FRUS 1944, Vol. V, The Near East, South Asia and Africa, the Far East, p. 165.
[84] MacVeagh to Stettinius (189), December 27, 1944, FRUS 1944, Vol. V, The Near East, South Asia and Africa, the Far East, pp. 171–2.
[85] MacVeagh to Stettinius (190), December 27, 1944, FRUS 1944, Vol. V, The Near East, South Asia and Africa, the Far East, pp. 172–3.
[86] Roosevelt to King George of the Hellenes, December 18, 1944, FRUS 1944, Vol. V, The Near East, South Asia and Africa, the Far East, p. 177.
[87] Churchill to Roosevelt (863 and 864), December 29 and 30, 1944, FRUS 1944, Vol. V, The Near East, South Asia and Africa, the Far East, p. 178.

Britain was extremely critical of Churchill and the British army for repressing what they believed was a popular movement that had heroically resisted the German occupation. However, once reports of mass abductions and killings and photographs of dead bodies began to circulate, that support diminished.[88] In Britain, some Labour Party MPs were extremely critical of the Greek government, referring to Plastiras as "reactionary" and the Greek government as "totally unrepresentative" and harbouring "monstrous aims" of continuing the conflict. On January 15, 1945, two days before the fighting ended, in a meeting with Churchill, a member of the Labour delegation, Jim Griffiths, described the importance of Greece to the Labour Party and the party's vision for the post-war world: "it was immediately [about] the situation in Greece, but it is much more than that," referring to how the post-war world would be structured.[89]

By the end of January, the attention that the Greek conflict had been receiving was diminishing; the bad press that the EAM/ELAS had been given for its treatment of prisoners during the *Dekemvriana* forced the rest of the Labour Party (i.e., those not in the cabinet with Bevin and who had previously been highly critical of the British government) to join the government in its condemnation of the EAM/ELAS and vindicated many of Churchill's statements and policies.[90] The situation in Greece also had the benefit of further cementing the Anglo-US relationship. Illustrating the deepening relationship between Washington and London, in February 1945, the US State Department noted that the US Embassy in London had become one of the "largest and most important offices" overseas.[91] This view led to a steady increase in embassy staff numbers in the early post-war years, and the embassy played a key role in the formation of US-British policy going forward.[92]

---

[88] Woodhouse, *The Struggle for Greece*, p. 135, and Ryan, pp. 139–45. See also: Winant to Stettinius (451), January 13, 1945, FRUS 1945, Vol. VIII, The Near East and Africa, p. 103, and MacVeagh to Stettinius (70), January 19, 1945, FRUS 1945, Vol. VIII, The Near East and Africa, p. 107.

[89] Labour delegation to Prime Minister, January 15, 1945, quoted in: Thorpe, p. 1105. Emphasis and brackets added. The situation in Greece was about the present, but it was also about the future of socialism in Britain.

[90] Thorpe, pp. 1097–8, and Thorpe, p. 1095, citing Labour Party records from various electoral ridings.

[91] National Archives and Record Administration (NARA II), College Park MD, Record Group (RG) 59, Records of the Office of British Commonwealth and Northern European Affairs, 1941–1953, Lot 54D224, Box 22, "Information for the Survey Group Proceeding to London," February 24, 1945.

[92] Coleman, pp. 339, 360.

The Varkiza Accord

In much the same way as was expected after the signing of the Lebanon accord, the British hoped that Varkiza would mark the end of armed uprisings in Greece. British policy in Greece at this time was therefore focused on establishing a government that included members of the country's moderate political groups, and the British hoped that the Varkiza accord would help accomplish that objective. One of the first conditions of the treaty required the EAM/ELAS to surrender its weapons in order to be able to participate in the political process. Partial clemency for those who had participated in the December uprising, the formation of a new non-political Greek Army, an Allied-supervised plebiscite, and, crucially, elections to follow within a year were also included in the treaty.[93]

In a discussion at the British Embassy in Athens on February 15, 1945, Ambassador Leeper claimed that the Varkiza accord represented the vindication of British foreign policy in Greece despite the criticism that the British had been subjected to both at home and abroad. This sense of optimism and vindication was echoed in a speech that Churchill delivered the same day. He spoke of Greece's bright future and said that the efforts of the British and Greek governments had been misunderstood in many parts of the world.[94] Eden also delivered a short speech expressing his belief that Greece had found internal peace, unity, and strength. The ambassador, prime minister, and foreign secretary were anxious to close this chapter and focus on defeating Germany.

By early 1945, conditions seemed to be right for Greece to begin to overcome its social schism and recover from the effects of the occupation. The optimism that the British expressed officially was mirrored by the EAM after the Varkiza accord, and it seemed that the KKE was finally prepared to participate in the new Greek government. On February 15, 1945, the ELAS Central Committee ordered the demobilization of its remaining forces while reminding its "fellow fighters" to remain vigilant to ensure that the government honored the articles of the Varkiza accord.[95] Just before Churchill returned to Britain, the Central Committee of the EAM sent a message thanking him for his role in the ceasefire and pledged to work for peace and reconciliation in Greece: "counting on

---

[93] Leeper to Eden, (Doc R 3056/4/19), February 7, 1945, BDFA, Series F Europe, Part III, Vol. 25, 1945, pp. 72–5. At Varkiza, the British agreed to hold the plebiscite before the elections, but they later reversed that decision. See also: Woodhouse, *Apple of Discord*, pp. 229–30.
[94] Leeper to Eden (R 3559/4/G), February 15, 1945, BDFA, Series F Europe, Part III, Vol. 25, pp. 75–8 and (R 4224/4/, 19), ibid., p. 87.
[95] EAM (National Liberation Front), *The White Book*: "Document No. 118," pp. 120–1.

Great Britain's aid we shall struggle for our country's immediate and complete restoration." Not long afterwards, however, the likelihood of Varkiza meeting its lofty objectives was seen to be diminishing. Ambassador MacVeagh advised the State Department that the KKE was already rebuilding its "cells" in Athens, forming an organization to subvert the Greek armed forces, impeding government authority and preserving the military and political aspects of its "revolutionary machine."[96]

The likelihood of an immediately peaceful future for Greece was challenged again on March 3, 1945, when the EAM Central Committee sent a letter to the Greek government and to American Ambassador MacVeagh complaining that the articles of the Varkiza accord were not being honoured.[97] Prior to the signing of the treaty, the main threat to the British objective of establishing a parliamentary democracy in Greece had come from the left. However, once the accord had been signed, the main threat came from the forces of the right. While confronting the left had been a straightforward objective for the British government, confronting the right was far more complicated. KKE members were relatively easy to identify, but members of the extreme right were not. The right dominated the armed forces, the civil services and the government, and the British could not remove them without dismantling the state machinery that they had been attempting to rebuild.[98] Therefore, as the communists were recovering from the defeat of ELAS in Athens, the British attempted to work with the Plastiras government, but extreme right forces began to undermine the Varkiza accord, mainly by increasing their attacks—both physical and ideological—on the left.

In London, various Labour MPs who had been critical of Churchill's policy in Greece, nonetheless supported the prime minister over the Americans' criticism. However, both the British and the Greek government found it insulting that the Americans had taken such a critical stance when they were not involved themselves and were not sharing the burden in Greece.[99] There was also concern that the Plastiras government might be unable to fully implement the Varkiza accord and, as a result, would delay the economic measures that were needed to avoid another financial crisis.[100] However, although Soviet pressure on the

---

[96] MacVeagh to Stettinius (185), February 16, 1945, FRUS 1945, Vol. VIII, The Near East and Africa, pp. 115–16.
[97] MacVeagh to Stettinius (256), March 10, 1945, FRUS 1945, Vol. VIII, The Near East and Africa, pp. 116–18.
[98] Kirk to Stettinius (882), March 8, 1945, FRUS 1945, Vol. VIII, The Near East and Africa, p. 116. See also: Alexander, p. 247.
[99] Thorpe, p. 1097.
[100] Winant to Stettinius (2630), March 14, 1945, FRUS 1945, Vol. VIII, The Near East and Africa, pp. 119–20.

British to begin to withdraw their troops from Greece was mounting, MacVeagh advised that it was better for them to stay, at least for the time being, to prevent destabilization.[101]

The British also damaged the perception of the Varkiza accord as the roadmap to peace in post-war Greece when Ambassador Leeper recommended that the plebiscite should be delayed in light of the current instability and the intense ongoing debates in the Greek government over the constitution. He informed the Foreign Office that a premature plebiscite could be detrimental to the parties that supported the return of the monarchy and that it would be wise to delay it until the people were in a more "normal" state of mind, capable of viewing the future of their country with less "jaundiced eyes."[102] This was the first significant shift in British policy since the signing of the Varkiza accord, reflecting the domestic volatility in Greece.

Already suspicious of the lack of control over mounting right-wing attacks against it, the KKE perceived this shift as another signal that the Varkiza accord might not be honored.[103] An analysis of the dispatches regarding this issue shows that the British desire to reverse the previously agreed order was based on the perceived risk that a prematurely held plebiscite could pose beyond Greece's borders. The plebiscite would be a vote for the type of state that the Greek people wished to have (a republic or a constitutional monarchy), and if elections were held first, they would represent a de facto recognition of the pre-existing system.[104]

The ability of the British to deal effectively with the growing tension in Greece was undermined once again by developments on the international front. The USSR, having been invaded twice in the previous thirty years through Poland and needing it as a buffer state, invaded and occupied it on March 15, 1945.[105] This increased Anglo-American suspicion of the Soviet Union and focused US attention on communist action in Greece.

However, the American assessment of conditions in Greece was still based largely on British reports; the US held that any activity in which it engaged regarding the supervision of the plebiscite and elections would be very difficult

---

[101] Kirk to Stettinius (946), March 12, 1945, FRUS 1945, Vol. VIII, The Near East and Africa, pp. 118–119.
[102] Leeper to Foreign Office (R 5105/4/19), March 17, 1945, BDFA, Series F Europe, Part III, Vol. 25, 1945, p. 89. As a result of the atrocities that ELAS had committed against the people of Athens at the end of December 1944, many Athenians viewed the return of the monarchy as their only defense against the communists. See also: Alexander, pp. 92–6.
[103] Gardner, pp. 225–30.
[104] For a full analysis of the decision to reverse the order of the elections and plebiscite, see: Paravantes: "A Tale of Two Referenda."
[105] Gardner, pp. 225–30.

given the current widespread political and social divisions in the country. International conditions were also affected by Soviet policy toward Eastern Europe and Poland, and by American plans for Germany.[106] Oscar Cox, General Counsel of the Lend-Lease Administration, commented in Washington on the situation in Greece: "Already, for example, as you are well aware, some of the people on the Hill are asking why lend-lease supplies should be used to kill some of our Greek friends."[107]

Even members of the American Congress were taking notes and becoming critical of how the British were handling affairs in Greece. Internationally, the USA was giving signs that the wartime alliance was dead, cutting off lend-lease to the Soviets on the day that Germany surrendered and to the British shortly thereafter.[108] On May 10, 1945, Truman signed JCS 1067. Those responsible for its implementation ensured that JCS 1067 was interpreted as strictly as possible to reduce the German standard of living and began the process of stripping Germany of what was left of its industry.[109] While the economy of the Western occupation zones of Germany temporarily stabilized at the end of June 1945, the British also succeeded in persuading the United States to share responsibility for the supervision of the Greek plebiscite and elections.

The British also advised that the Greek government should invite the Soviets to participate in Greece so as to encourage the USSR to invite the British and Americans to supervise elections in Soviet-controlled countries. However, the British believed that the Soviets would refuse to participate for the very reason that they did not desire Anglo-American participation in elections in the territories they controlled.[110] Two days later, the Soviets replied that Allied supervision of the Greek elections constituted interference in Greek internal affairs, but the United States said that based on the Yalta Declaration, it was part of its (and the Allied) duty to supervise elections in recently liberated countries to guarantee free and fair elections.[111] This exchange was another sign that the wartime alliance was breaking down.

---

[106] British aide-mémoire to Stettinius (868.00/6-1645), April 24, 1945, FRUS 1945, Vol. VIII, The Near East and Africa, pp. 126–8.
[107] Gardner, p. 218, quoting: "Cox to Hopkins, December 19th 1944."
[108] Childs, pp. 554–5.
[109] Petrov, pp. 228–9. Petrov further concludes that the Allies "delayed by several years the economic reconstruction of the war torn continent, a reconstruction which subsequently cost the U.S. billions of dollars."
[110] British Embassy to US State Department, June 27, 1945, FRUS 1945, Vol. VIII, The Near East and Africa, p. 128.
[111] "US participation in the supervision of Greek elections" (868.00/6-2945), June 29, 1945, FRUS 1945, Vol. VIII, The Near East and Africa, pp. 128–30.

Although the Soviets had signed the Yalta Declaration, from this point on they would refuse to honor its commitments to Central and Eastern Europe with regard to holding elections.[112] Furthermore, after the death of FDR on 12 April 1945, the new American president, Harry Truman, adopted a more rigid stance in opposition to the Soviets than that of his predecessor, and he moved United States policy closer to that of Britain. In a memorandum sent to President Truman on 4 July 1945, new Secretary of State James F. Byrnes endorsed US participation in the supervision of elections in Greece with or without the full participation of the Yalta signatories and suggested that perhaps France should also be invited by the Greek government to supervise the elections.[113] The State Department then sent a message to the British Embassy in Washington to advise the British of US participation in the Greek elections and to affirm that the United States did not consider Allied supervision of the elections to constitute interference, as the Soviets had asserted.[114]

By ensuring that Greece could sustain itself and that the communists could not assume power by force, the British would be able to retain Greece as a sphere of influence without having to maintain a strong (and expensive) military presence there. However, these few months were the last period of the Churchill government's foreign policy decisions for Greece.

Throughout the course of the war, Churchill had dedicated himself to doing everything in his power to defeat Germany. Flying around the world, meeting with Allies, and formulating Allied policy had left him little time to deal with domestic issues in England. He had entrusted that responsibility to his Labour Party Deputy Prime Minister, Clement Attlee.[115] Since autumn 1944, the British Parliament had been setting its sights on an election in 1945 once Germany had been defeated.[116] The coalition government, which had set aside political differences to unite the country to fight the Axis, had begun to splinter once the defeat of the Third Reich appeared imminent. One of Churchill's last acts as prime minister was to advise President Truman to use the atomic bomb to end the war in the Pacific, but before he could play a more major role in the Potsdam Conference, he was replaced by Clement Attlee. This change, combined with a

---

[112] This will be shown in the rest of the book.
[113] Byrnes to Truman (868.00/7-445), July 4, 1945, FRUS 1945, Vol. VIII, The Near East and Africa, pp. 130–1.
[114] State Department to British Embassy (868.00/6-1645), July 5, 1945, FRUS 1945, Vol. VIII, The Near East and Africa, pp. 132–3.
[115] Harris, p. 244.
[116] Pelling, p. 548.

new president in the United States and rising tension between the Soviet Union and the West, meant that a shift in world politics was imminent.

New Players at the Table: Truman and Attlee Take Over

In Greece, the KKE hoped that after the British elections, British foreign policy would become more accommodating to them. When Labour Party leader Clement Attlee replaced Churchill as prime minister, many in both Greece and Britain expected British-Soviet-Greek relations to improve.[117] KKE Secretary-General Zachariadis was quoted in the official KKE outlet *Rizospastis* as saying that "the British elections will change the system of (foreign) intervention."[118] However, the publicly expected pro-left shift did not occur with Attlee's election and the new Labour government, and British policy in Greece actually became even more hostile to the Greek communists. This occurred not only because of international developments but also because the status of the EAM/ELAS as an ally had been granted by the previous British administration. With the change in government, there may have been less pressure to adhere to wartime agreements.

The hostility to the KKE was also bred out of the realities of what the Second World War had done to Europe. France had been deeply divided by the German occupation. Germany had been defeated and left broken and defenseless. Italy was bankrupt, Eastern Europe was rapidly being swept into the Soviet sphere of influence, and the new Labour government in Britain believed that it was in British interests to participate in the anti-communist rebuilding of Western Europe.[119]

Greece therefore became even more important to the British as a means of supporting their strategic interests in the Eastern Mediterranean. But this meant that the "special relationship" between Britain and the United States had to be expertly manipulated so that the USA would also support British objectives in the Eastern Mediterranean. The new British Foreign Secretary, Ernest Bevin, would continue to encourage a significant level of British involvement in American policy decisions.

Bevin had grown up in poverty, led trade unions, and been Minister of Labor during the war, and although he was characterized by others and himself as a socialist, he had no love for communists.[120] During the war,

---

[117] Morgan, p. 47.
[118] Norton to Foreign Office, July 1945 (R 13134/4/19), BDFA, Series F Europe, Part III, Vol. 26, p. 44.
[119] Morgan, pp. 233–4.
[120] Murphy, pp. 222–3. Murphy wrote of Bevin, "He never forgets that he belongs to the working class and to the people with whom he has worked."

Bevin had been outspoken in his support of the Churchill government's policy of opposing the EAM/ELAS movement in Greece. He was also a supporter of the Commonwealth and of a British military and economic presence in the Middle East.[121] To secure British access to Persia through the Suez Canal, a non-communist Greece was important, and it offered the added bonus of having the potential to cut the Soviets off from the Mediterranean if the need arose. In mid- to late 1945, Bevin increased British involvement in Greece with the objective of maintaining a British presence in Europe. However, as conditions worsened in both Greece and Britain, he sought a policy that would solve the two countries' economic difficulties without compromising their national security interests. His chosen course of action was to maneuver the United States into assuming responsibility for Greece. This would take some work since in the summer of 1945, although Greece was vitally important to the British, it was less so for the United States.

The Americans' main concern was now the defeat of Japan, and even after the Japanese surrender on September 2, they remained focused on the Pacific theatre. The new threat looming for the United States in the Pacific was the possibility of a communist China, as Mao Tse-tung was embroiled in a civil war against the nationalist Chiang Kai-shek. Soon after the armistice with Japan was signed, the United States began to focus on rebuilding the Japanese economy and government. Following the Allied example of rebuilding efforts in Western Europe to oppose communist expansion, the United States government believed that the most effective barrier to communism in the Pacific would be an economically powerful Japan.[122] While these developments diverted American attention away from Greece at the time, the communist threat in the Pacific would ultimately aid the British in securing greater American involvement in European affairs.

The post-war administration of Harry Truman was operating quite differently from the wartime administration of Roosevelt,[123] and Stalin appeared to be comfortable with allowing events to unfold on their own.

---

[121] Morgan, pp. 235–6.

[122] Morgan, p. 234.

[123] Glantz, pp. 1, 179–80. In order to implement his policies toward the Soviets, which often met with fierce resistance from the various bureaucracies in his administration, FDR had reorganized the key departments that dealt with the USSR. But by summer 1945, the reorganized departments were being replaced by a new bureaucracy that was determined to stand against further Soviet expansion. This shift occurred for many reasons, primarily US support for global "open door" trade, a shift in public opinion against the USSR, and Soviet action in the Middle East and Eastern Europe.

Although a communist Greece would have been beneficial, Stalin was not willing to jeopardize his claim to Eastern Europe by provoking the Allies and openly helping the KKE. Therefore, from the Popov mission in early 1944 to September 1945, he continually advised the Greek communists to participate in the elections and in the government, and he answered their repeated requests for weapons and other supplies with vague statements of future support, giving them enough hope to keep fighting but not enough resources to actually sustain their efforts.[124] On the other side, the British, who had promised and delivered weapons and funds for Greece in the past, were experiencing increasingly severe financial and material hardships and would be able to offer no promises for the future for Greece; moreover, the ongoing conflict in the country was a major risk to the significant investments, both economic and political, that Britain had made in the Greek government. A solution was needed to protect those investments and to secure British interests.

---

[124] Iatrides, "Revolution or Self-Defence?," pp. 18–20.

2

The Aftermath of Varkiza and Inter-Allied Confrontations

Although Article 9 of the Varkiza accord provided for Allied assistance in holding elections in Greece, the Soviets refused to accept Allied participation. As a result, the US State Department recommended proceeding with British and American supervision, notifying the French and Greek governments to secure their approval and keeping the Soviets fully informed of all developments.[1] This recommendation was an important development for the British, since by the end of the summer of 1945, elements of the American government seemed intent upon freeing the US from its wartime alliance with Britain, leaving the UK to face an expanding USSR alone. As a result, the Labour government was looking for an issue that would keep the United States involved in European affairs. However, it was difficult for the British government to reconcile British public opinion, which at the time desired close relations with the USSR, and American political opinion, which was beginning to perceive the USSR as an increasing threat.[2] These tensions were exposed at the Potsdam Conference (July 16 to August 2, 1945), when the Allies were unable to come to an agreement regarding German the Second World War reparations. They merely agreed that reparations would be taken from Germany, and they addressed the issue of the surrender of Germany and Japan.

These international conditions began to take the shine off the idea that "socialist ideals" could bridge the gap between Britain and the USSR or, when it came to affairs in Greece, convince the Communist Party (KKE) and its affiliates to participate in the Greek government. After the British election

---

[1] Byrnes to Winant, UK (6704), August 9, 1945, FRUS 1945, Vol. VIII, The Near East and Africa, pp. 134–5.
[2] Anstey, p. 435.

held in summer 1945, Winston Churchill and Anthony Eden were replaced by Clement Attlee and Ernest Bevin, and whereas Atlee had, at least officially, been attempting to extricate the UK from Greek affairs, Bevin decided to commit more resources to maintaining Greece in the British sphere of influence. The year 1945 would therefore be one of extreme turmoil for Greece. Britain's policy decisions of 1945 were taken against a backdrop of Soviet aggression and expansion, and UK officials would have to decide whether to expend the resources necessary to stabilize Greece against the rising violence that was taking place.

The "White Terror" drove many members of ELAS (the Greek People's Liberation Army) and left-wingers into the mountains, where they banded together for protection. The British Ambassador to Greece, Reginald Leeper, believed the only solution was for the British to assume executive power in Greece because, in his view, the country was incapable of generating the type of leadership necessary to help it deal with the ongoing cycles of violence and crisis. As the Labour government came to power in August 1945, it implemented a policy that attempted to combine the non-intervention advocated by Churchill and the assumption of control favored by Leeper.[3] The Churchill administration's support of the Greek monarchy had stemmed from the king's staunch loyalty to Britain at the beginning of the war, but Bevin's support of the monarchy was more linked with the post-war economic and social realities that he was facing. In a memorandum that he presented to the cabinet on August 14, 1945, Bevin stated that it was vital for the British to maintain their influence in Greece to safeguard their strategic interests in the Middle East.[4] Later in August, at the Labour government's first foreign policy debate in the House of Commons, former British Foreign Secretary Anthony Eden clearly demonstrated that Bevin supported the Churchill government's policies:

Eden: During that period, there were many discussions on foreign affairs. I cannot recall one single occasion when there was a difference between us. I hope I do not embarrass the Foreign Secretary when I say that.
Bevin: No.
Eden: There were no differences on any important issues of foreign policy.[5]

---

[3] Alexander, p. 248.
[4] Alexander, p. 129.
[5] Cabinet Papers, "Foreign Policy Debate," London, August 1945.

Eden went on record regarding the similarities between the new Labour Foreign Secretary and the previous Conservative government. For those who had expected a change in British dealings with communists, both in Greece and abroad, this statement demonstrated how closely aligned Bevin was with Churchill's policy and foreshadowed how he would shape policy in the future. On August 11, 1945, Bevin went on record as follows: "We must maintain our position in Greece as a part of our Middle East policy and unless it is asserted and settled it may have a bad effect on the whole of our Middle East position."[6]

Bevin's biographer, Alan Bullock, states that there were two main reasons for his consistency with Churchill's policy. First, the Foreign Office was still full of the officials who had staffed it during the war, and second, Bevin was known for his constant and long-standing anti-communism.[7] So Bevin's consistency with Churchill's policies continued, even as foreign observers, including some from the United States, complained that the right-wing forces in Greece were being allowed to consolidate their power and attack the Greek left.[8]

In spite of the ongoing violence in Greece and criticism of British policy there, the British and Americans moved forward with plans for elections in the country. The British pushed the United States to agree to the elections being held before the plebiscite and to the two governments simultaneously issuing similar statements about their role as supervisory powers. On August 18, 1945, the Greek government officially approved the supervision of the elections by the Allied powers.[9] The US Secretary of State James F. Byrnes then sent a telegram to the Soviet Foreign Office stating that as a result of the Crimea and Potsdam conferences, the United States had agreed to assume responsibility for assisting "the Greek people to express their will freely at the polls." Byrnes also expressed "US government regret that the Soviet government could not see its way clear to participate," but added that he hoped that the Soviets would "adopt a friendly attitude toward this duty being undertaken by three of its Allies."[10] This period

---

[6] Bevin Cabinet Paper, August 11, 1945, CAB 093 3645.
[7] Alan Bullock, *Ernest Bevin, Foreign Secretary, 1945–1951*. 3 vols (London: Heinmann, 1983), Vol. 3, p. 160.
[8] Saville, pp. 18–19.
[9] Telegrams between Foreign Office and Department of State, August 13 to 18, 1945, FRUS 1945, Vol. VIII, The Near East and Africa, pp. 141–43. MacVeagh also informed Secretary Byrnes that the few communist and EAM (National Liberation Front) representatives who had been part of the Greek government had begun to resign. This was possibly because of the Soviet government's refusal to participate in the supervision of the Greek elections and may have been interpreted as a sign that the Soviets would assist these representatives, at least indirectly, by not supporting the current government or the Anglo-American plans for Greece.
[10] Byrnes to Harriman, USSR (1861), August 18, 1945, FRUS 1945, Vol. VIII, The Near East and Africa, p. 143.

marked an important change in relations among the Big Three, as it was over the issue of Allied supervision of the Greek elections that the United States took an anti-Soviet position and aligned itself fully with Britain. Although the language used by Byrnes was conciliatory and hopeful, from this point on the Americans would gradually align themselves much more closely with British policy, through a combination of British pressure and rising Soviet intransigence.

On August 23, 1945, the Soviet newspaper *Izvestiya* (News) printed a column regarding the proposed Allied observation of the Greek elections. The newspaper asserted that any observation in fact constituted control of and interference in the domestic affairs of foreign nations and that the Soviet refusal to participate was based on Soviet foreign policy of "respect for other states large or small" and "faith in democratic forces and rights of people, whether they be small or large." The column argued that Britain had imperialistic designs upon Greece since it was a key strategic point for access to the Eastern Mediterranean and the Suez Canal.

The Soviets asserted that the Americans had misinterpreted Allied responsibilities to liberated countries (as outlined by the Yalta Conference, also known as the Crimea Conference): since the conditions outlined in the Yalta communiqué for the establishment of democratic institutions did not exist in Greece, the observation of elections there "corresponded neither in letter nor in spirit to the Crimea declaration." In conclusion, the Soviet editorial stated that the duty of the Allies was to ensure that the conditions for democratic elections existed, and once that was accomplished, supervision would be unnecessary.[11] On August 28, 1945, again using the Soviet media, the Soviet government publicly rejected any participation in the supervision of elections.[12]

---

[11] Harriman, USSR, to Byrnes (3015), August 23, 1945, FRUS 1945, Vol. VIII, The Near East and Africa, pp. 148–9. The Yalta communiqué (February 1945) stated: "The establishment of order in Europe and the rebuilding of national economic life must be achieved by processes which will enable the liberated peoples to destroy the last vestiges of Nazism and fascism and to create democratic institutions of their own choice. This is a principle of the Atlantic Charter – the right of all people to choose the form of government under which they will live – the restoration of sovereign rights and self-government to those peoples who have been forcibly deprived of them by the aggressor nations. To foster the conditions in which the liberated people may exercise these rights, the three governments will jointly assist the people in any European liberated state or former Axis state in Europe where, in their judgment conditions require them, (a) to establish conditions of internal peace; (b) to carry out emergency relief measures for the relief of distressed peoples; (c) to form interim governmental authorities broadly representative of all democratic elements in the population and pledged to the earliest possible establishment through free elections of Governments responsive to the will of the people; and (d) to facilitate where necessary the holding of such elections."

[12] Harriman, USSR, to Byrnes (3090), August 28, 1945, FRUS 1945, Vol. VIII, The Near East and Africa, p. 150.

Meanwhile, in September 1945, there was rising domestic pressure for the Labour government to extricate Britain from Greece. However, as a result of Soviet involvement in Poland and US involvement in Italy, Bevin still believed that British presence in Greece was crucial for Britain to maintain its position in the post-war world order. Attlee and Bevin, committed Labour Party socialists with a Labour Party bureaucracy behind them, saw elections as a possible solution to their problems in Greece, which, if solved, could allow them to reduce their military commitments in Greece and help them to deal with the Soviet Union.[13] However, since Greece was once again in the throes of a massive economic crisis, the issue of holding the plebiscite before the elections was under review. Secretary Byrnes urged the US Ambassador to Greece, Lincoln MacVeagh, to meet with Archbishop Damaskinos—regent of Greece—and to "discuss most confidentially" with him the idea of holding the plebiscite after the elections, despite the provision in the Varkiza accord that the plebiscite would be held first. Byrnes said that for some time, the State Department had felt that "Greek political stability" would benefit from first installing a representative government, which could then itself "prepare questions for submission to [the] Greek people in [a] plebiscite." Although he explained that the United States did not wish to dictate to or manipulate the Greek government, he felt that such a suggestion might help the regent to "crystallize Greek thinking into some formula acceptable to most political factions."[14] A few days later, Archbishop Damaskinos flew to London and proposed to Bevin that the British and Americans support a plan to delay the plebiscite for three years.

However, the British and Americans wanted the Greek people to decide whether they wanted a democracy or a left-wing dictatorship (i.e., capitalism or communism), not whether they wanted a constitutional monarchy or a republic. The objective was to prevent the "decoupling of the notions monarchy and democracy." The two concepts had to remain linked because if the Greek people were given the opportunity to separate them, then there was a risk that similar events could occur elsewhere, namely, in Italy and Belgium, which also had strong communist parties and upcoming elections.[15]

After almost a year of Britain lobbying the United States to assume a more active role in Greece, the Americans had twice since July 1945 taken a strong

---

[13] Murphy, pp. 1-16.
[14] Byrnes to MacVeagh (898), September 1 1945, FRUS 1945, Vol. VIII, The Near East and Africa, pp. 150-1.
[15] For a more detailed analysis of the British and American decision to hold the plebiscite at this time, see: Paravantes, "A Tale of Two Referenda," pp. 243-57.

stand on Greek political issues; first in relation to the supervision of elections and second by directly attempting to influence the Greek regent. Not surprisingly, the decision to reverse the order of the plebiscite and the elections provoked a strong reaction from the communist press abroad, which condemned the Greek government and the "foreign powers" that were supporting it.[16]

In contrast to the previous month, when both the British and the Americans had attempted to include the Soviets in discussions about Greek political developments, by September 7, 1945, when it came to the decision to change the order of the plebiscite and the elections, British Under-Secretary Sir Orme Sargent recommended to Byrnes that the Soviets should not be included.[17] British Foreign Secretary Bevin then met with American Secretary of State Byrnes to determine the American position on the issue. Byrnes stated that although he was reluctant to delay the plebiscite for three years, he would assume joint responsibility with the British for the proposal—a position which was not completely surprising since he had asked MacVeagh to propose it to the archbishop.

On September 12, 1945, the USSR sent a memorandum to the Council of Foreign Ministers asserting that the conditions in Greece were not appropriate for the holding of elections and a plebiscite, especially since the Greek government had still not been formed in the way agreed by all parties at Varkiza. The Soviets also stated that the current conditions posed a grave danger to the Greek people and Greece's neighbors and that the presence of foreign observers served only to "obscure" the internal situation in Greece.[18] In spite of this strong Soviet protest, the British and Americans continued to move forward with their plans to hold and observe elections and to delay the plebiscite.[19] However, the decision did not improve conditions in Greece, and economic and political disorder grew to such levels that Ambassador Leeper believed that the British had to assume executive power to save the country.[20]

---

[16] Harriman, USSR, to Byrnes (974), September 5, 1945, FRUS 1945, Vol. VIII, The Near East and Africa, p. 152. For the British and the Americans, the media in communist countries were viewed as expressing official government policy, while in contrast, the media in England and the United States, if not reflecting public opinion, were at least catering to it.

[17] Winant, UK, to Byrnes (9163), September 7, 1945, FRUS 1945, Vol. VIII, The Near East and Africa, pp. 152–3.

[18] Soviet memorandum, translated and reported to Byrnes, September 12, 1945, FRUS 1945, Vol. VIII, The Near East and Africa, pp. 156–7.

[19] There are numerous dispatches related to the Anglo-American-French involvement in the supervision of Greek elections and the statements that these governments drafted regarding their participation. See: FRUS 1945, Vol. VIII, The Near East and Africa, pp. 157–60.

[20] Rosie, p. 92. Simultaneously in Indo-China, the British were using Japanese troops to maintain order against Vietnamese nationalists and communists until the French could return to govern. They also actively intervened by helping the returning French troops seize Vietnamese government buildings.

King George himself protested the decision to hold elections before the plebiscite, informing Secretary Byrnes that the proposal violated the Varkiza accord and risked creating greater problems in Greece.[21] The British were also pressing the Americans to work with their "British and French colleagues" to force Greek politicians to cooperate in the forthcoming elections, and the Americans again gave in, with MacVeagh acknowledging Byrnes' orders on the matter by September 26.[22] Meanwhile, negotiations with the Greek government over the specific date for elections continued until the end of September 1945. The Americans wanted a fixed date to be set, while the British were increasingly concerned over the rising right-wing influence in the government.[23] Therefore, while Anglo-American policy continued to support the creation of a centrist coalition government, both countries either failed to recognize or refused to acknowledge that the Greek political system was too fragmented for this to occur.[24]

At the beginning of October 1945, partly as a result of the failure of the Council of Foreign Ministers in London and partly owing to widening mutual suspicion, political conditions in Greece worsened. According to Ambassador MacVeagh, both left- and right-wing newspapers were reporting that since the Council of Foreign Ministers had failed, the likelihood of tripartite (i.e., joint Anglo-American-Soviet) agreement in Greece had virtually disappeared, contributing to the likelihood of renewed armed conflict.[25] However, internationally, the British were able to use growing antagonism toward the Soviets to their advantage. On 14 October, 1945, the Foreign Office stated that Soviet "intransigence" was greatly aiding British efforts to bring the United States around to the British way of thinking.[26]

---

[21] King George to Byrnes (CFM Files – Lot M 88, Box 31), September 22, 1945, FRUS 1945, Vol. VIII, The Near East and Africa, pp. 160-1. It is possible that because the Allies did not fully adhere to the Varkiza accord, the signatories in Greece may have felt free to disregard it as well.

[22] MacVeagh to Byrnes (1082), MacVeagh to Archbishop Damaskinos (Athens Embassy Files, 800 Elections), September 27, 1945, FRUS 1945, Vol. VIII, The Near East and Africa, pp. 164-5.

[23] Winant to Byrnes (9875), September 24, 1945, MacVeagh to Byrnes (1077 and 1078), September 25, 1945, FRUS 1945, Vol. VIII, The Near East and Africa, pp. 161-4. See also: Lagani, "Les Rapports De La Grece Avec Ses Voisins Balkaniques."

[24] Various documents, September to November 1945, DBFA, Vol. 5, 1945, Series F Europe. Between September and November 1945, the Greek government was re-constituted three times. Acting Prime Minister Admiral Voulgaris resigned on October 9, 1945, and until the first week of November 1945, no one could be convinced to form a coalition government. Themistoklis Sophoulis formed a government that lasted only two days, and the regent then assumed the premiership until November 2. See also: Woodhouse, *Apple of Discord*, pp. 252-3.

[25] MacVeagh to Byrnes (1121), October 4, 1945, FRUS 1945, Vol. VIII, The Near East and Africa, pp. 167-8.

[26] Foreign Office to British Embassy in Washington (371/44538/AN 3159), October 14, 1945, BDFA, Series C North America, Part III, Vol. 25 (1945).

Despite becoming involved in the supervision of the elections and the delay of the plebiscite, the Americans largely continued to defer to the British in their dealings with the Greek government. For example, the leader of the Socialist Party, George Papandreou, asked US Ambassador MacVeagh to intervene to keep the Voulgaris government in power. MacVeagh refused, stating that his orders were only to encourage party leaders to work together, not to "intervene [in] local affairs," to which Papandreou replied that MacVeagh's "British colleague" (Leeper) "regularly engaged [in] such intervention."[27] One notable exception occurred in November 1945 after Archbishop Damaskinos threatened to resign as regent. Ambassador Leeper "begged" Ambassador MacVeagh to see the regent and to try to convince him not to resign. MacVeagh said that although he had no "instructions or desire to intervene" in Greek domestic affairs, as a "friend of Greece," he felt that the regent's resignation could only hurt the country when the elections and Allied observation were imminent. After meeting with MacVeagh, the regent decided to remain in office.[28] The fact that this unofficial intervention by the State Department received the "full agreement" of President Truman also indicated the "changing currents" within the administration in favor of a form of American intervention that increasingly resembled previous British intervention.[29]

The first general elections in Greece in a decade were scheduled for January 20, 1946, in a climate of rising anti-Soviet sentiment. The Greek government stated that it was in favor of maintaining the pre-existing proportional representation system. After a few weeks spent choosing the various personnel to head the British, French, and American missions, and in accordance with Bevin's plan to hold elections as quickly as possible, advance parties of the Allied Mission for the Observation of Greek Elections (AMFOGE) arrived in Athens at the end of November 1945. Their preliminary report illustrated the growing role that the Americans would play in the future of Greece.

However, the arrival of AMFOGE representatives did not guarantee the endorsement of the elections by the KKE. On 12 December 1945, the KKE declared that it would abstain from participation in the committee for the

---

[27] MacVeagh to Byrnes (1138), October 8, 1945, FRUS 1945, Vol. VIII, The Near East and Africa, pp. 171–2.

[28] MacVeagh to Byrnes (1354), November 26, 1945, FRUS 1945, Vol. VIII, The Near East and Africa, p. 183.

[29] Byrnes to MacVeagh (1204), November 28, 1945, FRUS 1945, Vol. VIII, The Near East and Africa, p. 184.

registration of its members; then it declared that it would refuse to participate in the elections. The KKE's objective in abstaining was to make it difficult for the British to show Greece's communist neighbors that the elections were fair and open.

However, when the Greek government unilaterally changed the date for elections from January 20 to March 31, 1946, the Americans were not pleased. The Greek government publicly hinted that the date had been changed in response to pressure from AMFOGE officials, but the State Department ordered MacVeagh to publicize the fact that the Greek government had changed the date on its own. In response, the Greek Ambassador to the US informed Secretary Byrnes that the British had pressed the Greek government to fix a date "not later than March."[30]

As 1945 drew to a close, the British and Americans had succeeded in planning elections for Greece (although the date continued to be subject to revision), but domestic conditions in the country did not create a sense of optimism. In his summary of 1945 in Greece, Sir Reginald Leeper described British and Greek sentiment as he saw it:

> I do not think that the Greeks yet appreciate how much has been done for them by their British Allies. This arises partly from the fact that they feel we are here primarily in our own interest because Greece is necessary to us ... and Anglo-Greek relations have on the whole become less cordial during the past year. The British troops resent the fact that the Greeks do so little to help themselves and expect so much to be done for them by us ... It says much for the patience of the British temperament that things have gone as well as they have during the past year ... If I believed that Greece was to continue as at present for many years to come, I would take a very bleak view of her future, but I believe that the Greek people are very much better than their present politicians and that if we can help them to stand on their feet again they may produce better men to conduct their affairs.[31]

---

[30] Diamantopoulos to Byrnes (868.00/12-1045), December 10, 1945, FRUS 1945, Vol. VII, The Near East and Africa, p. 191. Sluggish economic recovery in Greece was a major obstacle to political progress; partly because of the lack of reparations awarded to Greece at the Paris Peace Conference, the government was left with the choice of raising taxes and/or taking foreign loans. See: Acheson to MacVeagh (24), January 8, 1946, FRUS 1946, Vol. VII, The Near East and Africa, p. 88. See also: Byrnes to Caffrey (5244), November 9, 1945, FRUS 1945, Vol. III, European Advisory Commission, Austria, Germany, pp. 1377-8. Given Italy's inability to pay reparations, Byrnes stated that only Greece and Yugoslavia, which had suffered tremendously at the hands of the Germans, would be able to link their claims against Italy with their pursuit of some share of German reparations. However, as the conference continued, it became clear that Greece would not receive enough reparations to have a significant impact on its economic recovery. See the above volume, pp. 1378-1506.

[31] Leeper to Foreign Office, December 1945 (R 245/1/19), BDFA, Series F Europe, Part IV, Vol. 5, p. 56.

1946: January to September

In contrast to the previous year, by January 1946, the US was poised to increase its intervention in Greece. External threats, namely the territorial violations of Greece's northern frontiers by Albania, Bulgaria, and Yugoslavia, reflected the rapidly growing antagonism between the Soviet Union and the US. As such, 1946 would also be a year of profound change for the world and a year of extreme change in British and American relations. In both Britain and the United States, there were extensive debates over how demobilization and reconstruction should take place in the transition from wartime to peacetime economies.

Additionally, the British were in tenuous positions worldwide, not only in Greece, and as post-war tensions between the West and the Soviet Union continued to rise, signs of the coming Cold War showed themselves. In the United States, the general public increasingly placed part of the blame for this state of affairs on the British; as a result, the British kept detailed records of American public opinion and how it could affect their policy implementation. As late as December 1945, a British Foreign Office communication acknowledged that, at least for the time being, Britain and the Commonwealth might be forced "to play the role of the second-class power." However, the Foreign Office believed that Britain still had a monopoly on "competent political leadership" as well as the immense asset of "the fundamental unity" of the British people and their willingness to abide by the decisions of their elected leaders, in contrast to the United States.[32] The British Embassy in Washington informed the Foreign Office that although diminished American expectations of British power were damaging to British morale, they could be used to Britain's advantage if America's *belief* in diminished British power encouraged the US to take an increasing role in dealing with rising Soviet pressure worldwide, and especially in the Eastern Mediterranean and the Middle East. The embassy added that just as Britain was experiencing a kind of identity crisis, so too was the United States, which was described as "a troubled spirit" conscious of its power and keenly aware that it lacked the gift of leadership in many significant fields as it confronted its own severe domestic issues.[33] Therefore, for the time being, in spite of their diminishing influence, the British maintained their physical presence in Greece.

---

[32] Foreign Office to Washington Embassy (No. 2, AN 2851/763/45), BDFA, Part IV, Series C, North America, Vol. 1, p. 7.
[33] Embassy in Washington to Foreign Office (No 2, AN 205/5/45), BDFA, Part IV, Series C, North America, Vol. 1, pp. 8–9. "Domestic issues" refers to post-war social, political, and economic troubles.

Bevin believed that the holding of elections and the establishment of an independent parliamentary democracy would allow the British to maintain their position of influence in Greek affairs. Once the elections were held, the British could deal with the plebiscite for the return of King George, which would represent the successful implementation of their longest-standing policy objective for Greece: the restoration of the Greek monarchy. However, the Americans demonstrated their increasing interest in Greek affairs on January 12, when the US government granted Greece a $25 million loan in an attempt to mitigate the economic crisis and create a favorable atmosphere for the successful holding of national elections.[34]

Following the news of the economic aid that the United States had provided to Greece, the British Ambassador to the United States, Lord Halifax, reported to the Foreign Office on January 19, 1946 that he had learned that the US military would pursue its demobilization. However, he felt that the rapid pace at which it was being completed had damaged America's international prestige and crippled the US military's effective fighting strength.[35] This was a major concern for the British, who were already in a difficult situation with their overseas armed forces and were still in need of American loans to stabilize their own (let alone the Greek) economy. With the rapid US demobilization came the prospect of Britain having to maintain its military presence in Greece at the same (unsustainable) level.[36] The British needed international developments to work in their favor, and they needed the Americans to become more involved in Greek affairs.

In connection with its loan to Greece, the United States government agreed to participate in the Greek Currency Committee, which represented another step in the deepening US involvement in the country.[37] The British followed with a £10.5 million loan to stabilize the drachma on January 24, 1946. Bevin stated that

---

[34] (No. 12, R 868/1/19), January 11, 1946, BDFA, Series F Europe, Part IV, Vol. 5, p. 93, and (No. 10, R 650/2/19), January 12, 1946, p. 58. See also: Byrnes to Tsouderos (868.00/1-1546), January 15, 1946, FRUS 1946, The Near East and Africa, pp. 95–6.

[35] Halifax to Foreign Office (AN 193/1/45), January 19, 1946, BDFA, Part IV, Series C North America, Vol. 1, pp. 47–51.

[36] Kirby, p. 396, and Anstey, pp. 420–8. A key obstacle to the approval of American loans was British "socialism," as many American politicians labelled it. Programs of wage and price control, in addition to health care and pensions, were viewed as socialism by many US politicians, who considered these policies dangerously close to the Soviet model. The British had to engage a substantial amount of their post-war propaganda efforts in convincing both American officials and the US general public that socialism in Britain was democratic and was similar to American economic and social values.

[37] Acheson to Winant (309), January 10, 1946, FRUS 1946, The Near East and Africa, pp. 89–90.

this was necessary to stabilize the Greek economy before the elections could take place, but he warned the British Parliament that all the financial assistance it was providing would be of value only as part of a larger economic plan. However, this economic aid to the Greek government provoked another Soviet demand on January 22, 1946 for Britain to withdraw its troops, which the Soviets claimed were preventing the Greeks from obtaining and exercising their freedom.[38] The Soviets lodged an official protest with the United Nations and reiterated their demand for British withdrawal.[39]

Meanwhile, the British had begun to provide the US State Department with assessments of current and possible future conditions in Greece. In addition to these reports, US Army Captain William Hardy (WH) McNeill, who had arrived in Athens following liberation, produced reports for the US War Department. At this time, he was serving as a military attaché to the American Embassy in Athens, and he wrote a report that was endorsed by Ambassador MacVeagh and then sent to Under Secretary of State Acheson for consideration. In the report (foreshadowing the logic of the domino theory), McNeill predicted that the worsening Greek economy, coupled with a British troop withdrawal, would lead to a right-wing dictatorship, which would inevitably result in more civil unrest, foreign intervention, and an eventual communist takeover. This last stage, he argued, would invariably bring Greece, like the countries of Eastern Europe, under the Soviet sphere of influence.[40]

In the weekly summary for February 1946, Ambassador Halifax stated that the continued Soviet attacks on Britain's action and presence in Greece (he also mentioned Iran and Indonesia) had drawn allies to Britain, since the British had responded with "open-handedness," in contrast with the Soviets' methods.[41] Stalin, though still keen to avoid a direct confrontation with the United States, also wished to keep the Americans out of the Eastern Mediterranean, and he advised the KKE to seek a compromise with the Greek government. He was also fearful that Yugoslavian support of the KKE could contribute to an escalation of

---

[38] (No. 11, R 1352/2/19), January 25, 1946, p. 59 (No. 12, R 868/1/19), January 11, 1946, p. 94, (No. 20, R 1375/1/19), January 19, 1946, p. 98, and (No.40, R 2196/1/19), February 2, 1946, p. 105. *BDFA Series F Europe, Part IV, Vol. 5, 1946.*

[39] Iatrides, "Revolution or Self-Defense?" p. 18. See also: United Nations, official Records of the Security Council, First Year, First Series, Supplement No. 1, p. 73.

[40] MacVeagh to Byrnes (2100), January 19, 1946, FRUS 1946, Vol. VII, The Near East and Africa, pp. 97–9. This report may be interpreted as yet another British effort to prepare the United States to continue to assume greater involvement in, if not yet responsibility for, Greece in the near future.

[41] Halifax to Foreign Office (AN 299/1/45) February 1946, BDFA, Part IV, Series C North America, Vol. 1, pp. 56–60. The Soviet methods, whatever they may have been, are not mentioned.

Western intervention in Greece, so he sought ways to limit Yugoslavian aid and involvement in Greece as well.[42]

In response to the Soviet demand to remove the remaining British troops from Greece, the Greek Ambassador to London issued a statement to the British press that the British troops were in Greece at the request of "successive Greek Governments." Leeper believed that the Soviet statement would encourage the Greek communists even more because they would interpret it as a message from the Soviets that the KKE had become a major foreign policy priority for them.[43] The USSR's demand therefore generated considerable fallout, and the KKE received powerful ammunition for its escalating propaganda campaign against the British and Greek governments.[44] It is also possible that the Soviet Union's statements encouraged the National Liberation Front (EAM) to boycott the elections, as KKE General Secretary Nikos Zachariadis had been claiming it would do since September 1945.

In February 1946, the Soviets continued to condemn Britain's presence in Greece within the UN. The US representative to the UN, Edward Stettinius, reported to Under Secretary Acheson that Bevin had stated that while British troops would be withdrawn at the earliest possible opportunity, they were there at the request of the Greek government to preserve peace and security and to create and maintain the necessary conditions for the holding of "fair elections." Bevin also attacked the communist anti-British propaganda that was circulating in Greece, which he claimed the Soviets were continuing to provide to the KKE. He then asked the members of the Security Council to give a "definite yes or no answer" as to whether British actions had endangered world peace and security. Stettinius reported that he believed that Bevin's statement was sound and likely strong enough to prevent further Soviet protests, at least for the time being. American support for British actions was demonstrated the next day, when Stettinius met privately with the Soviet representative to the UN and informed him that the United States saw nothing in British actions that had endangered

---

[42] Stavrakis, "*Moscow and Greek Communism*." The author mentions many examples of Soviet pressure on the KKE to avoid military confrontation. See pp. 48–51, 104–7, 110–12, 120–1, 123–6, 125–8, 139–40.

[43] Leeper to Foreign Office (no. 53, R 2528/1/19), February 7, 1946, BDFA, Series F Europe, Part IV, Vol. 5, pp. 108–9.

[44] Iatrides, "Revolution or Self-Defense?" p. 18. The comments referred to here are from Stalin's speech of February 9, 1946, in which he declared that "peaceful coexistence with the West was infeasible."

world peace and security.⁴⁵ On February 5, 1946, the UN Security Council met to further discuss the "Greek issue," and the British and Soviets again clashed over the British troop presence in Greece and what it actually represented. The Soviets asserted that while the troops themselves did not represent a threat to world peace and security, their presence created the *conditions* that could lead to such a threat. The solution agreed on was to officially publish the views of all the Security Council members on the effect of British troops in Greece and then to leave the matter alone.⁴⁶

The Americans worked to keep the Soviet allegations against Britain from culminating in a Security Council vote or a General Assembly resolution, and Stettinius reported that Britain seemed to have been "cleared of the charges." While Bevin agreed that the British would not seek a formal resolution to clear their name, he did ask for an official statement from the chair of the Security Council to support Britain's continued presence in Greece. However, the Soviets threatened to veto any statement that exonerated the British and instead demanded a resolution ordering a British withdrawal.⁴⁷ Though no resolution was passed and no veto occurred, these problems in the Security Council foreshadowed more to come. The news from Greece was not much better as the Greek government considered postponing the elections once again. However, under combined British and American pressure, no delay was accepted, and regent Damaskinos signed several decrees at the end of February 1946 that defined the total number of seats in the parliament, outlined the electoral districts and confirmed the time and date of the vote.⁴⁸

Meanwhile, in Washington in early March 1946, the British Embassy continued to monitor public and congressional statements relating to a possible formal military alliance between the United States and Britain.⁴⁹ Equally

---

[45] Stettinius to Byrnes (1275), February 2, 1946, and Memorandum of conversation between Stettinus (USA) and Vyshinsky (USSR) (USSC 46/13, Conv. 2), February 3, 1946, FRUS 1946, Vol. VII, The Near East and Africa, pp. 104–8. If actions were deemed to constitute a "threat to peace and security," they triggered immediate Security Council action, which was why such importance was placed on determining unequivocally whether the British military presence in Greece constituted such a threat.

[46] Memorandum of Security Council meeting, Stettinius to Acheson (USSC 46/9, report 13), February 5 and 6, 1946, FRUS 1946, Vol. VII, The Near East and Africa, pp. 108–12. Italics added. This exchange is interesting from a legal and international relations perspective, as it demonstrates how countries argue "diplomatically." Note the shift in definitions used by the Soviets; i.e., the "conditions" that could endanger world peace and security.

[47] Stettinius to Byrnes (1465), February 6, 1946, FRUS 1946, Vol. VII, The Near East and Africa, pp. 112–15.

[48] Rankin to Byrnes (277), February 28, 1946, FRUS 1946, Vol. VII, The Near East and Africa, p. 116.

[49] Washington Embassy to Foreign Office (No. 7, AN 649/4/45), March 1946, BDFA, Part IV, Series C North America, Vol. 1, pp. 29–30.

important to the British was American economic support, since the Soviets had all but blocked Eastern Europe to Western trade. The British were also troubled by the possibility that German trade might never be allowed to fully recover as a result of Soviet interference.[50] For these reasons, Bevin, with the support of the Foreign Office and the Chiefs of the General Staff, continued to pursue the policy of rebuilding British strength by leaning on the United States and maintaining a British presence wherever possible, particularly in the Middle East, to preserve Britain's strategic interests. However, an important difference of opinion between the British prime minister and the British foreign secretary regarding these policies soon came to light.

On 2 March 1946, Prime Minister Attlee distributed a brief to the Defense Committee stating that the British could no longer expect to dominate the Mediterranean and should withdraw troops from the rest of the Middle East, including Egypt and Greece. He concluded by stating that the British should design their foreign policy based not on sentiment but rather on a rational assessment that the new strategic center of the world was America, not Britain as "a power looking eastwards through the Mediterranean to India and the East."[51] The Chiefs of Staff rebutted Attlee's arguments, reiterating their belief in the importance of the Middle East for securing communication and trade routes and oil supplies. Bevin supported the Chiefs of Staff, stating that Britain had to have a strong enough military to make its foreign policy credible. Under this combined pressure from the Chiefs of Staff and Bevin, upon whose influence Attlee depended in the cabinet, the Prime Minister backed down.[52] The British would be staying in Greece, at least for the time being.

By early March 1946, it was clear that the Greek left would boycott the elections. Both the regent and the American Ambassador explained to the State Department that this choice was being encouraged "from abroad in order to sabotage the elections, gain time to build up strength and when ready, to seize power."[53] This interpretation was strengthened when the Greek Ambassador to the US informed the Secretary of State that the Soviet Ambassador to Greece had approached the Greek government regarding increasing trade between the USSR and Greece, saying that such trade could be facilitated by ceding Greek ports to the Soviets. Prime Minister Themistoklis Sophoulis rejected

---

[50] Foreign Office to Washington Embassy (No. 9, AN 719/36/45), BDFA, Part IV, Series C North America, Vol. 1, pp. 37–9.
[51] Attlee, quoted in Bullock, *Ernest Bevin*, Vol. 3, p. 242.
[52] Attlee, quoted in Bullock, *Ernest Bevin*, Vol. 3, p. 340.
[53] Rankin to Byrnes (317), March 8, 1946, FRUS 1946, Vol. VII, The Near East and Africa, pp. 118–19.

the proposal, informing the Soviet Ambassador that Greek ports already had the facilities necessary to handle increased Soviet-Greek trade and that such "ceding" was unnecessary. However, concerned about what the Soviet proposal could mean in terms of Soviet designs on the Dodecanese, the Greek Prime Minister ordered the ambassador to inform the State Department of the Soviet proposal.[54] Therefore, by March 1946, it seemed as though the British and American suspicions of Soviet territorial ambitions for Greece had been confirmed. The British and Americans interpreted the Soviet trade proposal as further expression of the Soviet intention to expand south into the Mediterranean.

As early as 1939, the USSR had attempted to gain influence over the Dardanelles, inviting the Turkish Foreign Minister to Moscow and attempting to persuade Turkey to sign a mutual defense treaty with the USSR in which both countries would assume responsibility for the defense of the Dardanelles. Turkey rejected this proposal, but seven years later, Soviet attempts to assume or at least share control of the Dardanelles remained. By February 1946, the USSR had moved troops to the Bulgarian-Turkish border and was pressing for greater control over and access through the Dardanelles. In response to Soviet pressure, the United States sent the battleship *Missouri* and two destroyers to Constantinople (officially renamed Istanbul in 1930, but still referred to in the BDFA as Constantinople), officially to repatriate the remains of the Turkish Ambassador to the US but mainly to demonstrate American determination to block or at least limit Soviet access to the Eastern Mediterranean.[55] Countering any further Soviet expansion was still vital to former British Prime Minister Churchill, as exemplified by his speech at Westminster College in Fulton, Missouri, on March 5, 1946.

Churchill recommended a close Anglo-American alliance to combat the expansion of the "atheist" Soviet regime.[56] Though initially skeptical of such religious terminology in the politically charged atmosphere, many in Truman's inner circle subscribed to the British plan. This was demonstrated by the declaration of Vaughn Taylor, US Ambassador to the Vatican, that "the cause of

---

[54] Diamantopoulos to Acheson (958), March 9, 1946, FRUS 1946, Vol. VII, The Near East and Africa, pp. 119–20.

[55] Vali, pp. 58–9, 69–71. This struggle would continue well into the 1960s, as the USSR attempted to assume greater influence over the Mediterranean nations. In the 1950s and 1960s, NATO increased its presence in the region in response. For more information, see Paravantes, "The issue of NATO 'out-of-area' operations"

[56] Churchill's Fulton Speech, quoted in: Kirby, p. 391, full text available at: www.historyguide.org/europe/churchill.html

Communism versus Christianity and Democracy transcends minor differences in Christian creeds. It is the *Great Issue* of the future and thus of today."[57] However, despite these arguments and a shared anti-communist position, the British Labour government continued to be branded as too socialist by various groups in the United States.

To counter these accusations, the Foreign Office advised Prime Minister Attlee, Deputy Prime Minister Herbert Morrison and Foreign Secretary Bevin to understate or even deny the policy differences between the Labour Party and the previous Conservative government when communicating with American press and officials. The Foreign Office advised that it would be preferable to educate the American public and policy-makers about Britain in general and the values it shared with the United States rather than emphasizing the differences between the Labour Party and the Conservative Party. It was seen as being much more beneficial for Britain to show continuity with the Americans rather than alarming them with implications that change and major domestic economic intervention were on the horizon.[58] As a result, owing to external considerations as much as domestic concerns, British policy remained relatively consistent from the defeat of Churchill in the previous year's elections to the spring of 1946.

It may be argued that Britain's anti-communist stance, both in Greece and elsewhere, was also a way for the British to divert American attention from Britain's efforts to manipulate its own economy in an attempt to more rapidly assist its recovery (in stark opposition to American economic policy). Moreover, since 1943 the Foreign Office had consistently espoused the need to focus on British interests, rather than the British way of life, in order to distance Britain from socialists both domestically and abroad and to insulate the government from accusations that could endanger American economic aid.[59] The Foreign Office went so far as to attempt to silence anyone whose views could alienate the American public and policy-makers.[60]

In Greece, joint Anglo-American pressure was applied to the Greek government, which was still trying to delay the elections. The British and Americans argued that the consequences of such a delay would outweigh the

---

[57] Taylor to Truman (WHCF Box 44), June 11, 1946, Truman Papers. Emphasis in original.
[58] J.C. Donnelly to Patrick Gordon Walker, May 14, 1946 (FO 371/51639 AN 1413/15/45).
[59] Anstey, p. 425.
[60] Anstey, p. 426, Conant, Photo # 23, pp. 202–3. An indication of British success manipulating the Americans and hiding their actions, was that the head of their US spy ring, William Stephenson, was given a medal by the government upon which he had been spying. Stephenson, the chief British spy in the United States, received the Medal of Merit, the highest civilian award the United States could confer, for his "valuable assistance to America in the fields of intelligence and special operations."

consequences of holding the elections as planned. This argument was seized upon by the Soviets as a reason to claim that the election lists and the procedure for the pending elections were fraudulent.[61] When the election was held on March 31, the boycott by the left resulted in a decisive victory for the right.[62] The decision to boycott the poll proved costly to the KKE. Zachariadis had made the success of the Greek left dependent upon outside factors that he could neither predict nor control (namely, the support of the Soviets or other communist nations) and had not properly assessed the rising US interest in the Mediterranean and the Middle East.[63] For his part, though Bevin maintained that the Greeks had to form their own government, he also believed that the British should have a say in its composition. He instructed the new British Ambassador, Clifford Norton, to inform Tsaldaris that the most suitable government for Greece would be a broad coalition.

Though the election had taken place in relative calm, the results spelled disaster for Greece. As Woodhouse stated in reference to the 1945 governments that excluded the communists, the KKE's boycott of the election once again exempted its members from taking responsibility for the well-being of their nation, and shortly thereafter they made it clear that they were in favor of returning to an armed struggle to achieve their political objectives.[64]

In April 1945, Zachariadis boasted to his potential supporters in the USSR and Yugoslavia that by eluding the provisions of the Varkiza accord, the Greek People's Liberation Army (ELAS) had retained a considerable volume of machine guns, rifles, and other military equipment.[65] These statements were supported by a report from the head of the British police mission, whose units had apprehended a group of communists transporting weapons after attacking the northern Greek town of Katerini.[66] Throughout March and April 1946, Zachariadis attempted to enlist the support of Tito and the Yugoslav Communist Party, since the KKE hoped to field an army of 15,000 to 20,000 armed guerrillas

---

[61] Kennan to Byrnes (867), March 19, 1946, Rankin to Byrnes (370), March 20, 1946, Bevin to Byrnes, March 20, 1946, Byrnes to Rankin (352), March 21, 1946, Byrnes to Rankin (365), March 22, 1946, Rankin to Byrnes (383), March 23, 1946, FRUS 1946, Vol. VII, The Near East and Africa, pp. 122-8.
[62] Iatrides, "Revolution or Self-Defense?" p. 21.
[63] Smith, p. 100.
[64] Woodhouse, *Apple of Discord*, p. 253, and Smith, p. 96.
[65] Iatrides, "Revolution or Self-Defense?" pp. 20-2.
[66] Rankin to Byrnes (449), April 3, 1946, quoting Charles Wickam, BPM Head, FRUS 1946, Vol. VII, The Near East and Africa, p. 130.

but needed substantial foreign aid to do so.[67] However, the KKE was dismayed and impeded in its efforts in April, when Stalin ordered it to search for a compromise to prevent "an untimely armed intervention by the British."[68] Stalin still believed that the British were determined to hold on to Greece, and Bevin's continued interference in the Greek government seemed to support this theory.

The USSR continued to attack the British as imperialist, pointing to their substantial military forces stationed around the world, namely in Palestine, Iraq, and Greece, but at the Paris Council of Foreign Ministers in May 1946, Soviet hostility toward the British began to shift more and more toward the United States. International tension was further heightened by the Soviet refusal to sign up to a twenty-five-year non-aggression pact with the Western powers. The situation in Germany was deteriorating as well, as the British and American zones in Berlin began to unify in reaction to the instability in the Soviet zone, and the British and Soviets remained entrenched in their virtually irreconcilable positions.[69] A few members of the US government, suspicious of official British policy, stated publicly that in Germany, the British were engaging in a program that was designed to bring them into conflict with the USSR. The only encouraging international news for the British at this time was that the French constitution, which the British believed was largely sponsored by the communists, was rejected by the French electorate.[70] This was a welcome development for the British and the Americans, who had intervened against the communists in France. In the spring of 1946, the British increased their use of religious organizations to provide another avenue through which they could influence American public opinion, if not directly in their favor then at least against the Soviet Union (as they had previously done in Italy and France to counter communist influence). Reiterating the message emphasized during the war against the Germans, the propaganda

---

[67] Smith, p. 96. Smith states that there is no concrete information about the specifics of the agreements made with the Yugoslavians and that the information he cites comes from Zachariadis' recorded statements from the Seventh Plenum in 1957. In terms of the estimates of the size of the army, Smith cites a "Report on the Situation in Greece, 12 September 1946" that was sent to the communist parties of the USSR, Yugoslavia, and Bulgaria. Smith does clearly state, however, that the report contains no evidence that assistance "had already been discussed and agreed upon."
[68] Iatrides, "Revolution or Self-Defense?" p. 21. Zachariadis would later choose to ignore the order, submitting an official request for weapons to the Soviets on September 12, 1946. The KKE requested 8,000 rifles, 15 heavy mortars, 50 light mortars, 250 machine guns, 10,000 grenades and, 150,000 dollars per month.
[69] Morgan, pp. 246–8.
[70] Halifax to Bevin, May 13, 1946 (AN 1515/1/45), BDFA, Series C North America, Part IV, Vol. 1, pp. 157–9.

machines in both Britain and the United States portrayed the USSR as the enemy of "Western Christian civilization."[71]

Additionally, in the spring of 1946, as reports of border violations in Epirus and the terrorization of the Greek population there arrived from the American and British missions in Albania and Greece, threats to Greece's sovereignty were increasingly being noted. The reports also stressed the virtual indefensibility of Greece's northern frontiers should Yugoslavia and Bulgaria attempt to force their territorial demands.[72] Therefore, by May 1946, the British and Americans were confronted with what they believed to be very real communist designs for Greece manifested by increasing Soviet pressure at the UN/international level, threats to northern Greece by Greece's communist neighbors at the regional level and an armed revolutionary force at the domestic level.

On May 13, 1946, with the approval of the British, the Tsaldaris government announced that the plebiscite would take place on September 4, 1946.[73] Perhaps believing that it had made a mistake in not participating in the March elections, the KKE began to urge its members to register to take part in the plebiscite. However, this measure was taken too late to make much of a difference, since the forces of the right were firmly in control, and the British appeared to be continuing their preparations to leave.[74]

At the request of the Greek government, the United States agreed to send observers to supervise the plebiscite.[75] Though the British and Americans agreed to participate in this supervision, the French did not accept, and Canada was nominated as a replacement. The British and Americans were adamant that more than two nations should participate in order to prevent protests at the results. Additionally, the British and Americans favored the plebiscite being a question of monarchy or republic rather than simply whether the monarchy should return. For many of those opposing the Greek monarchy, including republicans and other non-KKE-affiliated left-wing groups, there was no contradiction between voting against the monarchy and maintaining a democracy in Greece.

---

[71] Kirby, p. 309. Referring to Churchill's speech of March 5, 1946.

[72] Rankin to Byrnes (2531), April 18, 1946, FRUS 1946, Vol. VII, The Near East and Africa, pp. 139–43. There is no mention of Albanian security concerns in the report, nor is there any specific information about the origin of the quotation except to say that some Albanian commanders had been overheard.

[73] Byrnes to Rankin (516), April 19, 1946, Acheson to Rankin (571), May 4, 1946, FRUS 1946, Vol. VII, The Near East and Africa, pp. 144–5, 155. The Americans initially did not favor such an early date for the plebiscite but after consulting with the British they changed their position and supported it.

[74] Richter, p. 521.

[75] Acheson to Truman (868.00/5-746), May 7, 1946, Acheson to Rankin (620), May 16, 1946, FRUS 1946 Vol. VII, The Near East and Africa, pp. 157–8, 162–3.

The great unpopularity of the monarchy and the current Greek government and their inability to effectively deal with the ongoing economic and social crises had done much to discredit them, and a vote in favor of the monarchy was by no means certain. By holding elections before the plebiscite, the British were able to accomplish three objectives. First, an implicit acceptance of the form of the pre-existing Greek state, a constitutional monarchy, was gained from all those who voted. Second, the KKE abstention skewed the results of the election, seeming to indicate an even greater acceptance by the Greek people that they should remain within the Western sphere of influence. The results could therefore be interpreted as an open declaration by the population that they accepted Greece's place in the West. The third objective was realized with the holding of the plebiscite in September 1946. The overwhelming result in favor of the return of the monarchy was a vindication of British policy. Britain could now argue that it was the will of the Greek people and that the plebiscite was further proof that they were committed to remaining with the West. The Greeks had publicly demonstrated that they were on a path that kept them in the sphere of the West.

By successfully manipulating the order of the election and the plebiscite and interpreting the results in a way that corroborated their policy, the Western powers had ample justification for the steps they had taken to achieve those results. The resumption of hostilities shortly after the election, the mass persecution of leftist "fellow travellers" and the inclusion of former collaborators in the government, the police and the armed forces were all justifiable sacrifices in pursuit of anti-communism, which would prevent Greece from falling under the Soviet sphere of influence. Anti-communism became the accepted blanket justification for all the persecution and suffering heaped on the Greek people; by the end of 1947 almost a million Greeks remained homeless.

Also of significance, not only for Greece but also for all nations that would require American funds to finance reconstruction efforts, was a statement by John Foster Dulles. Dulles, at the time serving as the US Ambassador to the UN, stated that the Kremlin regarded military force as the core of sovereignty. This American belief greatly aided the British in securing continued support for their post-war Mediterranean and European grand strategy. The British had been carefully monitoring US public opinion and the efforts being made by the US government to stop the spread of Soviet power.[76] The timing could not have been much better.

---

[76] BDFA, Series C North America, Part IV, Vol. 1, 1946, Inverchapel to Bevin (no. 1446, June 29, 1946), paragraph 6, pp. 197–8 and Inverchapel to Bevin (no. 1927, 15 August, 1946), paragraph 10, p. 212.

In a reversal of the position that the British had attempted to hold in Greece since the end of the Second World War, they were now forced to break with the policies of the past because they could no longer afford to maintain many of their overseas military commitments, including in Greece. Britain could no longer continue to manage its affairs as it had through nearly seven years of heavy involvement in the country. The majority of the decisions that the British would now make concerning Greece were designed to facilitate their exit.[77] Other developments outside Greece worked to Britain's advantage as well; in May 1946, the Soviets sent troops to Manchuria to help the Chinese communists fight the Kuomintang. This development further widened the gap between the Americans and the Soviets, and even pro-Soviet newspapers in the United States began to blame the USSR for the failure of the Paris Council of Foreign Ministers.[78] In June 1946, the results of the French and Italian elections gave hope to the British that some peoples in Europe feared a communist takeover and would take action to vote against them.[79] The British used these results to persuade the Americans that only with continuing aid could Greece, where conditions were worse than in France and Italy, remain in the Western sphere of influence. Britain wanted to continue to link British plans with American intervention. On June 4, 1946, Bevin gave a speech to the British House of Commons in which he stated that it was vital for Britain and the USA to continue to work along parallel lines in terms of their foreign policy and foreign intervention.[80] This statement was made not only to secure US intervention in Europe but also to help secure an American loan to the British government, which was in an increasingly desperate domestic economic situation.

The US loan was critical for the British economy, although a key condition for securing it was Britain's commitment to "de-imperialize" and to reduce Britain's Commonwealth preferences.[81] The British were reluctant to agree since they

---

[77] Morgan, p. 252.
[78] Halifax to Bevin, May 13, 1946 (AN 1636/1/45), paragraph 17, BDFA, Series C North America, Vol. 1, p. 169. Stephen Kotkin has claimed that this development was the United States' "greatest failure of the Second World War and the early post-war years"; not forcing Stalin to support Chiang Kai-shek and help wipe out the Chinese communists. He argues that Stalin had such great designs for Eastern Europe that the Western powers could have acted pre-emptively to have him wipe out Mao's forces, and in so doing they could have altered the post-war history of the Far East. See: "David Kennedy, Andrew Roberts and Stephen Kotkin Discuss the Big Three of the 20th Century"
[79] Inverchapel to Bevin, June 8, 1946 (AN 1770/1/45), paragraph 6, BDFA, Series C North America, Vol. 1, p. 176.
[80] Foreign Office to Washington Embassy, June 8, 1946 (AN 1770/1/45), Paragraphs 10–12, BDFA, Series C North America, Vol. 1, p. 177.
[81] Inverchapel to Bevin, August 15, 1946 (no. 1927), paragraph 11c, BDFA, Series C North America, Part IV, Vol. 1, p. 213.

were heavily reliant on government control to maintain the economy, prevent its collapse, and perhaps restore some of their lost power.

In Greece during June and July 1946, as fighting between the communists and various right-wing groups was escalating, Tsaldaris met with British and American diplomats in an attempt to secure bigger foreign loans to rebuild Greece, gain further support for its territorial claims and assure the Western allies of Greece's commitment to them.[82] However, the dramatic increase in right-wing violence in Greece had destabilized the country to such a level that increasing British investment was not likely.[83] At the end of July 1946, the Chancellor of the Exchequer informed Prime Minister Attlee that the British "had reached a point where we could do no more," and "for the next year or so we should have to deny our friends, including the Greeks, any future credits."[84] Britain had reached the financial breaking point, and though the British wanted to be sure that their policy in Greece since October 1944 had not been a complete failure, they were caught in the post-war economic crisis. Shortly thereafter, the Greek government began to look more to the United States for financial assistance. Tsaldaris feared that the British would be offended by his approaching the US for financial assistance, but the Chancellor of the Exchequer replied that far from objecting, "he would welcome such a step" because the Americans were in a better financial position than the British.

At the Paris Peace Conference, the Foreign Secretary spoke with US Secretary of State Byrnes about future loans for Greece from the Export-Import Bank, and Byrnes replied that if the bank began to run low on funds, he would ask the US Congress for more.[85] From this point on, the Greek government would increasingly be aided by the United States. Securing greater levels of American financial intervention in Greece, and through it (the British hoped) also in Western Europe and the Middle East, was a significant achievement for British policy in Greece, and another indication that the Americans were following the path the British had laid out for them.

---

[82] Acheson to Rankin (739), June 14, 1946, Rankin to Byrnes (790), June 18, 1946, FRUS 1946, Vol. VII, The Near East and Africa, pp. 170–1.
[83] Alexander, pp. 202–6.
[84] Bevin to Norton (497), July 20, 1946, BDFA, Series F Europe, Part IV, Vol. 6, 1946, Doc R 10729/8523/19, Enclosures 3–5, pp. 38–40.
[85] Bevin to Norton (497), July 20, 1946 (R 10729/8523/19), Enclosure 4. BDFA, Series F Europe, Part IV, Vol. 6, p. 39. This promise was not a guarantee that more funds would be available but simply that Greek requests would be evaluated. See: Acheson to Harriman (5358), July 13, 1946, FRUS 1946, Vol. VII, The Near East and Africa, pp. 181–2.

The decision to award the Dodecanese Islands to Greece on June 27, 1946 was another important indicator of Western support of Greece. Soviet pressure against Turkey and Greece over the Dardanelles, was decisively rebuffed by the British and Americans when the Dodecanese were returned to Greek control.[86] Additionally, the British continued to press the United States to respond to the growing Soviet influence in Greece, and this pressure was having the desired effect. On August 31, 1946, the British Ambassador to Washington noted that the Americans had developed a growing tendency to link events in one part of the world with actions against the US or its allies elsewhere, and to lay the blame for such undesired events on the USSR.[87]

This was not a difficult connection to make, especially in Greece, as conditions there worsened and showed no signs of improvement. On August 13, 1946, Bevin received a dispatch informing him that the first efforts of the Greek government to coordinate large-scale anti-communist action between the army and the gendarmes had been largely unsuccessful, mainly owing to a lack of communication and a failure to define which group would have situational control over the other. Bevin's chargé d'affaires, D. W. Lascelles, then informed Bevin that Greek forces in northern Greece were enforcing martial law, but the Greek government would not admit to this because it did not want it known that conditions were unsuitable for holding the plebiscite. Bevin was therefore understandably concerned with the international reaction to the plebiscite.[88] Realizing its error in boycotting the elections the previous year, the KKE urged its members to register for the plebiscite. Further complicating matters in August 1946 was continuing Soviet pressure on Turkey for greater influence in the Dardanelles.[89] As a result, maintaining control in Greece was seen as being of even greater immediate importance for the West. This dramatically increased international tensions in the areas around Greece—a situation that was not helped when the Yugoslavians shot down an American fighter plane.[90] The Yugoslavian attack, though not sanctioned by the Soviets, was further evidence of perceived communist aggressive intentions in the Balkans.

---

[86] Report of Meeting in Paris (868.00/7-146), July 1, 1946, FRUS 1946, Vol. VII, The Near East and Africa, pp. 174–5.
[87] Inverchapel to Foreign Office, August 31, 1946, no. 2657, FO 371/51609.
[88] Quoted in: Close, "The Changing Structure of the Right," pp. 134–7.
[89] Inverchapel to Bevin, August 18, 1946 (No. 570), paragraph 14, BDFA, Series C North America, Part IV, Vol. 1, p. 265.
[90] Inverchapel to Bevin, August 23, 1946 (No. 581), paragraph 1, BDFA, Series C North America, Part IV, Vol. 1, p. 268.

Despite its reluctance in early July to grant Greece any new loans "in the foreseeable future," on August 7, 1946, the US Export-Import Bank granted a $175 million reconstruction loan to Greece in addition to a July 31 UNRRA grant to Greece of $293 million.[91] The Americans were clearly taking a greater interest in Greece. However, the British and Americans were still not fully prepared to antagonize the USSR, so they proceeded cautiously with the organization of the Greek plebiscite.[92]

Soviet concerns regarding Greece were expressed on August 24, 1946, when the Ukrainian representative to the UN, raised an allegation against the Greek government under Article 34 of the UN Charter, claiming that its actions against Albania (moving soldiers to the border and threatening to invade), facilitated by the continuing British troop presence in Greece, were creating conditions that could threaten the peace and security of the Balkans.

In contrast to the more conciliatory tone used by the Americans the previous year, at the end of August 1946, the American representative to the UN stated that the Ukrainian allegations were "frivolous." Although the State Department acknowledged that every country had the right to bring an issue before the Security Council, it also noted that it seemed strange that the Ukrainians were "pleading Albania's case" and that they should at least "state reasons why Albania was itself not in a position to do so." The State Department said that this fact in itself might be used as justification for dismissing the Ukrainian allegations. The Americans instructed their representative to the UN to point out that the Ukrainian allegations against Greece were only "part of the picture" and that more information was required from both sides to fully address the territorial and border issues between Greece and Albania. The Americans also countered Ukrainian allegations that the right in Greece was engaging in nationalist propaganda by claiming that the center and left-wing media were advocating Greece's territorial claims in Northern Epirus. Finally, in defense of the British presence in Greece, the US rejected the Ukrainian allegations as "[reviving a] similar charge made by the USSR against the United Kingdom in January"; it

---

[91] Acheson to Harriman (5358), July 13, 1946, Acheson to Truman (868.51/8-746), August 7, 1946, FRUS 1946, Vol. VII, The Near East and Africa, pp. 181–2, 187–8. The US loan was heavily balanced in favor of Greece using the funds to purchase American manufactured goods, particularly war materiel.

[92] Though the Big Three were not cooperating as they had during the war, they were not yet at the antagonistic levels they would reach the next year.

maintained that no new information had arisen that could implicate the presence of British troops in the current situation.[93]

The following week, the State Department instructed the US representative to the Security Council, Herschel Johnson, to respond to the Ukrainian allegations, specifically those alleging that the March elections had been fraudulent. The State Department pointed out that the UK, the USA, and France had observed the elections, signed the report, and sent copies to the UN and that the copies were "available to anybody who will take the slightest trouble to read them." Acheson also instructed Johnson to remind the Ukrainians that as part of the USSR, they had been invited to observe the March elections and had declined to participate. Furthermore, the United States had no reason to believe that the results of the plebiscite threatened international peace; the results supported the presence of British troops in Greece as contributing to the peace and security of the country and the region. With regard to the border dispute between Greece and Albania, far more investigation was required before any blame could be attributed to either side; Acheson authorized Johnson to support the formation of a subcommittee in New York, but not on the ground, to investigate the matter further.[94] Though the United States was still using cautious rhetoric regarding Greece to deal with the allegations from the Soviets and their satellites, it was clearly aligning itself against the USSR.

For the British, although Bevin was outspoken in his criticism of the USSR—he had stood up in parliament to say that the Soviets "wanted to go right across the throat of the British Empire" and had spent much of his tenure as foreign secretary opposing Soviet expansion and influence at every step[95]—he had proceeded cautiously with regard to the plebiscite to ensure that there could be little or no objection from the Soviets. Fortunately for Bevin, the plebiscite took place without significant incident, and the result was an overwhelming victory for the royalists.[96] Though the plebiscite took place in relative calm,

---

[93] Attitude to Ukrainian complaint against Greece (501.BC/8-2746), August 27, 1946. Acheson to Johnson (174), August 28, 1946, Acheson to Johnson (179), September 5, 1946, FRUS 1946 Vol. VII, The Near East and Africa, pp. 194–200. This period also provides an opportunity to reflect on how two sides in a conflict perceive security. What was "Northern Epirus" for Greece was "Southern Albania" for Albania.

[94] Acheson to Johnson (183), September 7, 1946, FRUS 1946, Vol. VII, The Near East and Africa, pp. 202–4.

[95] Murphy, p. 232.

[96] Norton to Bevin (261), September 13, 1946 (R 14061/1/19), BDFA, Series F Europe, Part IV, Vol. 6, pp. 58–9. In the village of Kotili in Western Macedonia, a garrison of gendarmes and soldiers was overcome; twenty-two were killed and twenty-one were captured. The plebiscite saw 68.9 percent of the electorate vote in favor of the return of King George, cited in (R 16571/1/19), BDFA, Series F Europe, Part IV, Vol. 6, p. 285.

the overwhelming results in favor of the monarchy's return, while provoking suspicion as to the declared results, also finally convinced the left that the democratic path to power was lost. British reports of the levels of violence after the plebiscite showed that clashes were increasing in Thessaly, the Peloponnese, and Western Macedonia and that the communists were reinforcing their armed bands. Although the British believed that the gendarmes seemed to be managing the situation well, they observed that the same "could not be said" of the Greek army, which "appear[ed] to have had little heart for the arduous, dangerous, and often disappointing operations necessary to round up Communist guerrillas during the summer."[97] Furthermore, on September 16, 1946, the British received reports that Albanian and Russian troops were massing on the Greek border.[98] The US received similar reports and took measures to strengthen Turkey since "the Soviet Union appears to be pursuing of [or?] endeavouring to undermine the stability and obtain control of … Greece, Turkey and Iran." The measures included approving loans and the sale of military equipment to "strengthen the will and ability" of those nations to resist Soviet pressure. The State Department also emphasized continuing Soviet efforts to destabilize the Middle East, and although the USSR had placed no demands on Greece or Iran, as it had on Turkey, it was vital for US interests that the "independence and territorial integrity of Greece and Iran"[99] be maintained.

The week before the Greek monarch returned to Greece, the American representative in Albania, Joseph Earle Jacobs, informed the Secretary of State that over the past six weeks, the Albanians had mobilized between 60,000 and 100,000 troops with Soviet and Yugoslavian advisors and materiel. Jacobs also reported that Albanian army leaders were "reliably reported to have said 'we must attack Greece.'"[100] These reports, however accurate they may or may not have been, further helped the British convince the US of communist intentions toward

---

[97] Norton to Bevin (206), July 11, 1946 (R 14232/1/19), BDFA, Series F Europe, Part IV, Vol. 6, p. 66. There was also talk of cutting diplomatic ties with Franco in Spain as a result of Soviet and left-wing pressure against the fascist regime; however, this was opposed by the British, who stated that "an eventual general rupture of diplomatic relations with Spain should be rejected since interference of this kind in the domestic affairs of another country has not proved effective in the past."

[98] Inverchapel to Bevin, September 16, 1946 (No. 606), paragraph 21, BDFA, Series C North America, Part IV, Vol. 1, p. 287.

[99] Clayton to Byrnes (711.68/9-1246), September 12, 1946, FRUS 1946, Vol. VII, The Near East and Africa, pp. 209–13.

[100] Jacobs to Byrnes (487), September 21, 1946, FRUS 1946, Vol. VII, The Near East and Africa, p. 222. Though Jacobs states that the inexperience of the Albanian Army made it a negligible threat to Greece, its size and recent movements, which represented a significant economic drain on the Albanian economy, could also mean that an Albanian attack was imminent. He also notes the strong presence of Soviet and Yugoslavian military advisors and equipment in Albania.

Greece. Secretary of State Byrnes therefore reported that the United States had amended its previous policy and would now provide aid based not only on need and ability to repay, but also on whether the recipients' strategic and political objectives were aligned with those of the USA. Byrnes stated that in the previous months, the situation had "so hardened" that in his view, aid must be provided to "our friends in every way" and denied to those who for any reason opposed "the principles for which we stand." Byrnes then met with Foreign Secretary Bevin and suggested that the British provide military materiel to Turkey, while the United States would provide financial and technical assistance. Finally, while the political system of Turkey was "more satisfactory" than that of Greece, Greece's strategic position was "equally great."[101] The State Department proceeded to produce an analysis of the military, political and economic situation and needs of Greece and Turkey that, once completed, was submitted to President Truman.[102] This analysis would become the basis for the Truman Doctrine.

After nearly two years, the British, aided simultaneously by their own efforts in the US and by Soviet actions within the UN and in the Middle East, had convinced the United States of the importance of maintaining Greece, Turkey, and Iran in the Western sphere of influence. What had to be accomplished next was a concrete guarantee of action by the US government to achieve this objective. On September 28, following this policy success, King George II made his formal entry into Athens. Ambassador Norton felt that it would be difficult to integrate the king into the new Greek political structure because the royalists would probably become disillusioned with him, as he preferred to associate with "British officials" and his "English friends" and to read his English newspapers.

In addition to the return of the king, September 1946 was the worst month for acts of violence directed against the state since the signing of the Varkiza accord.[103] Although during the previous year, British policy had moved toward the creation of a parliamentary democracy in Greece and a national army to support it (the holding of the elections and plebiscite and the reformation of the justice system and the economy were key parts of that plan), these measures became a mechanism not only for greater British control but also to draw the United States further into Greek affairs.

---

[101] Byrnes to Clayton (4787), September 24, 1946, FRUS 1946, Vol. VII, The Near East and Africa, pp. 223–4.

[102] Clayton to Byrnes (711.68/9-2546), September 25, 1946, FRUS 1946, Vol. VII, The Near East and Africa, pp. 225–6.

[103] Norton to Bevin (R 15177/1/19), September 28, 1946, BDFA, Series F Europe, Part IV, Vol. 6., pp. 281–282 and (R 15503/1/19), ibid., p. 282.

The British were aided once again by reports of "provocations" on Greece's northern borders, which US Ambassador MacVeagh claimed were masterminded by "Soviet puppets" to provoke Greece to take action that would then justify "Soviet claims that Greece is a menace to peace." MacVeagh also stated that the Turkish Ambassador to Greece, sharing MacVeagh's view of the military threat to Greece, had said that a British troop withdrawal would be followed by a "Yugoslav Army Corps ... in Salonika within 24 hours."[104] The threat to Greece, whether or not it actually existed, was at that time clearly perceived by Anglo-American policy-makers, and the USSR's continued linking of Anglo-American policy to the "fascist monarchist regime" in Greece[105] illustrated how the widening gap between the wartime allies would expand into the Cold War.

1946: October to December

By October 1946, the Foreign Office had outlined its concerns regarding the popularity of the USSR in Britain and the lack of concern felt by some members of parliament and the general public over Soviet actions.

> In Great Britain a general realisation of the pattern of Soviet policy will come about slowly, and while it is forming, every allowance will be made to the Russians and none to the Foreign Office. The result of this will be a split in public opinion between those who blame the Russians and those who blame the Foreign Secretary. If we are to keep this split to the smallest possible proportions – and this we must do if we are to reduce the effectiveness of communist propaganda inside this country – we shall have to show patience, forbearance and a strict correctness in all our dealings with the Russians. We cannot afford to be in the wrong.[106]

At the British Embassy in Washington, Ambassador Inverchapel stated that the West had to oppose Soviet influence in Greece and Turkey.[107] Furthermore, though they acknowledged American financial and military superiority, the

---

[104] MacVeagh to Byrnes (1307), September 30, 1946, FRUS 1946, Vol. VII, The Near East and Africa, pp. 226–7.
[105] Dubrow, USSR, to Byrnes (3802), October 10, 1946, FRUS 1946, Vol. VII, The Near East and Africa, p. 233.
[106] Brimelow, minute, September 9, 1946 (FO 371 56835).
[107] Inverchapel to Bevin, November 5, 1946 (No. 2640), BDFA, Series C North America, Part IV, Vol. 1, pp. 301–3.

British had already clearly expressed their doubts about America's ability to make good use of this superiority.

> America is herself a troubled spirit: Conscious that she has attained greatness but ruefully aware that she is inadequately equipped with gifts of leadership in many fields and confronted with serious domestic problems of her own. Here in itself is an opportunity for Britain to set an example of greater steadiness and sanity to the English-speaking world.[108]

The British were also extremely concerned about the rapid US demobilization in Europe; according to the embassy in Washington, this demobilization reflected the fact that increasing numbers of US policy-makers favored financial over military intervention.[109] In response to what appeared to be concrete US action to invest heavily in the reconstruction of Europe, after the return of King George II the British continued their troop withdrawal from Greece. It was a slow process for many reasons, not least of which was the right-wing tendencies of the Greek government and the rapidly escalating violence between left- and right-wing forces in Greece. Additionally, the Yugoslavians had finally decided to help the KKE directly with money and supplies in October 1946, though this aid had taken six months to secure and commenced only after British troop reductions had begun in September.[110]

As well as the increasing violence in Greece, the ongoing communist support for the Democratic Army of Greece (DSE) and the composition of the Greek government initially made it difficult for the British to obtain assurances of aid for Greece from the United States. The Americans had serious concerns about worsening conditions in Greece, both internally and along its northern frontiers, and the State Department said that it was "prepared to take suitable measures to support the territorial and political integrity of Greece."[111] However, the United States also communicated to the Greek government that although it regarded Greece "as of vital interest to the United States" and would provide "substantial

---

[108] Balfour to Mason (AN 205/5/45), January 11, 1946, BDFA, Series C North America, Vol. 1, pp. 8–10.
[109] Washington Embassy to Foreign Office, BDFA, Series C North America, Part IV, Vol. 1, pp. 370–1 (paragraphs 13 and 19). See also: Byrnes to Clayton (4787), September 24, 1946, FRUS 1946, Vol. VII, The Near East and Africa, pp. 223–4, relating to the US favoring financial over military intervention.
[110] Smith, p. 97. Smith states that the Yugoslavians tried to "cultivate the impression that they had decided to support the KKE… and that their support was motivated by international solidarity." He bases these assumptions on the article "The Yugoslavs and the Greek Civil War, 1946–49" by Elizabeth Barker, who based her study exclusively on Yugoslavian sources.
[111] Acheson to MacVeagh (1336), October 15, 1946, FRUS 1946, Vol. VII, The Near East and Africa, pp. 235–7.

aid" to protect Greece's sovereignty and independence, this aid would be granted only if the Greek government could demonstrate to the American people that it was not "oligarchic or reactionary, that the democratic institutions were functioning and that the Greek people, apart from the communists, were united."[112] Furthermore, Ambassador MacVeagh, speaking to Ambassador Norton, said bluntly that "the American Government could hardly be expected to rush to the help of Greece while extreme Right-wing elements ... held important positions in the government."[113] So as the Greek government applied for more loans from the American and British governments, liberal and left-wing media (not specified in the dispatch) wrote that such loans should be granted only if the Greek government broadened its political platform. However, the escalating violence throughout the country prevented any change in political approach and also continued to create high levels of anxiety, especially as anti-government guerrillas seemed to be operating out of neighboring countries with increasing frequency.[114]

Despite American reservations about conditions in Greece, the State Department was by this time convinced that the Soviet Union was "aggressively attempting to bring under its control an ever-increasing number of nations," and it stated that "the strategic importance of Greece to US security lies in the fact that it is the only country in the Balkans which has not yet fallen under Soviet hegemony."[115] These statements clearly indicate the US position and highlight Britain's success in persuading US officials to adopt it. However, despite the success of British foreign policy, the rising violence on both sides in Greece did little to ease domestic criticism of British policy in Greece and Britain's relations with the United States.[116]

Meeting in Paris in November 1946, Foreign Secretary Bevin and Secretary of State Byrnes agreed that Britain would continue to supply arms to the Greek government since British troops were still in Greece, and the United States did

---

[112] Lagani, "US Forces in Greece in the 1950s," p. 310.
[113] Norton to Attlee (311), November 9, 1946, BDFA, Series F Europe, Part IV, Vol. 6, Doc R 16571/1/19, p. 285.
[114] Norton to Bevin (277), November 19, 1946, BDFA, Series F Europe, Part IV, Vol. 6 Doc R 16958/1/19, pp. 299–300. See also: Iatrides, "*Ambassador MacVeagh Reports*" pp. 701–3.
[115] Memorandum regarding Greece (868.00/10-2146), October 21, 1946, FRUS 1946, Vol. VII, The Near East and Africa, pp. 240–5. See: Chapter 1, pp. 30, 40–1, 44, 47–51.
[116] In November 1946, R. H. S. Crossman, who had become well known as one of Bevin's strongest opponents, stated in a House of Commons debate that Britain had become far too closely connected to the American system. His criticism broadened into the "keep left" movement, which called for Britain to be positioned somewhere between the United States and the Soviet Union and independent of both. This movement made it even harder for the British government to work toward closer US-British relations. See: Saville, p. 95.

not want to give the impression that it was "carrying on a provocative policy with regard to the Soviet Union and its Balkan puppets."[117] This decision indicated first that the British wanted to show the US that they intended to maintain a presence in Greece (whether they actually did or not) at least for a little while longer, and second that the United States was not yet expecting a British withdrawal.

Anglo-American policy in Greece was also influenced when the Greek government forwarded reports to the British and Americans that a Yugoslavian general had been dispatched from Belgrade to "take charge of all bandit groups operating in Greek territory." Furthermore, the Americans received information that the communists intended to sever northern Greece from the south, which would contribute to the growing anarchy and endanger the peace of the region.[118] However, within the UN, plans were being laid to set up a committee to investigate the situation along Greece's northern frontiers. The US again proposed a multinational committee that would send observers to northern Greece and report back to the UN under Article 34.[119] Simultaneously, Ambassador MacVeagh reported that the various "bandit groups" in Greece had been re-formed into a "self-declared 'army.'"[120] The DSE had formed, and the "third round" of the Greek Civil War was under way.

On December 12, 1946, Prime Minister Papandreou, admitting that Greece was again embroiled in civil war, said that appeasement was impossible and that "the question was now whether Greece should defend herself against the KKE or submit to it."[121] The Americans reiterated their belief in Soviet and Yugoslavian designs on the Dardanelles and Thessaloniki, respectively.[122] By December 1946, the Americans had demonstrated much greater levels of interest and involvement in Greek and European affairs, but British Prime Minister Attlee was still unsure

---

[117] Acheson to MacVeagh (Top Secret 868.24/11-846), November 8, 1946, FRUS 1946, Vol. VII, The Near East and Africa, pp. 262–3.

[118] MacVeagh to Byrnes (1604), November 18, 1946, FRUS 1946, Vol. VII, The Near East and Africa, p. 265.

[119] Hiss (UN) to Acheson (501.BC Greece/11-2146), November 21, 1946, FRUS 1946, Vol. VII, The Near East and Africa, pp. 266–7. Article 34 of the UN Charter allows the Security Council to investigate any situation or dispute that may lead to "international friction." It was preferred to Article 33, which was more specific, requiring that a dispute be proven to exist before the Security Council could investigate. See also: Memorandum (501.BC/11-2546), Undated, FRUS 1946, Vol. VII, The Near East and Africa, pp. 268–9.

[120] MacVeagh to Byrnes (1628), November 23, 1946, FRUS 1946, Vol. VII, The Near East and Africa, p. 268.

[121] Norton to Bevin (R 143/4/19), December 12, 1946, BDFA, Series F Europe, Part IV, Vol. 5, pp. 117–18.

[122] Incidents on Northern Greek Frontier (501.BC/12-946), December 9, 1946, FRUS 1946, Vol. VII, The Near East and Africa, pp. 276–7.

whether any foreign intervention could change conditions in Greece or whether the US would assume the role that the British hoped it would.

At the end of 1946, Attlee stated that in his opinion, the nations bordering the Soviet Union could not become strong enough to form a barrier that would withstand the Soviets should they decide to invade, nor did the British have the resources to boost these countries' strength. Furthermore, he said that it was difficult to know to what extent Soviet policy was dictated by fear of attack from the United States and Great Britain and to what extent it was influenced by expansionism; he suggested that perhaps the British should attempt to reach an agreement with the USSR to mutually disengage from these "border" nations.[123] However, Bevin vigorously opposed Attlee's suggestion (and was later proved right). Bevin believed that to withdraw from Eastern Europe and the Middle East would be "Munich over again, only on a world scale with Greece, Turkey and Persia as the first victims in place of Czechoslovakia." Bevin added that a withdrawal would also be very damaging to British-American relations, since the British were now economically and militarily dependent upon the United States and had taken great pains to persuade the United States that the maintenance of the British position in the Middle East was also in its strategic interests. Furthermore, Bevin believed that being linked to the United States would enable the British to negotiate with the Soviets from a position of strength.[124] Because he needed Bevin's support in the cabinet and influence with the trade unions, Attlee gave way.[125] So by the end of 1946, Britain's plan to maneuver the United States into assuming support for British interests in Greece and, by extension, in the Middle East and Eastern Europe had been almost fully revealed. However, it was not fully manifested until three months later.

In late 1946, Britain's plan to cling to American power to fulfil British foreign policy objectives came into focus. In reviewing government policy from the start of the Second World War to the start of the Cold War, it becomes clear that, rather than comparing Labour and Conservative policy on Greece, it is more appropriate simply to refer to "British policy." It was a policy that cut across party lines, one that was designed to preserve British interests at the expense of anyone except the British. The social, economic, and political costs of this policy were

---

[123] Attlee to Bevin, December 9, 1946, "Private Collections," *Foreign Office, Public Records Office* (London), FO 800, p. 475.
[124] Bevin to Attlee, January 9, 1947, "Private Collections," *Foreign Office, Public Records Office* (London), FO 800, p. 476.
[125] Weiler, pp. 161–2.

particularly high in Greece. Despite individual differences of opinion, British policy continued on its anti-communist path and drew along the Americans, who followed based both on the information and policy fed to them by the British and on the dynamics of domestic politics in the United States, where individuals and parties readily used the Soviet threat to advance their own agendas.

On December 1, 1946, Attlee wrote to Bevin, who was in New York for a meeting with Secretary of State Byrnes to lay out the plans for increasing American involvement in Europe. Attlee stated that in his opinion, the British position in the Middle East was only an "outpost position" and that he doubted whether the Greek "game" was worth the British effort.[126] Attlee was not sympathetic to the communists—quite the opposite—but he was more pragmatic than Bevin in his assessment of British capabilities in relation to foreign expenditure, and he was particularly aware of Britain's domestic situation, which meant that he was less willing than Bevin to maintain expensive foreign commitments.[127] Bevin rejected Attlee's arguments, stating that Attlee's proposal would showcase British weakness, which he saw as extremely dangerous considering how tenuous Britain's economic and military situation was. He said that when both the economic and military positions were "consolidated" and "it has finally become clear to the Russians that they cannot drive a wedge between the Americans and ourselves, we shall be in a position to negotiate with Stalin from strength." He concluded that there was no hurry to alter British foreign policy since the United States was becoming more involved and the United Nations Organization (UNO) was gaining strength; therefore, the British could "hold on to essential positions and concentrate on building up the UNO." The next week, Attlee and Bevin had a meeting in which Bevin declared that his Greek policy would continue and no British troops would be withdrawn.[128]

The last statement is particularly interesting, first because it represented a highly unusual relationship between a prime minister and foreign secretary

---

[126] Attlee, quoted in Bullock, p. 340. "Outpost position" meant that Attlee viewed Britain's position in Greece as temporary and non-vital. This was in stark contrast to Bevin, who strongly believed that a British presence in Greece was vital to British strategic interests and used his considerable influence in the cabinet to overrule the prime minister. For an earlier example of Attlee's view, see chapter 2, March 2, 1946, when he came into conflict with the British Chiefs of Staff over Greece's strategic importance.

[127] Harris, pp. 297–9. Later, in 1947, Attlee would comment on how inexperienced he believed the Americans to be in their understanding and appreciation of Stalin and Soviet objectives. Into early 1947, Attlee continued to call for a serious re-assessment of British Middle Eastern strategic objectives, and he strongly criticized the arguments of the Chiefs of Staff. However, he remained unsuccessful in changing the course of British policy.

[128] Clement Attlee, quoted in Bullock, pp. 342–50.

who in practice seemed almost to have reversed roles. Second, despite Bevin's assertion that British policy would continue and that no troops would be withdrawn, his statements in February 1947 to the United States indicated the opposite. This point is crucial to the central argument of this book. The statements indicate that the British deliberately misled and manipulated the United States into assuming responsibility for Greece, and through it for Western Europe, and that this was what led to its subsequent worldwide effort to contain communism.

Given the cabinet forces and considerations aligned against him, it is unlikely that Attlee could have changed the course of British policy, particularly as he continued to rely heavily upon Bevin's support in the British cabinet to remain as prime minister.[129] Notwithstanding their promise to withdraw from Egypt, the British were not prepared to jeopardize their position in the Eastern Mediterranean.[130] In spite of their internal differences of opinion, it is important to keep in mind that the British were convinced of Soviet intentions to control Eastern Europe and expand westward.

In Greece, the general communist threat perceived by the West appeared again when the Bulgarians claimed Western Thrace and the Yugoslavians claimed parts of Macedonia to be incorporated into the Yugoslav People's Republic of Macedonia (PRM). This convinced Greek policy-makers that the communists were determined to attempt a takeover of at least northern Greece, if not the whole country.[131] According to the French Ambassador in Athens, the Greek government had already renewed its repression of political adversaries, and its actions in the field in northern Greece, limited as they were at the time, worsened the relations between Greece and her northern neighbors.[132]

As 1946 drew to a close, conditions in Greece were barely more promising than they had been a year earlier, but in terms of British plans for American policy, success seemed tantalizingly close. The Attlee-Bevin government had worked for a year and a half to keep Greece under its influence. However, the

---

[129] Harris, p. 286, and Bullock, p. 352.
[130] Previously stated in: Halifax to Bevin, May 13, 1946 (AN, 1515/1/45), BDFA, Series C North America, Vol. 1, p. 159.
[131] Hatzivassiliou, p. 8. The alliance of the Bulgarian and Yugoslav governments was perceived as a major threat to Greece until the Tito-Stalin split in June 1948, which turned Bulgaria and Yugoslavia into adversaries.
[132] Lagani, "*Les Rapports De La Grèce Avec Ses Voisins,*" p. 246. Quoting reports of the French Consul in Thessaloniki, AEP, Greece, Z 177-1, vol. 155, no. 54, Salonique (Consul Raoul Duval, a AEP., August 26, 1946).

international conditions created by rapidly declining British power and the widening gap between the wartime allies contributed to Britain's inability to fully meet that objective. As a result, Greece was as divided and unstable as it had been since liberation, if not more so.

As another new year approached, there was little to encourage a sense of optimism. In a dispatch to Foreign Secretary Bevin on December 28, 1946, referring to the constantly changing political and military situation in Greece, Ambassador Norton said, "Nothing in Greece seems to stay put for very long, except the Acropolis."[133] The state of the British economy was also worsening, and it seemed to many US observers that the situation in the UK was as desperate as the British claimed.

The Chancellor of the Exchequer could lend no more money, and people in Britain were still using food stamps. Even as the violence in Greece worsened, the British continued to remove its troops, and everything they had worked for since October 1944 was in jeopardy. Because Greece was the only Balkan/Eastern European nation (not including Turkey) to have a (somewhat) diverse, democratically elected government, it became an important symbol for the West, and the Americans would have to make an almost immediate decision on whether to support it.

As tensions between the USSR and the United States continued to escalate, US reservations about helping Greece began to dissipate in spite of Greek governmental problems.[134] For the United States, the Greek Civil War provided evidence of the aggressive intentions of the USSR to control "an ever-increasing number of nations" whose value in strategic terms was crucial to American interests. As a result of this belief, the Office of Near Eastern and African Affairs in the State Department recommended that the US government "firmly oppose the USSR's 'manoeuvres and machinations ... to expand its power by subjecting Greece to its will, and then using Greece as an important stepping-stone for a further expansion of Soviet power.'"[135] At this time, US hostility to the Soviets was so high that Secretary Byrnes

---

[133] Norton to Bevin (R 143/4/19), December 28, 1946, BDFA, Series F Europe, Part IV, Vol. 5, pp. 117–18.
[134] Incidents on Northern Greek Frontier (501.BC/12-946), December 9, 1946, FRUS 1946, Vol. VII, The Near East and Africa, pp. 276–7. See also: Ole L. Smith, p. 98.
[135] Memorandum by the Office of Near Eastern and African Affairs of the State Department, October 21, 1946, FRUS 1946, Vol. VII, The Near East and Africa, p. 242.

refused a Greek proposal to hold a meeting between US, Soviet and British representatives to solve the northern frontier issue, despite support by Molotov and Bevin support for the proposal.[136]

The Americans perceived the Soviets as operating behind the scenes, encouraging Greece's communist neighbors to act aggressively. The United States was convinced that there was a real possibility of "all out revolution" in Greece by April 1947 and, foreshadowing the reversal of the British and American roles in Greece, agreed to supply military transport aircraft to the Greek military to aid it in combating the insurgents.[137] Furthermore, in response to what it saw as a slow British response to the pressing needs of the Greek military, the United States advised Britain to create a list of all other military equipment needed by the Greek military that the British were unable to supply and to forward it promptly to the US.[138] The United States' reluctance to supply arms to Greece had dissipated along with Britain's ability to supply them. Interestingly, this decision was reached as the Security Council unanimously agreed to form a committee to investigate conditions on the Greek border.[139] Though this seemed a positive step toward a possible resolution of the dispute, the committee would instead reflect the widening gap between the Soviet Union and Britain and the United States.

---

[136] For a more complete picture of British perceptions of US-Soviet tensions at this time, see: Bevin to Foreign Office, December 6, 1946, no. 17677, FO 371/58891. Interview between Bevin and Tsaldaris, 6 December 1946, no. 18531, FO 371/58892. Bevin to Foreign Office, December 7, 1946, no. 17689, FO371/58891. Warner to Williams, December 11, 1946, no. 18129, FO 371/58891. Record of conversation between Bevin and Molotov, December 9, 1946; minutes of a conference between Bevin and Byrnes, December 9, 1946. Note by Dixon, December 19, 1946. Minutes by McCarthy, December 19, 1946, no. 18129, FO 371/58891.

[137] Note 63 in Acheson to MacVeagh (1583), December 13, 1946, FRUS 1946, Vol. VII, The Near East and Africa, pp. 278–9.

[138] MacVeagh to Byrnes (1721), December 16, 1946, FRUS 1946, Vol. VII, The Near East and Africa, pp. 282–3.

[139] Johnson, UN, to Byrnes (983), December 19, 1946, FRUS 1946, Vol. VII, The Near East and Africa, pp. 284–5.

3

A New Era of American Intervention: The Truman Doctrine, the Marshall Plan and the Beginning of the Cold War

January to March 1947

"While Soviet power is impervious to the logic of reason, it is highly sensitive to the logic of force."[1] Though written in February 1946, these lines can be said to sum up the fundamental American attitude toward the USSR by 1947. The ongoing disputes over Greece's northern frontiers took on a life of their own, making their way to the UN Security Council and then to the General Assembly. How the issue was used by the US and USSR in these arenas highlights the change in their relations and the role played by the British in influencing American policy. It was also another year of economic calamity for Greece, and the continuing economic instability went hand in hand with the ongoing political, social, and military crises in the country.

Since late 1944, the British had been unable to resolve the economic situation, and as the Americans began to play a greater role, they too would be faced with a very difficult task in the economic sphere. As a result, 1947 became a year of profound change in Greece because of the change in British, American, and Soviet relations. This change was clearly reflected in the work and findings of the UN Special Committee on the Balkans (UNSCOB), which was formed and sent to Greece to evaluate the validity of the Greek government's claims regarding its northern neighbors' violations of the border in support of the KKE and the DSE since the end of 1945. Although tasked with resolving the situation in Greece,

---

[1] Kennan to Byrnes (511), February 22, 1946, FRUS 1946, Vol. VI, Eastern Europe and the Soviet Union, pp. 696–709.

UNSCOB did little more than reflect the deepening division between Britain, the United States, and the Soviet Union. However, it allowed the British to secure American military and economic intervention in Greece.

On the international front, by January 1947, the United States had almost completed one of the most rapid demobilizations of armed forces in history.[2] This was in part because of the desire of the Truman administration to reduce armed forces expenditures, the Americans believing that their possession of the atomic bomb would serve as a sufficient deterrent to curtail further Soviet encroachment in Europe. Additionally, the Americans foresaw economic development as a key tool to prevent further communist expansion.[3]

The implementation of economic containment in Greece was initiated through the Porter Economic Mission, which arrived in Athens in mid-January 1947 and initiated talks with hundreds of Greek engineers, businessmen, farmers, workers, organization spokesmen, and economists in order to assess the current Greek economic situation.[4] Porter concluded that the situation was worse than expected and that the country was on the verge of bankruptcy owing to numerous factors, such as politics permeating every facet of Greek life, the black market, the lack of long-term investment or reconstruction programs (largely because of a lack of confidence in the government), and the dependence mentality of the Greek people—they felt that the Allies were obliged to help them because of the suffering they had endured during the Second World War.[5] Porter even argued that Greece was not truly a state according to the Western definition. He described a "loose hierarchy of individualistic politicians" who had no interest in reform owing to their preoccupation with their own power; in his opinion, the greatest threats facing the country were economic.[6]

However, Ambassador MacVeagh disagreed with Porter's assessment and argued that the greatest threat to Greece was the military situation along the northern border. He believed that if that situation was resolved then the economic and political issues could be dealt with.[7] Although both views later proved to be more or less accurate, the UN had already endorsed the American plan to

---

[2] Ambrose, pp. 76–7. The army was reduced from 8 to 1 million men, the navy from 3.5 to less than 1 million, and the air force from 200 combat groups to less than 50.
[3] Ambrose, p. 89. This superiority would only be short-lived, since on August 29, 1949, the Soviet Union conducted its first successful weapon test.
[4] Jones, p. 29.
[5] Jones, p. 29.
[6] Porter to Clayton, February 14, 1947 and Porter to Truman, March 3, 1947, Porter Papers, Truman Library, pp. 2–5.
[7] Jones, p. 30.

form an international committee to investigate the military situation on Greece's northern frontiers.⁸ While Attlee had been seeking to disengage Britain from some of its international obligations since mid-1946, by January 1947, the first areas where he felt he could do so were Greece and Turkey because he believed that the US could be persuaded to assume Britain's role in these countries.⁹ The British intended UNSCOB to prove to the Americans, and also to the rest of the world, that the Soviets intended to take over Greece and were acting through the KKE and Greece's communist neighbors to do so. UNSCOB was declared to be independent, but not surprisingly, the Big Three dominated its activities, thereby ensuring that its conclusions reflected their respective positions.¹⁰

The idea of forming a UN commission to investigate Greece's allegations against its communist neighbors was proposed in the UN Security Council by the United States; shortly thereafter, both the British and the Americans began to pressure the Greek government to broaden its composition and to unite the centrist parties to isolate the KKE. They also wished to limit the increasing extremism of the Greek government in light of the international exposure that would be generated by the creation of UNSCOB.¹¹ Additionally, while the KKE expected UNSCOB to settle the domestic situation and enable it to participate in the government, the British and Americans wanted the commission to cut off the KKE's foreign support and pursued a policy that they hoped would prevent the communists from replenishing their armed forces by closing Greece's northern boundaries. They believed that the sooner the DSE and the military threat it represented were exhausted, the sooner the Greek government could begin to assert its authority more effectively and, in so doing, foster a sense of legitimacy.¹²

---

⁸ Letter from the Acting Chairman of the Delegation of Greece to the Secretary-General, 3 December 1946, and Enclosed Memorandum, no. 18181, FO 371/5889.
⁹ Harris, pp. 299, 304. Although Attlee initially intended to keep to the "short and arbitrary deadline" of March 31, after Truman's declaration on March 12, he consented to delaying the complete removal of Britain's armed forces until American aid had begun. Attlee ordered Foreign Secretary Bevin, who was in Moscow, to inform Marshall that the British would stay in Greece past the March 31, 1947 deadline to facilitate the transition. For the complete dispatch, see: BDFA, Series F Europe, Part IV, Vol. 12, Doc R 3708/50/G and Doc R 3935/50/G, pp. 142–3.
¹⁰ Sfikas, pp. 244–5.
¹¹ This is a summary of many documents that outline the British hopes and objectives at the time. Listed next are some of the most demonstrative dispatches. Memorandum by Sargent, July 11, 1945, *Documents on British Policy Overseas* (hereafter DBPO), Vol. 1, no. 102 (London: HMSO, 1984). See also Bullock, *Bevin*, pp. 5–6, Interview between Harvey and Aghnidis, December 28, 1946 (no. 33, FO 371/66994). Inverchapel to Foreign Office, January 1, 1947 (no. 77, FO 371/66994). Norton to Bevin, December 28, 1946 (no. 143, FO 371/66994). Norton to Tsaldaris, January 3, 1947 (no. 520, FO 371/67049). Tsaldaris to Norton, January 10, 1947 (no. 832, FO 371/67049). Foreign Office to Norton, January 8, 1947 (no. 113, FO 371/67049). Foreign Office to Norton, January 19, 1947 (no. 715, FO 371/66996).
¹² Ibid., and Sfikas, p. 250.

The UN commission arrived in Athens on January 30, 1947, and the issue of whether the domestic situation in Greece fell under its jurisdiction was immediately raised. The British and Americans claimed that UNSCOB's only role should be to rule on Greece's northern frontier violations, while the Soviet, Bulgarian, Yugoslav, and EAM representatives argued that only conditions in Athens and southern Greece should be examined.[13]

The commission partially acceded to the demands of the Balkan representatives by urging the Greek government to suspend executions of left-wing prisoners. The British were not pleased with the "independent" policy pursued by UNSCOB, but US Secretary of State Marshall supported its conclusions, arguing that not supporting the commission's recommendation would play into the hands of the Soviets. On February 9, 1947, the UN Secretary-General issued UNSCOB's recommendation to the Greek government, which reluctantly complied.[14] Now, the American Economic Mission to Greece had been keeping the US government informed of developments since early 1947, and its members had more negative comments about the Greek situation than UNSCOB. On February 17, 1947, Paul Porter informed the US government that "it is characteristic of these people not to take corrective measures until absolutely necessary, and then, only to take a minimum."[15] His reports also noted complete disorganization and an inefficient bureaucracy that was incapable of dealing with the slightest government initiative. Porter added that the short working week enabled many civil servants to hold other jobs, further reducing efficiency and increasing corruption.[16] There was also almost no way to protect the UNRRA supplies that were arriving in Greece from disappearing into the black market.

On the military question, earlier in the year Bevin had requested that the United States provide military aid and training to the Greek armed forces in the

---

[13] Norton to Foreign Office, February 5, 1947, no. 1809 (FO 371/66999). Peck to Chancery (Athens), February 5, 1947 (no. 2096, FO 371/67062). However, Britain was experiencing severe economic hardship by mid-February 1947, and the British began to see the commission as a way to facilitate their exit with or without American guarantees. UNSCOB was temporarily allowed to pursue solutions to Greece's internal political situation. See: Minutes by Selby and Williams, February 17–19, 1947 (no. 1975, FO 371/67000).

[14] Norton to Bevin, February 18, 1948, Annual Report 1947 (no. 51 R 2576/31/19), February 18, 1948, BDFA, Part IV, Series F Europe, Vol. 17, pp. 72–94. Peck (Thessaloniki) to Athens, February 5, 1947 (no. 2096, FO 371/67062). MacVeagh to Marshall (169), February 7, 1947, FRUS 1947, Vol. V, The Near East and Africa, pp. 817–18. Marshall to MacVeagh (146), February 8, 1947, FRUS 1947, Vol. V, The Near East and Africa, pp. 818–20.

[15] Paul A. Porter to the US Department of State, February 17, 1947, University of North Carolina Library, Chapel Hill, Ethridge Paper Number 3842.

[16] Paul A. Porter, "Our Chances in Greece," August 7, 1947, University of North Carolina Library, Chapel Hill, Ethridge Paper Number 3842.

event that the communists violated the ceasefire or the UN commission failed to find a solution to the border violations. He wanted the Greek government forces to be prepared and trained for guerrilla warfare.[17] Consistent with Porter's observations months later, the British wrote that the intense anti-communism, corruption, and incompetence of the army, the police and the bureaucracy were so pervasive that no government could make a difference.[18]

Even so, by the spring of 1947, the only significant remaining British military presence was a small military mission that became responsible for training and acted mainly in accord with the American Military Mission (AMM) in Greece. Since 1945, the British Military Mission (BMM) had been responsible for training the new Greek army, but with few positive results. Owing partly to a lack of resources and partly to a lack of urgency, British training proceeded slowly and was made even less effective by the failure to provide training in counter-guerrilla tactics; instead, recruits were trained in conventional warfare.[19] Another blunder by the foreign military missions was their inability to rapidly and accurately assess how many troops were needed to pursue the enemy and to protect communications, civilians, and installations. For example, in early 1947, the Greek army had approximately 100,000 men, but less than half were combat-ready, and even at full strength it would have been hard-pressed to accomplish all of its objectives.

Although the military situation was dire, the Americans believed that the most pressing concern was still the weakness of Greece's economy. They were well informed of the economic situation, and they believed that without emergency aid and "long-range" economic planning, Greece would collapse and endanger American access to Middle East oil and attempts to constrain Soviet expansion.[20] The American forecast and objectives for Greece, the Eastern Mediterranean and the Middle East increasingly resembled Britain's objectives in the immediate post-war period.

By this time, Britain's coal reserves, manpower and assets, both at home and overseas, had been significantly diminished, while its liabilities had increased.

---

[17] Memorandum by Bevin, "Policy toward Greece and Turkey," January 25, 1947, no. 34, CAB 129/16/CP (47). See also CAB 128/9/CM 14 (47), January 30, 1947. See also: Bevin to Norton (384), February 19, 1947 and Bevin to Inverchapel (1634), February 19, 1947, BDFA, Series F Europe, Part IV, Vol. 12, 1947, pp. 122–5.

[18] Lascelles to Foreign Office, January 25, 1947 (no. 1138, FO 371/66997). Norton to Bevin, December 28, 1946 (no. 143, FO 371/66994).

[19] It was not until the latter phases of the Civil War in 1949 that anti-guerrilla tactics were taught at all—at the very moment that Nikos Zachariadis ordered DSE commanders to switch to conventional warfare.

[20] Jones, p. 26.

Its industries were outdated, and British exports were negligible. In addition, with unemployment at 15 percent in 1947, extreme domestic weather conditions leading to property damage and crop failure, and a severe fuel shortage, Britain was in a desperate condition.[21] The economy was reeling, and Bevin said that if Britain were to survive, it would need to coordinate its foreign policy with that of the only country capable of exerting significant economic power: the United States.[22] Although Attlee had been elected in the near-euphoric period immediately following the defeat of Germany, by 1947, that enthusiasm had almost disappeared as the British government finally began to see the results of its anti-Soviet policy, and the people of both Britain and the United States began to believe that the greatest threat, not only to Britain but to the West as a whole, was the Soviet Union. Three days before the British announced their withdrawal from Greece, Permanent Under-Secretary Sir Orme Sargent encouraged the British government to continue to use the fear of the Soviets to secure American involvement, first in Greece and then in Europe, thereby guaranteeing the protection of British interests.

At the beginning of 1947, these conditions were well known to the American government, and there was a fear that Britain could go bankrupt. Britain faced so many challenges worldwide that bankruptcy was a real possibility if its government continued to attempt to play the full part of a world power. The winter of 1946/47 was very severe, causing significant damage to crops across Europe and particularly in Britain. As a result, Britain's industrial, food, and coal reserves were almost exhausted, as were whatever funds remained in the treasury, and these issues were compounded by government expenditures that further demonstrated Britain's inability to reconcile its domestic needs with its international obligations.[23]

Britain's energy crisis was compounded by its antiquated manufacturing and industrial sector, which had not undergone a substantial, rigorous modernization for over a century. So although "the gap between policy and resources was not created by the February 1947 energy emergency," the crisis

---

[21] Jones, pp. 31–2.

[22] Ernest Bevin, "The Effects of our External Financial Position on our Foreign Policy," February 12, 1947 (FO 371/62420 UE 678/176/53).

[23] Bullock, *Bevin*, p. 381. In March 1947, Bevin met with Joseph Stalin in Moscow and attempted to convince him that Britain's stated shortage of coal reserves was real. These issues had been plaguing Britain to some degree since the end of the Second World War, but by 1946/47, they had become more pressing. See the earlier section on British food supply problems in 1946. Page 111, note 240 (Halifax to Bevin, April 27, 1946 (AN 1269/1/45), BDFA, Series C North America, Part IV, Vol. 1, pp. 151–2). See also references to Britain's coal crisis: Doc. 57, February 15, 1947, BDFA, Series F Europe, Part IV, Vol. 10, France, 1947.

ensured that it "was driven home with a force that could not be denied."[24] It soon became apparent that the British might not be able to meet their obligations, and the Americans were extremely concerned about how Britain's economic weakness might hinder its foreign policy. That weakness was exposed by the ongoing crisis in Greece: British Ambassador Clifford Norton advised London that Greece was in such dire straits that it would not be able to successfully oppose the communist threat unless it received substantial economic and military aid. At this point, Foreign Secretary Bevin had to admit that Britain could do no more.

The British were aided in their efforts to persuade the Americans to assume responsibility for Greece by the crisis in Poland, where the communists had seized power, and subsequent communist victories in Romania and Bulgaria.[25] Moreover, the Bulgarian Prime Minister openly told Britain's acting political representative in Sofia that "opposition politicians were saboteurs obstructing the building of a better Bulgaria" and that they would "deserve the preventative medicine" he was preparing for them.[26] These events would coincide to help President Truman sell his program of economic and military anti-communism to the United States Congress. The British had succeeded, at least for the time being, in securing a firm commitment of substantial American economic and military support for British interests in Greece, and through it the Eastern Mediterranean, Europe and, they hoped, soon the Far East.

On 15 February in Washington, Secretary of State Marshall stated that "it is to the interest of the United States and of all the United Nations that Greece be assisted to maintain her independence and national integrity."[27] Driven by their own economic problems, the British took advantage of the negative American Economic Mission reports and Marshall's statement. On February 19, 1947, Bevin decided that the time was finally right to force the United States to directly assume responsibility for British interests in Greece. He instructed the British Ambassador to the United States, Lord Inverchapel, to deliver a memorandum to the US State Department regarding the situation in Greece. It expressed Britain's desire for the United States to replace the British in assisting the Greek armed forces and economy, since Greece was on the verge of collapse. As the memorandum

---

[24] Bullock, p. 362.
[25] These crises occurred in the first two months of 1947.
[26] Bulgarian Prime Minister to British Embassy (32, R 2749/889/7), 17 February 1947, BDFA, Series F Europe, Part IV, south-eastern Europe, Vol. 12, pp.64–6.
[27] Washington Embassy to Foreign Office (UR 1248/25/851), February 15, 1947, BDFA, Series F Europe, Part IV, Vol. 12, p. 122.

explained, Britain's aid to Greece would expire on 31 March, after which point it would be unable to grant any further assistance. By all reports, the timing of this memorandum initially shocked the State Department, and it quickly decided to convince the American people and Congress of the need for the United States to assume a more significant role "in the direction of world affairs" and to seize the opportunity provided by Britain's decision.[28]

In Washington, the American response to the announced British withdrawal from Greece was rapid. The British declaration, made on February 21, 1947, was answered by the US State Department on February 26. Acheson's domino theory, as it came to be known, held that should one country fall to the communists, its neighbors would soon follow. On March 12, in a move that formalized US opposition to the expansion of Soviet influence, President Truman addressed the US Congress about "giving aid to Greece and Turkey. Truman informed the US congress that assistance is imperative if Greece is to survive as a free nation." After summarizing Greece's non-military needs and requests, Truman addressed the military situation in the country:

> The very existence of the Greek State is today threatened by the terrorist activities of several thousand armed men, led by communists, who defy the government's authority at a number of points particularly along the northern boundaries ... the Greek government is unable to cope with the situation. The Greek army is small and poorly equipped. It needs supplies and equipment if it is to restore the authority of the government throughout Greek territory. Greece must have assistance if it is to become a self-supporting and self-respecting democracy. The United States must supply that assistance.[29]

This announcement committed the United States to the role that the British had been playing in Greece since 1944, and the British thereby achieved their objective of handing over their responsibilities. The British government could no longer justify expensive foreign commitments, and when it reached its breaking point, it maneuvered the Americans into taking over as patrons of Greece. Attlee was anxious to extricate Britain from Greece so that his government could focus on rebuilding Britain and Germany. Since it appeared that the Soviets would ultimately control Poland, and considering that they already had a foothold in East Germany, Attlee believed that Britain's security depended on a

---

[28] Alexander, pp. 243–4.
[29] Truman's speech of March 12, 1947, quoted in: (R 3426/50/19), BDFA, Series F Europe, Part IV, Vol. 12, pp. 138–41.

non-communist Germany that could serve as a buffer against Soviet expansion into Western Europe.[30]

The Truman Doctrine made it clear to the Soviets that the Americans would not tolerate any direct intervention in Greece. Therefore, Stalin steadfastly maintained his advice to the KKE to seek a compromise, just as he had done a year earlier. However, the Soviets exerted some pressure by continuing to insist that the cause of the Civil War was the repressive right-wing nature of the national government, while the British and Americans continued to stress the external causes.[31]

Meanwhile, in Greece, UNSCOB arrived in Thessaloniki on February 25, 1947 to investigate and report on the violations of Greece's northern border. After failing to meet with DSE leader Markos Vafiadis, the commission returned to Thessaloniki on March 12, 1947, without the Polish and Soviet members, who remained to meet the DSE leader. When these members returned to Thessaloniki, they presented the commission with a report outlining the KKE's records of the "White Terror" that had followed the signing of the Varkiza accord and its proposals for an end to the Civil War. However, in the meantime, the commission had taken evidence from numerous Greek government witnesses about the Albanian, Bulgarian, and Yugoslav border violations, which the British reported as the focus of the commission's work. Though the Soviets had attempted to keep the commission in Athens to investigate the domestic causes of the Civil War, the British and Americans succeeded in persuading it to examine the external causes of the conflict. This point is crucial in understanding not only the objectives of the Big Three but also how they attempted to achieve them.

The British and Americans wanted to maintain Greece as a buffer state against further communist expansion and believed that the Civil War had to be contained and isolated from outside influences. The Soviets, also keen to contain the Civil War at this time, urged the KKE to seek reconciliation but also sought to direct attention to domestic causes and to achieve communist participation in the government, which they hoped could lead to a

---

[30] Harris, pp. 247–8. The United States followed Attlee's lead in this, reversing the previous policy that the German standard of living should be kept below that of the rest of Europe. Instead, through the Marshall Plan, and specifically the provisions on debt relief, the United States financed West German reconstruction, leading to the *Wirtschaftswunder* ("economic miracle"), as the Federal Republic's rapid recovery after the Second World War was described. See: Berger, Helge, Ritschl, and Albrecht, pp. 199–245.

[31] Multiple dispatches between Secretary of State Marshall and Ethridge (244, 19, 21, 111, 185), FRUS 1947, Vol. V, The Near East and Africa, pp. 823–30. The Americans even considered a population exchange of Slavophones as a possible solution to the communists' territorial claims on Macedonia. See: ibid., Number 244, p. 823.

future re-alignment of Greek foreign policy that was more favorable to them. All three sides attempted to use UNSCOB to support their policies for Greece and in so doing prevented the commission from actually helping to find a resolution to the conflict. As a result, the findings of UNSCOB did little more than reiterate these differences.

As the USSR continued to extend its control over Central and Eastern Europe, a clear distinction began to emerge between America's foreign and military policies. Although the Americans wanted to contain any further communist expansion, the only military deterrent they possessed was the atomic bomb, which seemed to have no effect on Soviet planning. It was clear that the Truman administration saw economic chaos as the key factor in facilitating the spread of communism. However, a debate arose as to whether solving the economic question would resolve the military situation, or whether the military situation had to be dealt with before the economic and political system could be fixed.[32] The former option, supported by George Kennan, was discarded in favor of military aid.

Interestingly, one of the most significant differences between the official British and American interventions in Greece was the degree to which the two countries were prepared to become directly involved in the decision-making process. Through late 1945 and into 1946, the British had become increasingly reluctant to order political and military action. Correspondingly, the Greek government was less and less inclined to listen to British recommendations. This tendency, combined with the inability of the Greek military to suppress the increasing insurrectionism and the massive power struggles between political parties, paralyzed the Greek government and drove the country deeper into chaos. The Americans held no such reservations.

What would later be called the "domino theory"[33] was the driving force behind the American belief that intervention in Greece was vital to prevent more "dominos" from falling. After the declaration of the Truman Doctrine, the Americans feared that failure in Greece could lead to the loss of Turkey and the Dardanelles, cut off access to the Middle East and then result in the loss of Italy, France, and Germany. They used this view to justify not only their support for the Greek government but also their increasing involvement in the Greek decision-making process.

---

[32] Ambrose, p. 88.
[33] First used by President Eisenhower in 1954.

When the Americans assumed Britain's role in Greece, they made it clear that continued aid was contingent upon government cooperation. In addition, the United States used the United Nations to investigate the aid that the Greek communists were receiving from Greece's communist neighbors.[34] Two months after Truman's speech of 12 March, the US Congress authorized 400 million dollars of aid to Greece and Turkey. However, at that stage the United States was in a position to offer only economic aid. It is important to examine the international issues confronting the Truman administration to place the ongoing official and unofficial British involvement in Greece in an international context.

On March 13, 1947, the day after the declaration of the Truman Doctrine, the British Embassy in Washington noted that there appeared to be a genuine desire among Americans in general to share their prosperity and wealth and to resist the Soviets.[35] Further assisting British efforts to secure greater American aid for Britain and Western Europe was the belief in the United States that the European economy would soon suffer a serious decline, meaning that Europeans would be unable to continue purchasing US products at their current levels. The increase in US production during the war had created a danger of export surpluses afterwards. This spurred the American business sector to lobby to maintain and then increase US foreign aid, which from 1945 to 1947 financed approximately 33 percent of American exports.[36] The desires of American business, combined with British objectives and the rise of US political anti-communism—highlighted by George Kennan's famous report on the Soviet Union in which he advocated containment—[37]created the perfect conditions for the British to secure American support for their strategic objectives, which were highlighted by the Truman Doctrine in March 1947 and the Marshall Plan in June 1947.

---

[34] Iatrides, "Britain, the United States and Greece, 1945–9," pp. 196–203.
[35] Inverchapel to Foreign Office, March 13, 1947 (FO371/ 67035/R3482). Inverchapel to Bevin (615 E), March 13, 1947, pp. 87–9. Inverchapel to Bevin (675), March 18, 1947, pp. 93–8, BDFA Part IV, Series C North America, Vol. 2. 1947. Ibid. **Note:** For an unexplained reason, page 85 (73), document number 17675, and page 86 (74), document number 17675, are **not** included in this volume of the confidential print series. It is simply stated that they are unavailable. Judging from the time period, they may have contained more dispatches related to the Truman Doctrine, but at this time, I can only speculate.
[36] Seville, pp. 23–24.
[37] Kennan to Byrnes (511), February 22, 1946, FRUS 1946, Vol. VI, Eastern Europe and the Soviet Union, pp. 696–709. This document was classified until 1947, when it was published in *Foreign Affairs* magazine in July. It subsequently became the basis for US foreign policy toward the USSR and was required reading for members of the State Department, despite the author's later statements that his meaning of "containment" had been misinterpreted and misapplied.

1947: April to December, A New Type of War

A new world order was emerging and, in a symbolic turn of events marking the end of the old Greek-British relationship, King George II died suddenly of a heart attack on April 1, 1947.[38] It was sadly ironic that so much blood had been shed in the years following the German occupation over the return to Greece of a king whose reign would last little more than six months. A few days later, UNSCOB met in Geneva, Switzerland, to assemble its report on Greece.[39] What happened next is a crucial point that clearly demonstrates the extent of British influence over US policy and highlights how the crisis in Greece had effects far beyond Greek borders in terms of relations between the USSR and the communist world and between the US and the non-communist world. Through their actions and discussions in the UN over the Greek issue, the two camps established the ways in which they would engage with each other throughout the Cold War.

At the UNSCOB meeting in Switzerland, the Soviet and Polish delegates requested that a translated report of the KKE and DSE positions on the causes and resolution of the Civil War be circulated to the other committee members. The British strenuously objected but were overruled by a vote of seven to four. The British Foreign Office was incensed and believed that the American representative, Mark Ethridge, had not objected to the Soviet and Polish proposal as firmly as he should have done. The Foreign Office asked its representative, Windell, whether Ethridge was likely to continue to act "contrarily." If so, it would make its objections known to the US State Department.[40] Simultaneously, the French representative attempted to convince the commission to refrain from reaching any conclusion of blame whatsoever and to allow amnesty and free elections in Greece. The British Foreign Office contacted the US State Department and urged the Americans to pressure the members of the committee to reject the French stance. Britain saw France's position as an acceptance of the Soviet line and an example of "meddling" in internal Greek affairs.[41] The British

---

[38] Norton to Foreign Office (no. 750, T6802/6802/379), April 1, 1947, BDFA, Series F Europe, Part IV, Vol. 12, p. 143.
[39] Acheson to Ethridge (89), April 1, 1947, FRUS 1947, Vol. V, The Near East and Africa, pp. 830–1.
[40] Windlel (Geneva) to Foreign Office, April 18, 1947, Foreign Office to Windel, April 23, 1947 (no. 5291, FO 371/67065), and Clutter (Geneva) to Williams, May 8, 1947 (no. 6644, FO 371/67068). See also an earlier dispatch regarding British instructions to the British representative on UNSCOB: Bevin to Windel (61), March 1, 1947, BDFA, Series F Europe, Part IV, Vol. 12, pp. 132–3.
[41] Inverchapel to Foreign Office, April 29, 1947 (no. 5742, FO 371/67066), Bevin to Inverchapel (4241), April 29, 1947, BDFA, Series F Europe, Part IV, Vol. 12, pp. 195–6, and Marshall to Ethridge (253), May 1, 1947, FRUS 1947, Vol. V, The Near East and Africa, pp. 837–8.

also pressured the State Department to force Ethridge to "toe the line," but he refused, stating that he believed that the "gangster-like methods" of the Greek government were responsible for the ongoing Civil War and northern border violations.[42] The British and the State Department, however, were anxious to spare the Greek government any blame, and when Ethridge included a proposal for amnesty for guerrillas and political prisoners in his draft report, they reacted accordingly.[43] Marshall urged Ethridge to remove the amnesty clause from the final report since the US believed that the guerrillas were acting under orders from the Soviets, and Ambassador Norton blamed "Ethridge's folly" for the Truman Doctrine getting off to a "bad start" in Greece.[44] In the end, the Foreign Office was successful in persuading the State Department to modify the commission's report to mention only that a new amnesty law was being considered by the Greek government.[45]

Though the final report satisfied the British and Americans as it contained statements regarding the Yugoslavian, Bulgarian, and Albanian provision of material and moral support (via the continuing border violations) to the KKE and DSE and the fomentation of separatist movements, it did attempt, at least on the surface, to meet the Soviet objective (though the Soviets refused to sign it) by stating that the domestic situation in Greece was also contributing to the situation.

In conclusion, the commission recommended that the UN Security Council should establish a new commission to monitor the situation at Greece's northern borders and that the four Balkan governments should strive to improve relations.[46] In reading the documents relating to the UNSCOB findings, the picture that emerges is of the British, Polish, and Soviet representatives refusing to deviate to any degree from their governments' positions, and the American, New Zealand, Australian, and other representatives attempting to accurately assess the causes of the problems in Greece. However, their voices were silenced, and their findings were modified.

---

[42] Ethridge to Marshall (274), May 8, 1947, FRUS 1947, Vol. V, The Near East and Africa, pp. 845–8. Marshall to Ethridge (349), May 10, 1947, FRUS 1947, Vol. V, The Near East and Africa, pp. 848–9.
[43] Draft Recommendations of US Delegation, May 2, 1947, no. 6129, FO 371/67066. Ethridge to Marshall (214), May 2, 1947, FRUS 1947, Vol. V, The Near East and Africa, pp. 838–9.
[44] Norton to Foreign Office, May 10, 1947 (no. 6345, FO 371/67067).
[45] Inverchapel to Foreign Office, May 10, 1947 (no. 6368, FO 371/67003). Foreign Office to Norton, May 13, 1947 (no. 6345, FO 371/67067). Inverchapel to Foreign Office, May 13, 1947 (no. 6749, FO 371/67067). See also: MacVeagh to Marshall (734), May 20, 1947, FRUS 1947, Vol. V, The Near East and Africa, pp. 174–5.
[46] Ethridge to Marshall (299), May 12, 1947, FRUS 1947, Vol. V, The Near East and Africa, pp. 850–60. Ethridge to Marshall (373), May 20, 1947, FRUS 1947, Vol. V, The Near East and Africa, pp. 863–4. The Report of the UNO Commission (no. 7244, FO 371/67069) and UNO/S C *Official Records, Second Year*, Special Supplement no. 2.

In short, the commission's conclusions simply reflected the positions of the Big Three without forcing any of them to change their methods of operation in Greece and its Balkan neighbors or changing the behavior of the Greek government. The current state of affairs was therefore destined to continue, and by failing to make concrete observations and take the KKE's position into consideration, the UNSCOB report demonstrated to the KKE and DSE that peace, reconciliation, and inclusion were options that were no longer open to them. This also reflected the international climate at the time, in which cooperation between the United States, Britain, and the Soviet Union was highly unlikely. Further reading of the relevant documents also shows that the British and Americans at this time made no distinction between the policies of Tito and Stalin. All the problems facing Greece were thought to emanate directly from the Soviet Union, and this belief turned international non-reconciliation with the Soviets into non-reconciliation with Tito or the DSE in Greece. However, the Soviet Union bore some responsibility for the Anglo-American failure to distinguish between Yugoslavian and Soviet policy. By refusing to acknowledge any external factors (i.e., the problems with Greece's northern frontiers), the USSR reinforced the British and American belief that the policy being pursued by Yugoslavia, Bulgaria, and Albania was of Soviet origin, even though studies of the Soviet archives indicate that this was not the case.[47] Finally, the fact that the British successfully put pressure on the United States to manipulate the findings of the first UN commission for the Balkans clearly illustrated the degree of influence that Britain was able to exert two years after the end of the Second World War.[48]

In mid-May 1947, when evaluating current British international capabilities, the State Department placed a high priority on obtaining complete knowledge not only of British intentions and capabilities but also of British "thinking on world problems." The United States particularly wanted to understand Britain's views on the defense of the Eastern Mediterranean and the continuing British presence in Palestine.[49] The American Ambassador to Britain, Lewis Douglas, responded that the British wished to be partners with the United States in

---

[47] See: Stavrakis, *Moscow and Greek Communism*, pp. 290–99.

[48] This could also be because of the wartime debates between Britain and the United States over the control of international aviation after the war. As discussed in Chapter 2, the British felt that the greater the territory in which they could exert their influence, the stronger their position in relation to the United States would be. Their anti-communism stance also helped them convince the Americans that Britain was an indispensable ally, which strengthened their position. See Bevin's speech of September 10, 1947 (AN 3096/61/45), BDFA Part IV, Series C North America, Vol. 2. 1947, pp. 223–5.

[49] Acheson to US Embassy in London (2155), May 17, 1947, FRUS 1947, Vol. I, *General; The United Nations*, pp. 750–51.

preserving peace until the UN was strong enough to do so and that, like the Churchill administration, the current administration saw the USSR as "the only important potential enemy." Douglas also pointed out that the British stressed that there could be no "Maginot line" mentality against Soviet expansion in the Mediterranean, that the Soviets had to be confronted and communist influence eradicated there.[50]

In keeping with their policy of sharing responsibility with the United States in Greece, at the end of May 1947, the British agreed to extend their police mission (BPM) for six months. This was a result of negotiations with the United States regarding Britain's continuing role in Greece. But by this stage, far from improving, the situation in Greece and the general state of security had actually worsened. By mid-June, the coalition government was still unable to effectively counter the insurgency in northern Greece, and the presence of the BPM in the northern frontier region only had a very temporary calming effect. In terms of the domestic situation, the British were still arguing that the Greek state was being undermined militarily and politically by the KKE with support from the communist parties in Yugoslavia, Bulgaria, Greece, Albania, and Russia.[51] The Americans had reached the same conclusion and informed their representative to the UN that in their opinion, the actions of Greece's northern neighbors constituted aggression, and if they continued, enforcement measures might be required to end them. However, the US did not believe that the aggression had yet reached a level that required intervention under Chapter VII of the UN Charter; it took the view that if Albania, Yugoslavia, and Bulgaria were to stop their actions, a peaceful settlement could be negotiated.[52]

Despite the harmony of US and British policy on the Greek frontier issue, the British were still concerned about when the effects of United States financial aid would be felt in Greece. The British hoped to secure American troops on the northern borders and to support the development of an effective United Nations body that could at the very least diminish the amount of aid being supplied to the communist army from across the borders. They felt that the situation in Greece was so desperate that only substantial, rapid, and concrete American military aid to Greece to prevent the infiltration of supplies and soldiers from across the northern border would prevent it from falling to the communists.[53]

---

[50] Douglas to Acheson (3173), June 11, 1947, FRUS 1947, Vol. I, *General; The United Nations*, pp. 751–58.
[51] Docs 25–27, May 8 to June 19, 1947, BDFA, Series F Europe, Part IV, Vol. 12, pp. 198–202.
[52] Marshall to Austin (252), June 9, 1947, FRUS 1947, Vol. V, *The Near East and Africa*, pp. 865–6.
[53] Norton to Bevin (260), June 19, 1947, BDFA, Series F Europe, Part IV, Vol. 12, pp. 202–4.

In light of British concerns and the recommendations made to the UN by UNSCOB, the State Department immediately began to pressure the Security Council to accept the recommendations and to take action to stop violations of the northern borders. The United States was convinced that with the support of the USSR, Greece's communist neighbors intended to separate Macedonia from Greece, turn it into a new Macedonian state and eventually set up a communist-controlled Greek government there that would force the country into the Soviet sphere of influence.[54] Therefore, Marshall instructed US representative Austin that the United States (like Britain before it) was not prepared:

> ... in any way to concede that Greece is guilty in any way of interference in the internal affairs of the other three nations. These three countries however are guilty of armed intervention in Greece and we cannot agree that any developments that may have taken place or are taking place in Greece can be regarded as any justification whatsoever for such intervention.[55]

Marshall concluded that a Soviet veto of a continuing investigative commission in Greece would be preferable to US support of the continuing presence of an investigative commission, since such a commission could investigate either Greek internal affairs or the actions of the American aid program to Greece.[56]

The terms of the American aid program to Greece stated that the Greek government had to do everything in its power to assist the United States in implementing the objectives of the aid program. It also stated that the Greek government was responsible for allowing United States officials to fully monitor the implementation of the program and for maintaining full and continuous publicity within Greece regarding the activities of the program.[57] This is significant because the program was much clearer in its instructions to the Greek government than any earlier British measures had been and because the aid to

---

[54] This was part of Tito's plan to establish a Slavic Balkan state with access to the Aegean. As mentioned earlier, the British and Americans did not distinguish between Tito's and Stalin's policies, so the Yugoslav plan, though in fact contrary to Soviet desires, reinforced the belief that the Soviets were determined to bring Greece under their sphere of influence. For greater detail, see: Marshall to Austin (280), June 26, 1947, FRUS 1947, Vol. V, The Near East and Africa, pp. 865–8. See also: Woodhouse, *Struggle for Greece*, p. 67 and Banac, pp. 259–60.

[55] Marshall to Austin (280), June 26, 1947, FRUS 1947, Vol. V, The Near East and Africa, pp. 865–8. This quotation clearly illustrates how the British and Americans drew no distinction between Tito's and Stalin's policies toward Greece.

[56] Marshall to Austin (280), June 26, 1947, FRUS 1947, Vol. V, The Near East and Africa, pp. 865–8.

[57] Details of US aid to Greece under the conditions authorized by the United States Congress (no. 28 R 8493/50/19), June 20, 1947, BDFA, Series F Europe, Part IV, Vol. 12, pp. 204–6. The failure of the Greek government to fully implement the conditions outlined in the aid package would later be used as justification by the second US aid administrator, also named Paul Porter (in mid-1949) to withhold funds from Greece.

Greece had been determined prior to the Security Council's consideration of the UN committee's report. Therefore, the Security Council's recommendations could not be allowed to differ dramatically from what the British and Americans were already planning to do in Greece. As a result, the British and Americans presented their position clearly to the Security Council, and their representatives received repeated instructions regarding what they were permitted to do and to support.[58] As an example of extra-United Nations pressure applied by the United States to foreign governments, the Americans even requested that the Colombian government support their proposals and instructed their ambassador to Colombia to voice Colombian support of the US position in the Security Council.[59] The Americans further hardened their position against the USSR by stating that if the Security Council was unable to protect the political and territorial integrity of a member of the UN, then that failure:

> ... would not, in the opinion of the United States Government, forbid or preclude individual or collective action by States willing to act, so long as they act in accordance with the general purposes and principles of the United Nations.[60]

This statement not only showed that the US was willing to bypass the organization it had formed if it did not reach conclusions that the US desired; it was also indicative of an approach that would have a far more long-term impact.

Marshall's statement represented the beginning of an American foreign policy that was first manifested in Greece in mid-1947, was repeated in Korea in 1950 and would continue throughout the twentieth and into the twenty-first century. It was a policy that would justify bypassing international treaties, organizations, and laws whenever they did not coincide with American policy objectives. This is why Greece and the role played there by the British are so significant. Both simultaneously represented, and were direct causes of, the new American foreign policy that was in evidence after the declaration of the Truman Doctrine. The *perceived* threat of the USSR and its expansion were so great that the US freed itself from adherence to any organization/body that restricted its ability to counter Soviet influence.[61]

---

[58] Marshall to Austin (298), July 7, 1947 FRUS 1947 Vol. V, The Near East and Africa, pp. 869–70.
[59] Marshall to the US Embassy in Colombia (354), July 9, 1947, FRUS 1947, Vol. V, The Near East and Africa, pp. 870–1.
[60] Marshall to Austin (308), July 11, 1947, FRUS 1947, Vol. V, The Near East and Africa, pp. 871–2.
[61] According to Marshall, the US perceived Soviet actions as a "world-wide communist effort to subvert governments and institutions not subservient to the Soviet Union." Marshall to Austin (280), June 26, 1947, FRUS 1947, Vol. V, The Near East and Africa, pp. 866–8.

Meanwhile, in the United States, the British were being attacked not only for their handling of affairs in Greece but also for their inability to manage their own economy. Britain's slow economic recovery was used by the Republicans to argue against further US aid to the country. The Foreign Office believed that the best way to counter the criticism was to explain that the current difficulties were direct and lasting effects of the war, again referring to the British stand against the Nazis and linking the past with Britain's future value as an investment and an indispensable ally against the spread of communism.[62] But the corollary of this view was that Britain also needed a strong Germany, not only as a buffer against the USSR but as a trading partner. In light of the rapidly changing international political climate, and after the Morgenthau Plan had managed to keep Germany crippled and in worse condition than in 1945 or 1946, the United States implemented a new German policy.

Until July 1946, the United States had pursued the industrial dismantling of Germany, in keeping with FDR's desire to punish the Germans for electing Hitler and causing the Second World War.[63] However, as a result of rising tensions with the USSR, Joint Chiefs of Staff (JCS) Order 1067, which had directed the American occupying forces to do nothing to aid the economic rehabilitation of Germany, was replaced by JCS Order 1779, which stated that a prosperous Europe was dependent upon a "stable and productive Germany."[64] According to the British, the French government largely agreed that it was necessary to change the pre-existing policy and to focus on rebuilding Germany, since, with a population of 66 million, it had huge potential for both the production and consumption of goods.[65] Bevin, aware of how such a dramatic change in Allied policy would be received, recommended that the new policy initially

---

[62] John Balfour to the Foreign Office, August 5, 1947, (FO 371/61002 AN 2661/1/45). See also: Anstey, p. 418.
[63] Weinberg, pp. 150–1.
[64] Petrov (quoting Hammond, *American Civil-Military Decisions*, p. 443), p. 236.
[65] Murphy to Marshall (1569), June 3, 1947, Caffrey to Marshall (2775), July 11, 1947, FRUS 1947, Vol. II, *Council of Foreign Ministers; Germany and Austria*, pp. 977–86. The British neglected to mention that it would have been political suicide for any French politician at the time to argue in favor of German reconstruction. It would take another three years before a solution could be found that would allow the French government to publicly support German reconstruction. The Schuman Plan is the name given to the proposal made by French Foreign Minister Robert Schuman on 9 May, 1950. Inspired and drafted by Jean Monnet, the plan proposed placing Franco-German production of coal and steel under a common high authority. The organization would be open to participation by other European nations, and the cooperation was designed to foster common interests between European countries, gradually leading to greater economic and then political integration. In his declaration, Schuman stated: "Europe will not be made all at once, or according to a single plan. It will be built through concrete achievements which first create a de facto solidarity. The coming together of the nations of Europe requires the elimination of the age-old opposition of France and Germany." See: The Schuman Declaration, available online at: https://europa.eu/european-union/about-eu/symbols/europe-day/schuman-declaration_en

be kept secret.⁶⁶ The communist members of the UN had predicted that the British and Americans would rebuild Germany rather than punish it, and those statements had resonated in France with opponents of the French government. The French lodged numerous complaints over the new Anglo-American policy for Germany but were not successful in changing it.⁶⁷

The British again took advantage of the change in American attitude, noting that the United States also feared standing alone against the Soviet Union. This indicated to the British not only that they had an opportunity to continue to play the role of the best and most reliable US ally, but also that they could profit from it.⁶⁸ From this point on, though they would disagree from time to time, Britain and the United States linked their foreign policy to a degree never previously seen between two world powers. Furthermore, because of their shared objectives, Britain's post-war weakness and the presence of a common foe, they switched positions as the premier world power without "firing a shot." As stated in the introduction, never before had two superpowers made such a change without armed conflict between them.

However, the American aid program to Greece was delayed, which meant that the entire summer of 1947 was virtually lost.⁶⁹ So UNSCOB's official *raison d'être* (i.e., to assist the Greek government and people in the reconstruction of their country) was subverted, and it was transformed into a vehicle through which the Big Three could sort out their post-war positions and policies in relation to each other. Accusing the Security Council of refusing to assign blame under Chapter VII of the UN Charter for the threat to peace posed by Greece's northern neighbors, the United States said that it would have to bring the issue before the General Assembly.⁷⁰ The US would use the same argument and procedure to justify its intervention in Korea three years later.

The US continued to argue that a Chapter VII violation was being perpetrated against Greece by Yugoslavia, Bulgaria, and Albania, since not only had UNSCOB and the subcommittee found evidence of their support of the DSE;

---

⁶⁶ British Embassy to Department of State (862.6362/7-1547), July 15, 1947, Marshall to US Embassy in France (2605), July 15, 1947, FRUS 1947, Vol. II, *Council of Foreign Ministers; Germany and Austria*, pp. 986–8. This decision would eventually lead to the British and Americans dismissing claims for war reparations against Germany and the US dismissing reparations against Japan. See: Franks to Bevin (399), May 23, 1949, BDFA, Part IV, Series C North American, Vol. 3, 1949, paragraphs 3, 5, and 6, pp. 177–9.
⁶⁷ Bidault to Marshall (711.51/7-1847 and 1947), July 17, 1947, Caffrey to Marshall (2863), July 18, 1947, FRUS 1947, Vol. II, *Council of Foreign Ministers; Germany and Austria*, pp. 991–6.
⁶⁸ Inverchapel to FO, August 23, 1947, Foreign Office Records, (61056/AN2982). Balfour to Bevin (2037), August 23, 1947, BDFA, Part IV, Series C North America, Vol. 2, 1947, pp. 219–22.
⁶⁹ Rapp to Bevin (no. 30), July 22, 1947, BDFA, Series F Europe, Part IV, Vol. 12, pp. 212–14.
⁷⁰ Marshall to Johnson (333), July 30, 1947, FRUS 1947, Vol. V, The Near East and Africa, pp. 875–7.

they had also denied the subcommittee the right to investigate conditions in their territory. The State Department argued that, as established by the Havana Convention of 1922 and various treaties concluded in 1933 between the USSR and other European states, assisting a rebellion in a foreign country constituted "an act of aggression or a threat to peace." The US concluded that in spite of these actions, the Security Council had refused to take action under Chapter VII, instead favoring a non-military solution prescribed under Chapter VI. The US had accepted the latter solution "in the spirit of conciliation," but the motion had been defeated by the Soviet veto. Therefore, the US maintained that in spite of the Security Council's decision, the UN still had a responsibility to act.[71] The next day, Marshall ordered UN Representative Johnson to propose a resolution that would clarify the Soviet position on Greece by placing the Soviet veto on the record.[72] The previous year, the State Department had wanted to find proposals to prevent a Soviet veto, but by August 1947, it was forwarding proposals designed to provoke a veto in order to force the USSR to publicly demonstrate that it would not cooperate internationally and thus to justify the increasingly "hard-line" approach to the USSR pursued by the British and Americans.

Given the ongoing impasse in the Security Council over the issue of passing a military resolution under Chapter VII, many "friendly members" questioned the United States' continued insistence on the point, "even as a build up to a case before the General Assembly."[73] So the US secretly contacted the Security Council representatives who had been voting with it in support of action under Chapter VII, first to explain why it was supporting the Greek government and second to reassure them that in spite of the Soviet veto, "we have a definite plan of action in mind." Marshall explained that far from being a useless gesture, continued support for intervention under Chapter VII, in spite of the repeated Soviet veto, would:

> ... demonstrate to the world the determination of nine of the eleven members to prevent aggression, whereas a failure by the Council to meet the issue squarely would be a signal to aggressors that they could act with impunity, secure in their belief that their actions would be tacitly condoned.[74]

---

[71] Marshall to Johnson (333), July 30, 1947, FRUS 1947, Vol. V, The Near East and Africa, pp. 875–7. According to Marshall: "That veto [from the USSR] does not remove obligations of members of the UN nor does it prevent them from supporting to the fullest extent purposes and principles of Charter."

[72] Marshall to Johnson (334), July 31, 1947, FRUS 1947, Vol. V, The Near East and Africa, p. 877.

[73] Austin to Marshall (712), August 6, 1947, FRUS 1947, Vol. V, The Near East and Africa, pp. 879–80.

[74] Marshall to Certain Diplomatic Missions (501.BC – Greece/8-947: Circular Telegram), August 9, 1947, FRUS 1947, Vol. V, The Near East and Africa, pp. 880–1.

Marshall reiterated how important it was for the majority of the Security Council to stand together on the issue because it would dramatically strengthen their arguments and the possible resolution if and when the issue was brought before the General Assembly. However, he added that at this point, the US must not yet "harden our thinking to the exact type of action that the General Assembly might take," since in his opinion, that action would depend largely on the course of events in Greece.[75] A State Department release on August 12, 1947 affirmed:

> It is the view of the United States government that Greece is in grave peril. This peril results from the guerrilla warfare now being waged against the Greek government by communist-led bands actively supported by Albania, Bulgaria, and Yugoslavia and by the Communist party of Greece. It is perfectly clear the governments of these three northern countries are working in close conjunction with the Greek communists with a common objective – the establishment in Greece of a minority totalitarian government which would be subservient to the communist-controlled countries.[76]

Though this statement clearly illustrated the Americans' new role in world affairs, British Foreign Secretary Ernest Bevin told Parliament that he rejected the view that Great Britain had ceased to be a great world power:

> We regard ourselves as one of the powers most vital to the peace of the world, and we still have our historic part to play. The very fact that we have fought so hard for liberty, and paid such a price, warrants us retaining this position; and, indeed, it places a duty upon us to continue to retain it. I'm not aware of any suggestion, seriously advanced, that, by some stroke of fate, as it were, we have overnight ceased to be a great power .... I must say, it has never occurred to his Majesty's Government, nor, I believe, to the British people. ...[77]

Bevin's remarks were corroborated by the role that the British would continue to play, not only in Greece but internationally. In terms of the military situation in Greece, in August 1947, the British projections for that year's remaining campaign against the insurgency were dependent upon the amount of foreign aid that would continue to be delivered across Greece's northern borders. The

---

[75] Marshall to Certain Diplomatic Missions (501.BC – Greece/8-947: Circular Telegram), August 9, 1947, FRUS 1947, Vol. V, The Near East and Africa, p.882.
[76] Department of State, p. 765.
[77] House of Commons debates (437), May 16, 1947 (fifth series, collection, 1965). This statement illustrated the continuity of British policy and in some ways foreshadowed British actions in the 1950s in Egypt.

British had very low expectations for the success of the Greek forces for the rest of 1947. They also expected no significant American economic help until the spring of 1948. Another problem facing the Greek armed forces was the misuse—in Britain's view—of the gendarmerie, which had been reorganized into a unit that ended up working in competition, rather than cooperation, with the Greek army. The British also recommended to the American Joint Chiefs of Staff that Greek forces should be increased.[78] However, the insurgents took advantage of the limited British troop withdrawals (which had the effect of removing British soldiers from the countryside) and the lack of immediate American military assistance and looted over 30 villages in central Greece between August 13 and 20. In the Security Council, the situation had also deteriorated.

The Syrian member of UNSCOB threatened to abstain from the vote in early August 1947, and the State Department moved quickly to threaten the Syrians with "corrective measures" if they did not vote in favor of the American/British initiative.[79] Though the Syrians quickly changed their stance, the Soviet veto of the American proposal on August 19, 1947 forced the United States to go to the General Assembly to pass its resolution. By August 29, 1947, the State Department had used its embassies in forty-four countries to convey the American "desire" for those nations' support in the General Assembly vote.[80]

---

[78] Reilly to Bevin (1486, R 10421/230/19), 29 July, 1947, BDFA, Series F Europe, Part IV, Vol. 12, pp. 214–15. This document demonstrates that after persuading the Americans to assume responsibility for Greece, the British still felt able and entitled to offer advice on how the Americans should proceed. They provided the United States with their recommendations regarding the size and equipment of the Greek army.

[79] The Acting Secretary of State (Lovett) to the Legation in Syria (178), August 18, 1947 FRUS 1947, Vol. V, The Near East and Africa, pp. 882–3. The US "reminded" Syria that it was acting to protect smaller nations from outside influence, implying that it was also setting a precedent to protect Syria from Soviet pressure.

[80] The Acting Secretary of State (Lovett) to Certain Diplomatic and Consular Missions (501.BC – Greece/8-2947: Circular Telegram), August 29, 1947, FRUS 1947, Vol. V, The Near East and Africa, pp. 883–5. Since 1947, the US has deferred to the General Assembly on only a few occasions and only when it has not been able to force resolutions through the Security Council. Interestingly, when the UN General Assembly has proposed resolutions which are non-binding under the UN Charter, the members of the Security Council have almost always ignored them. Members of the Security Council have used the General Assembly only as a mechanism to support their policies and never as a source for international consensus. The second time that a General Assembly resolution was considered binding was in 1950, when the US Secretary of State went to the General Assembly for a resolution that supported peacekeeping forces in Korea. Britain engaged in similar manipulation but tended to do so out outside the United Nations. For example, see the British actions related to the unification of Greece and Cyprus, discussed in Chapter 6, section: June 1950: The Implications of the Crises in Cyprus, China, and Korea.

The new world division that was reflected in the deliberations of the Security Council was expressed by the State Department as a regrettable but undeniable reality to which the United States had a duty to respond, not only for its own interest and wellbeing but also for those in the non-Soviet world.[81] This belief would lead the US to bypass the very organ that it had helped form (the Security Council) to safeguard what it perceived as an issue that was vital for the security of the "free world."

A few weeks later, the State Department drafted a resolution on Greece to be presented before the General Assembly. The draft resolution found Albania, Yugoslavia, and Bulgaria guilty of contravening the UN Charter and called on them to immediately desist their military and cross-border aid to the DSE. Furthermore, the resolution called for the Greek government and the governments of Albania, Yugoslavia, and Bulgaria to meet to find a peaceful solution to their disputes and to normalize relations. Marshall also called for the four governments to cooperate with a second UN special committee, thereby allowing the UN to carry out its prescribed functions.[82] Meanwhile, in Washington, the issue of aid to Europe as a whole was being examined with urgency.

As a result, by the end of September 1947, with the cooperation of the American government, which was equally anxious to persuade the US Congress to support the European aid program, the Foreign Office stressed the need to highlight the dangers of Soviet policy. Dispatches were sent to British embassies to be used in informal meetings with US diplomats and reporters, outlining the dangers of succumbing to Soviet pressure and stressing the vital role that the United States should play in European security to oppose Soviet influence.[83] This tactic was successful. It was also aided by the formation in Poland in September 1947 of the Cominform, which had members from most of the Eastern European nations and which attacked the French and Italian Communist Parties for not being revolutionary enough. This push for militancy was also taken up by the British Communist Party (BCP)[84] and aided the propaganda/public diplomacy arms of the British government, which pointed to communist subversives in its own country. As a result of the Labour Party's alliance with what British communists

---

[81] Memorandum of the Consular of the Department of State, August 30, 1947, FRUS 1947, Vol. I, *General; The United Nations*, pp. 763–5.
[82] Marshall to Lovett (868), September 23, 1947, FRUS 1947, Vol. V, The Near East and Africa, pp. 886–9.
[83] Lord Inverchapel to British Consuls in the United States, September 13, 1947 (FO 371/62416 EU 8789/168/53).
[84] Childs, pp. 555–6.

called "the imperialist camp," the BCP attacked the government's foreign and domestic policies.[85] The Labour government was able to use its opposition to the BCP to show the United States that it was staunchly opposed to communism both abroad and at home, shared the same core values as the Americans, and agreed with the American view of the threat posed by the communists. It responded to the BCP by purging the civil service and the Trade Union Council (TUC)—and even its own party—of communists or members who favored the BCP "line."[86]

In the United Nations, on September 25, 1947, the United States presented another resolution, this time to the General Assembly, proposing another UN special committee on the Balkans, UNSCOB II, and called on the Yugoslavians, Albanians, and Bulgarians to desist from any further aid to the DSE.[87] On October 21, 1947, the resolution was passed and UNSCOB II was formed. However, the communist members of the General Assembly refused to acknowledge the legitimacy of the resolution, and it had no effect on the situation at Greece's northern borders. As a result, UNSCOB II was "confined ... to findings and proposals similar to those of its predecessor."[88] The United States bypassed the Security Council and the power of the Soviet veto by using the General Assembly to pass its resolution.[89] Meanwhile, the British Embassy in Washington reported to the Foreign Office that the Americans were now more likely to support allies based on their ideological compatibility with the United States rather than their economic viability.[90] This was welcome news to the British, both for their domestic needs and in securing support for their ongoing commitments in Greece.

The American stance did not reflect a desire to provoke an open conflict with the USSR. Rather, it stemmed from the belief that communism would spread locally, through domestic communist groups, and that although the USSR would do everything it could to conceal its role, it would likely order the communists in France and Italy to "resort to virtual civil war." As a result, the United States

---

[85] Childs, p. 556.

[86] Childs, p. 557. In the United States, the Republican Party was attacking the Truman government for working so closely with the British, whose government, they argued, was little better than that of the Soviet Union. See also: "In defense of British Socialism" by Anstey.

[87] The Secretary of State to the Acting Secretary of State, September 23, 1947, editorial note, FRUS 1947, Vol. V, The Near East and Africa, pp. 888–9.

[88] Sfikas, p.260.

[89] This was a significant event. While the legal historiography of the UN refers to the triggering of Chapter VII in the General Assembly during the Korean War as the first time that the US had engaged in such practice to bypass the Security Council, this is not the case. The formation of UNSCOB II was the first time the US did so, although the Korean War was the first time it argued for Chapter VII to be triggered.

[90] Washington Embassy to Foreign Office, "Weekly Political Summary," September 4, 1947 (FO 371/61056 and AN 3069/40/45).

believed that Greece was in danger and that Czechoslovakia would be crushed when the USSR consolidated its hold on Eastern Europe. The US also believed that its economic intervention thus far was the main reason that the spread of communism to the West had slowed, and that the promise of continuing aid would further that trend. Though it acknowledged that its continued use of the UN to mobilize world opinion against the USSR could result in the Soviets leaving the organization, the US believed that it could "bring communist expansion to a halt" by continuing and expanding upon its political, economic, and military assistance/intervention plans.[91]

The tangible effect of the implementation of "containment" in Greece was the arrival of the first American troops in November 1947. The Greek army was reorganized and, with American aid, an additional 10,000 soldiers were permanently added, bringing the total to 120,000 men. However, the ongoing corruption, infighting, and favoritism of the Greek government plagued even the US military mission. The British maintained a strong position of influence as General Rawlins, Chief of the British Military Mission, and General Livesay, British military adviser to the American Mission for Aid to Greece, held discussions with the Greek government on the appointments of generals for the new armed forces.[92]

Notwithstanding these developments, by the end of 1947 Greece was in a worse state than it had been in 1946. The military and the government continued to be completely ineffective in dealing with any crisis whatsoever. The Americans pressured the Greeks to form a coalition government that would squeeze out many of the smaller parties, thereby further minimizing the possibility of finding a political solution to the recurring cycle of crises. On the other side of the equation, gross over-estimates of the size of the DSE, estimated at 300,000 members when in fact it was approximately ten times smaller, meant that funds that could have been injected directly into the economy were instead diverted to the Greek military.[93]

---

[91] Report by the Policy Planning Staff (PPS – 13), November 6, 1947, FRUS 1947, Vol. I, *General; The United Nations*, pp. 770–7. The planning committee also forecast severe troubles in Palestine and acknowledged that China had been lost to the West. This would provide major political ammunition for the Republican Party in the United States, which blamed the Democrats for being "soft" on communism.

[92] Norton to Bevin (no. 390 R15014/34/19), November 7, 1947, pp. 223–4, Norton to Bevin (no.132 R 14595/2219/19 – weekly summary), October 30, 1947, pp. 264–5. BDFA, Series F Europe, Part IV, Vol. 12, 1947.

[93] In addition to this estimate being more than ten times larger than the actual DSE strength at this time, it again illustrates the considerable role played by perception in Anglo-American decision-making. It is an example of the exaggerated perception of the actual danger presented by the communists and also provides an opportunity to reflect on the perception of Anglo-American intentions by the Bulgarian, Albanian, and Yugoslavian governments. Apparently, they too felt threatened by increasing Anglo-American criticism of their policies and involvement in the Balkans.

Also, the government policy of amnesty led mainly to the surrender of members of right-wing bands rather than members of the DSE. Additionally, though the government had begun to release political prisoners, this was done in such a haphazard and disorganized fashion that many of those released simply left prison and rejoined the bandit groups. British Ambassador Norton also doubted whether any Greek government, however it was composed, would be capable of rising above "considerations of selfish and sectional political interests" to deal with the daunting problems facing Greece. He was convinced that this was why the American mission had produced few or no visible effects up to this point. In his view, many Greeks believed that the United States was so heavily committed to Greece it could not afford to withdraw. Therefore, he argued, the Greeks believed that they could wait for the Americans to do all the work. The Ambassador also criticized the fact that the American economic mission had taken three months to present an economic program to the Greek government and had failed to adequately exchange information and policy with the British Economic Mission. He stated:

> Our invaluable experience was largely wasted in major and interesting difficulties that arose at the start. It was soon realized that the cost of the military operation would far exceed the original American estimates and that it would almost certainly be necessary to reallocate the military's funds earmarked for reconstruction.[94]

At that time, the Americans pressured the Greek government to reduce the civil service as part of the economic reforms. There was mass dissatisfaction with the scales of pay and conditions of work, including the abolition of overtime, that were drawn up in consultation with the American mission. Similar to events that would occur sixty years later, civil service strikes and demonstrations paralyzed an already ineffective government.[95] On December 13, 1947, two weeks before the communists formed the government of free Greece in Macedonia,[96] United States Ambassador Douglas contacted Bevin in London to raise the question

---

[94] Norton to Foreign Office (392), November 11, 1947, BDFA, Series F Europe, Part IV, Vol. 12, pp. 225–6.

[95] Norton to Bevin (392), November 11, 1947, Norton to Bevin (134), November 6, 1947, BDFA, Series F Europe, Part IV, Vol. 12, pp. 227, 264–5. In an interesting development, the Canadian Minister of Trade and Commerce, J. A. MacKinnon, visited Athens in late October 1947 to increase Canadian imports from Greece. Ibid., p. 265. What the Americans implemented in late 1947 echoed the present-day calls of the IMF and the EU in Greece.

[96] In Greece, Markos Vafeiadis formed a communist government in northern Greece in December 1947, but not surprisingly, the Americans and British did not recognize it.

of combining the two countries' military missions in Greece. Once again, the British had successfully altered American policy to suit their interests.

Bevin was reluctant to unite the missions, arguing that it was contrary to Ministry of Defense policy and that the British would prefer it if the Americans dealt with "supplies and operations and things of that character" so that they could confine themselves to training.[97] By maintaining separate missions, the British prevented the Americans from obtaining the ability to exercise control over British forces and kept cooperation reliant upon requests between the two governments.[98]

Interestingly, British intelligence continued to provide information to the United States about conditions in Greece (and would do so until the end of the Greek Civil War).[99] One explanation was that in the wake of the dissolution of the OSS, the newly formed CIA had not yet developed enough to take over intelligence responsibilities. It is also worth remembering that Britain, which greatly benefited from American involvement not only in Greece but also in Western Europe, continued to provide intelligence that would keep the United States involved. One of the most telling signs of this arrangement emerged from British activities at the American Embassy in London.

Before releasing documents to the US, British officials would present and explain them to senior members of the US Embassy staff a day in advance.[100] Though never given as an official reason, this method seemed to indicate that the British were determined to ensure that the documents would be interpreted in the "right" way. The British also paid close attention to the American Congress, which since the end of the war had come to play a much more significant role in the formation of policy, especially in financial matters. The British also secured official American support for anti-communist measures such as signing the NATO charter and implementing the Marshall Plan.[101]

With the British being criticized for their military mission's failure to properly train the Greek army for guerrilla warfare, the United States government decided to create a joint planning staff that would incorporate all American

---

[97] Douglas to Bevin (2159), December 13, 1947, BDFA, Series F Europe, Part IV, Vol. 12, p. 229.
[98] Norton to Bevin (139), November 13, 1947, BDFA, Series F Europe, Part IV, Vol. 12, pp. 267-8. Ironically, British training of the armed forces was criticized on November 13, 1947 by members of Minister Zervas' National Party, which stated that the British military mission had failed to properly train the Greek Army for guerrilla warfare and that the Greek army was overly subservient to the American mission.
[99] Close and Veremis. "The Military Struggle," p. 113.
[100] Coleman, p. 355.
[101] Anstey, p. 420.

armed forces personnel in addition to American military advisers and attach them to Greek army units. The British had been arguing for such a plan since the summer of 1947, but despite the poor performance of the Greek army to this point, the Americans refused to take over the training of the Greek armed forces.[102] Additionally, the economic situation continued to worsen, and there were rumors that the Greek government would resign if the United States did not allow it to resume the sale of gold by the Bank of Greece. The issue was resolved the following week when the United States government agreed to exchange gold for the Greek government; however, this gain was limited by increasing levels of public-sector anxiety. Threats of strikes were so high that the government enacted strike legislation that even imposed the death penalty should strikes result in violence.[103]

The situation certainly seemed dire as 1947 drew to a close. The belief that Britain could quickly overcome its post-war devastation, to resume its status as a great power seemed to be gone. Also gone was Britain's belief that it could remain separate from European economic recovery and still rebuild its economy quickly.[104] Most importantly, the belief that the British could independently determine their own destiny had disappeared. These beliefs were replaced by

---

[102] Greece: weekly summary (139), November 26, 1947, BDFA, Series F Europe, Part IV, Vol. 12, pp. 267–8. That is, until the British finally removed all of their remaining soldiers in November 1948. See the next chapter.

[103] Greece: weekly summary (143), December 11, 1947, BDFA, Series F Europe, Part IV, Vol. 12, pp. 269–70. Previously, in mid-December 1947, the United States had sent eight senior officers to Athens to establish the "advisory group on Greek army operations" as part of the military section of the American military mission to Greece. However, at the close of 1947, conditions in Greece (as in Britain) were much worse than they had been in 1946. The labor situation had improved slightly through civil servants receiving a bonus, although it was only half of what they would normally have received, and inflation continued to be a significant problem with 200,000 drachmas required to buy one gold sovereign. See: Norton to Bevin (146), December 24, 1947, BDFA, Series F Europe, Part IV, Vol. 12, pp. 270–1.

[104] Previous references to Anglo-American financial agreements are in Chapter 2. See: Anstey, p. 245, and Inverchapel to Bevin, August 15, 1946, (no. 1927), Paragraph 11c, BDFA, Series C North America, Part IV, Vol. 1, p. 213. For records of the amount of financial aid given to the UK by the USA in 1946, and available until March 31, 1947, see: Balfour to Bevin (No. 1776 E), July 22, 1947, BDFA, part IV, Series C North America, Vol. 2, pp. 210–13. It may also be argued here that this was at the root of British policy toward the European integration process and its pursuit of the European Free Trade Association (EFTA). The constant dilemma faced by British officials when contemplating post-war economic recovery was just how closely they could be tied to the continent. Numerous works broach this topic, from Gillinghams's "The EU: An Obituary" to René Leboutte's "Economic and Social History of the Construction of Europe." However, as the current Brexit crisis goes on, it may be safe to say that no British government has been able to decisively answer this question. For its part, this book can only say that these considerations first came to appear in the diplomatic record in 1946–7, in conjunction with discussions on British policy in Greece. This is perhaps a result of the way in which British involvement and expenditures in Greece, even after the declaration of the Truman Doctrine, threw the spotlight on their own economic woes and the difficulties that lay in solving them.

greater confidence in and growing dependence on American economic and military protection. The Americans, in turn, had now concluded that the:

> ... objectives of the European Recovery Program (ERP) are of such importance that they must be achieved by every means possible short of seriously depleting our own natural resources. [Furthermore,] National Security requires adequate reserves of strategic and critical materials .... There should be no restriction on increased production for United States requirements of these materials.[105]

The demobilization that had begun in 1946 was about to be reversed in dramatic fashion, as the British desired. They had successfully lobbied and maneuvered the US through their spies and influence in Washington and through events in Greece. Another factor that aided British policy was the split between Yugoslavia and Moscow, which earlier in the year had been dismissed as implausible at best but now was a reality. To the Soviets, Yugoslavia's aid and actions in support of the Greek communists had encouraged greater American intervention in the Balkans, which was exactly what Stalin had hoped to avoid, as demonstrated though testimony about the Popov Mission in 1944.[106] So it can be claimed that the success of British policy in Greece was also aided by Tito's foreign policy. These factors, combined with the perceived Soviet objectives, succeeded in persuading the Americans to commit to unprecedented levels of military spending and intervention from this point forward.

British policy in 1948 was also driven by the knowledge that Britain's financial dependence on the United States radically weakened its international leverage. As a result, the British began to pursue a new multifaceted foreign policy. On the one hand, they would draw closer in limited ways to continental Europe to aid economic reconstruction and mutual self-defense. On the other hand, they would continue to attempt to obtain American guarantees of military and economic aid, not only for themselves but also for the European nations that would serve as a barrier to communism—at this time namely Germany and Greece.

In December 1947, at the London Council of Foreign Ministers, the British held secret talks with the French and the Americans regarding opposition to any further Soviet expansion. In light of the situation in Greece, Eastern Europe

---

[105] National Security Resources board to President Truman, December 4, 1947, FRUS 1947, Vol. I, *General; the United Nations*, pp. 777–8.
[106] Zubok and Pleshakov. p. 127.

and the Far East, the policy was generally well received, although the French were still uncomfortable about the Anglo-American plan to rebuild Germany.[107] Bevin told US Secretary of State Marshall that he felt that Western Europe could be ideologically and spiritually united and outlined his plan for "not a formal alliance, but an understanding backed by power, money and resolute action," which could guarantee Western European security and prevent the Soviets from expanding further into Europe.[108] This was the groundwork for the Brussels Treaty Organization (BTO) and the North Atlantic Treaty Organization (NATO).

---

[107] The Schuman Plan of 1950 was a direct result of French attitudes toward post-war Germany as the French government needed a way to justify German recovery (economic, political, and military) to its people. For more, see René Leboutte "Economic and Social History of the Construction of Europe," and Paravantes, Spero "In for a penny: A Legal and Diplomatic History of Reparations and Their Impact on European (dis?) Integration."

[108] Anglo–US–French conversations, British memorandum of conversation, Top Secret, December 22, 1947, FRUS 1947, Vol. II, *Council of Foreign Ministers; Germany and Austria*, pp. 815–22, and: Gallman to Marshall (6585), FRUS 1948, Vol. III, *Western Europe*, pp. 1–2.

4

"Paved with Good Intentions": British Influence and American Intervention in Greece

1948: January to May

Though the Cold War began in 1947, it became firmly established over the following two years. The Czechoslovakian coup in 1948 essentially formalized the division of Europe, which was further demonstrated the following year by the de facto division of Germany and the founding of the Brussels Treaty Organization (BTO) and the North Atlantic Treaty Organization (NATO).[1] Based on the previous year's developments, the United States National Security Council (NSC) concluded that the security of the Middle East and the Eastern Mediterranean was vital to American security. Should any one of Iran, Italy, Turkey, or Greece fall under Soviet influence, it would threaten the security of the whole area. The NSC also concluded that the United States should use all of its economic assets, and possibly military assets, to guarantee the security of the region by strengthening the nations in question.[2] This conclusion was in line not only with British strategic interests for the area but also with future British planning. In January 1948, Bevin stated:

> It is not enough to reinforce the physical barriers which still guard our western civilisation. We must organize and consolidate the ethical and spiritual forces inherent in this western civilisation of which we are the chief protagonists. This

---

[1] NATO, legally and philosophically speaking, can be considered as the opposite of the UN, which was Roosevelt's vision for post-war international relations.
[2] Report to the National Security Council (NSC 5), January 6, 1948, FRUS 1948, Vol. IV, Eastern Europe; The Soviet Union (Multilateral Relations, pp. 1–732), pp. 2–8.

in my view can only be done by creating some form of union in Western Europe, whether of a formal or informal character, backed by the Americas and the Dominions.³

Bevin was clearly linking the future of Britain with the involvement of the United States and the remaining countries of the Commonwealth in guaranteeing European security. He also illustrated the role he saw for Britain, for which he and his government had been lobbying the United States, by saying that:

> Material aid will have to come principally from the United States, but the countries of Western Europe which despise the spiritual values of America will look to us for political and moral guidance in building up a counter-attraction to the baleful tenets of Communism within their borders and in recreating a healthy society wherever it has been shaken or shattered by the war.⁴

Bevin also asserted that Britain could harness American power and rebuild:

> Provided we can organize a Western European system such as I have outlined above, backed by the power and resources of the Commonwealth and of the Americas, it should be possible to develop our own power and influence to equal that of the United States of America and the USSR. We have the material resources in the Colonial Empire, if we develop them … we should be able to carry out our task in a way which will show clearly that we are not subservient to the United States of America or to the Soviet Union.⁵

Bevin could not have stated British objectives much more clearly. He shaped British foreign policy to direct the Americans to assume support for British interests, and Greece was a key part of his plan. Interestingly, just as US foreign policy was affected by domestic political conditions and Republican charges that the Democrats were "soft" on communism, Bevin had to resist charges that his government was allowing itself to be overtaken by American policy. He would later state that Britain must aggressively promote the British way of life and British policy. It was a policy designed by Bevin to align Britain with the United States without alienating his own party.⁶

---

[3] Bevin to the Cabinet, "The First Aim of British Foreign Policy," January 4, 1948 (CP (48)6, CAB 129/23).
[4] Bevin to the Cabinet, "The First Aim of British Foreign Policy," January 4, 1948 (CP (48)6, CAB 129/23) (Ibid.).
[5] Bevin to the Cabinet, "The First Aim of British Foreign Policy," January 4, 1948 (CP (48)6, CAB 129/23) (Ibid.).
[6] Anstey, pp. 432–5, and Kirby, p. 405.

Since the Marshall Plan had not yet been approved by Congress, the British still believed that it was only by continuing to stress the communist threat that British and American policy could remain aligned and the Americans could be encouraged to follow the British lead. In January 1948, Bevin commented on the threat posed by communism in the Far East:

> in the Middle East and possibly in certain Far Eastern countries such as India, Burma, Ceylon, Malaya, Indonesia and Indo-China, Communism will make headway unless a strong spiritual and moral lead ... is given against it, and we are in a good position to give such a lead.[7]

By convincing the Americans to commit to the defense of Greece, and through it Western Europe, the Middle and Far East could therefore also be guarded against further communist expansion. Bevin also advocated a more integrated Europe (for which Churchill had also been campaigning since leaving office), which appealed to the United States and was designed to encourage American aid to Europe generally and to Britain specifically.[8] Bevin also proposed the idea of a Western Union backed by the "power of the United States and the Dominions" to shore up the countries bordering the Soviet sphere in the East. In outlining his plan, Bevin clearly stated that both the USA and Britain should lead the proposed union and that those nations that had experienced Nazi occupation first-hand would likely be the most willing to support Anglo-American and, to a lesser extent, French leadership in such a union, whether or not it was formal.[9] So despite Anglo-American frustration over the day-to-day realities of the Greek situation, Greece was still seen as vital to their interests. For example, Bevin summarized the conditions in Greece:

> The Greek government are making great difficulties for their friends ... I am more alarmed by the dissension within the Greek ranks than by Markos (Vafiadis) and the rebels .... To sum up the Greek government is moribund .... Every day that passes is likely to increase the popular demand for a radical, i.e., semi-dictatorial

---

[7] "Future Foreign Publicity Policy," January 4, 1948 (CAB 129 23, CP (48) 8).
[8] (NSC 5) 6 January, 1948, FRUS 1948, Vol. IV, Eastern Europe, the Soviet Union, Multilateral Relations, pp. 2–8. Britain's success in persuading the Americans to support unity of policy with British strategic interests in the Eastern Mediterranean is shown in a secret National Security Council (NSC) document from January 1948. In the document, the NSC stated that for US security interests to be achieved, it would be vital for the US and Britain to work "along parallel lines." See also: Kirby, p. 407. Kirby reflects on whether Bevin had any real intention of following through on his statements and quotes Belgian Prime Minister Paul-Henri Spaak as stating that he was puzzled that Britain never followed through on and sometimes opposed European integration.
[9] Inverchapel to Marshall (840.00/1-1348), January 13, 1947, FRUS 1948, Vol. IV, Eastern Europe; The Soviet Union (Multilateral Relations, pp. 1–732), pp. 3–6.

solution. The present government is dying not so much from disunity or internal dissention as from inanition, senility ....[10]

However, the US Director of Near Eastern and African Affairs L. W. H. Henderson, stated that the United States' decision to protect Greece had to be stronger than the Soviet will to conquer it to prevent the outbreak of a new world war or at least the loss of the Middle East, the Eastern Mediterranean, and possibly even Europe. He therefore recommended that the US prepare "under certain circumstances" to send troops to Greece or elsewhere in the Eastern Mediterranean. His recommendation came in response to a declaration by the Greek Communist Army (*Dimokratikos Stratos Ellados* – DSE) of the "provisional democratic government of free Greece," supported by the communist Balkan governments and their ongoing violations of Greece's Northern borders and of UNSCOB II's directives. Henderson felt that clear and urgent direction from the United States was needed to restore Greek morale and to prevent the USSR from recognizing the provisional government—such was the perceived importance and symbolism of the struggle in and for Greece.[11]

Officially, blame for the poor domestic situation, delivered through the findings of UNSCOB II as well as the British and American Embassies, was assigned to the continuing material aid that the DSE was receiving from the communist Balkan states. Simultaneously, but unbeknownst to the British and the Americans, Stalin was exerting intense pressure on the Yugoslavians to desist in their aid to the Greek communists. He firmly believed that Great Britain and the United States would never permit a break in the lines of communication from the Mediterranean and that Tito's actions would only cause an escalation of Western intervention in south-eastern Europe.[12]

Referring to the provisional government as the "Markos Junta,"[13] the Americans swiftly moved to prevent any foreign recognition of it, which they believed would be disastrous, and reported that more American officers were being deployed to advise the Greek Army in its action against the guerrillas and

---

[10] Ernest Bevin/Foreign Office to Athens Embassy, November 8, 1948, FO 371/72249/R12662.
[11] Henderson to Marshall (711.69/1-948), January 9, 1948, FRUS 1948, Vol. IV, Eastern Europe; The Soviet Union (Multilateral Relations, pp. 1–732), pp. 9–14, subsequent letters, pp. 15–18. Though the US would decide that only clear and external military aggression against Greece would necessitate an armed American response, such aggression was still considered a real possibility. It is also important to bear in mind that there was still no distinction between Tito's policy and Soviet policy. Everything that took place with regard to Greece's northern neighbors was perceived as being dictated by Moscow.
[12] For a very detailed analysis of this period from the Soviet perspective, see: Stavrakis, *Moscow and Greek Communism*, pp. 127–85.
[13] Formed in December 1947.

train it in the use of new weapons. With regard to the aid to Greece and Turkey (and to Western Europe as a whole), they also emphasized that the American public needed to know "that the recipients of aid from this country [the USA] were doing the utmost to help themselves."[14] With American approval and the promise of a similarly strong statement in the near future, Bevin then issued a statement in the House of Commons saying that Britain, having already guaranteed Greece's territorial frontiers, "would take a firm stand now against any new attempt to dominate free and independent countries."[15] With this statement, the course of the third round of the Greek Civil War was set. A key step toward establishing an even stronger military in Greece was implemented a few days later when the head of the American Mission for Aid to Greece (AMAG) informed Secretary of State Marshall that unless the US supported the military effort, the economic and reform measures would not be successful.[16] The United States then decided that destroying guerrilla forces would have to become the top priority if American aid to Greece was to have the desired results. AMAG was therefore ordered to put other objectives to one side until the "rebel forces" had been completely destroyed.[17]

Despite this shift, the Americans were still frustrated by the lack of tangible results in Greece. Ambassador Clifford Norton explained that the failures were a result of the limitations imposed by Congress on the amount of money that the United States government could spend in Greece. He stated that the amount allocated by the American Congress for aid to Greece was no higher than the combined aid that Greece had previously been receiving from Britain, the United States and the United Nations Relief and Rehabilitation Administration. As a result, exactly the same percentage of funds was being distributed for military use, as for rebuilding efforts.[18] He argued that it was unreasonable to expect different results with the same level of funding. This shift in policy in Greece, reflecting the external US-Soviet hostility, was also

---

[14] Memorandum of Conversation (711.68/1-948), January 9, 1948, FRUS 1948, Vol. IV, Eastern Europe; The Soviet Union (Multilateral Relations, pp. 1–732), pp. 18–21. There was also continuing debate over whether the US was prepared to use American combat troops in Greece and whether it should make its decision public. See: Report by the Policy Planning Staff, January 10, 1948 (PPS/18), FRUS 1948, Vol. IV, Eastern Europe; The Soviet Union (Multilateral Relations, pp. 1–732), pp. 21–6.
[15] Inverchapel to Marshall (869.00/1-1648), January 16, 1948, Marshall to Inverchapel, January 20, 1948, FRUS 1948, Vol. IV, Eastern Europe; The Soviet Union (Multilateral Relations, pp. 1–732), pp. 30, 33.
[16] Griswold to Marshall (Amag 82), January 14, 1948, FRUS 1948, Vol. IV, Eastern Europe; The Soviet Union (Multilateral Relations, pp. 1–732), pp. 28–9.
[17] Marshall to Griswold (Gama 41), January 12, 1948, FRUS 1948, Vol. IV, Eastern Europe; The Soviet Union (Multilateral Relations), pp. 26–7.
[18] Norton to Foreign Office (51), February 18, 1948, BDFA, Series F Europe, Part IV, Vol. 17, p. 73.

noted in January 1948 in a meeting in the British cabinet. Bevin presented what he saw as the most pressing international problems:

> ... the United States proposals for assisting economic recovery appear to have crystallized the opposition of the Soviet government and closer organization of the democratic states of Western Europe; and it was clear that, although the recent Soviet attempts to stir up trouble in France and Italy had largely failed, some looser form of union should be created in Western Europe in order to resist the increasing penetration of Soviet influence.[19]

Bevin believed that Britain had to continue to exert its moral authority to cement anti-communist sentiment in Western Europe—not only because he believed that the Western nations held values closer to those of the British and Americans but also because he believed in the possibility of increasing Britain's own strength so that it might once again become an international power on more equal terms with the Soviet Union and the United States. Through the first half of 1948, Bevin would speak plainly, more so than before, about the methods employed by the Soviet Union—methods, according to Bevin, intended to limit opposition and to intimidate weaker neighboring states.[20] Again, though his assessment of the communist interest in supporting the insurgency in Greece was accurate, he mistakenly ascribed the primary support to Stalin and not to Tito. The effects of this ongoing misperception would be felt in numerous areas. Bevin also failed to understand that Stalin's anti-American strategy was based upon an effort to prevent Washington from expanding to areas and issues that were viewed as vital to Soviet interests while simultaneously maintaining the possibility of a "general agreement recognizing American predominance" in other areas and issues, such as the southern Balkans.[21]

To foster the impression that external threats were the exclusive reason for the domestic situation in Greece (as they had done a year earlier with the first UN committee in the Balkans), the British and Americans coerced members of UNSCOB to "correct" their reports or any suggestions that deviated from the British and American policy for Greece.

---

[19] CAB 128/12 (CAV 128/12 Cabinet minutes held at United Kingdom Public Record Office, Kew), CM 2 (48) 5.
[20] Bullock, *Bevin*, p. 519.
[21] Claudin, p. 493. See also: Stavrakis, "Soviet Policy in Areas of Limited Control," p. 227. Based on his research in the Soviet archives, Stavrakis argues that Soviet policy toward Greece was based on attempting to eliminate or at least reduce the "western presence in the eastern Mediterranean and the Near East."

In February, the Australian representative to UNSCOB II issued recommendations, strikingly similar to those proposed by the KKE in 1947, which, to the dismay of the British and Americans, included international administration of Western aid to Greece, amnesty for combatants and political prisoners, internationally supervised free elections, and consultations with Greece's Balkan neighbors to ease tension and improve relations. Secretary of State Marshall refused these recommendations, saying that it would be "unfair" to the Greek government since the KKE was perceived as being just a pawn of the Soviet Union.[22] However, Marshall advised the Greek government to begin to make reforms, especially in terms of prisons and the composition of the government. In the end, UNSCOB II was simply a tool used by the Big Three to justify their positions in Greece. Though members of the initial commission and later UNSCOB II saw that the domestic conditions were having a direct effect on the situation at the northern borders, the Big Three refused to accept any compromise solution. Furthermore, though UNSCOB II reflected the policies of the powers involved in its creation and failed to solve any of the issues facing Greece, it had a far more wide-reaching impact than might have been expected: It codified the split between the communist and non-communist worlds and set up the UN as an arena for their conflict. It also clearly illustrated the influence that the British could exert over American policy and how the two nations would continue to operate against the Soviets.

To continue to motivate the Americans into action, British intelligence sent a report to the American consulate in Thessaloniki in February 1948 that identified the state of affairs as a major contributing factor in the popularity of the communists, particularly in northern Greece. The report stated:

> It is hoped that Mr. Marshall's recent advice on social and economic reforms might curb the unnecessary and luxurious living in one district in Athens where the inhabitants live better than practically anywhere else in Europe and show little interest in the situation except to gamble on the gold market according to the ups and down of the "nerve war." This aspect of tactless and ostentatious display of vast limousines and quantities of luxury goods are definite factors contributing to communism and the bad feelings between northern Greece and the capital.[23]

---

[22] Drew to Secretary of State, February 3, 1948, FRUS 1948, Vol. IV, Eastern Europe and the Soviet Union (Multilateral Relations, pp. 1–732), pp. 225–6. The Secretary of State to the Embassy in Australia, February 5, 1948, FRUS 1948, Vol. IV, Eastern Europe and the Soviet Union, pp. 226–8.

[23] American Consulate in Thessaloniki to the US Secretary of State, "British 10th Infantry Brigade fortnightly Intelligence Report from 4th February 1948," US National Archives, Washington DC, 868.00/2-448.

The economic, political, and social conditions were still so poor that both Britain and the United States began at the very least to discuss, if not really to consider as an actual possibility, removing themselves entirely from Greek affairs.[24] However, the United States decided to adopt the view:

> ... that our policy with respect to Greece and Italy, and the Mediterranean area in general, should be based upon the objective of demonstration to the Russians that: a) the reduction of the communist threat will lead to our military withdrawal from the area; but that; b) further communist pressure will only have the effect of involving us more deeply in a military sense.[25]

The policy that would endure throughout the Cold War was therefore first codified in regard to the conflict in Greece. Though the actual American military intervention would never reach the level (in terms of soldiers fighting "on the ground") of the later US involvement in the Civil Wars in Korea and Vietnam, the precedents and justification for action there were established in Greece.[26] Furthermore, the US model of institution-building in third countries, particularly with regard to the military, was also shaped by the US experience in Greece.

The ongoing British effort to continue to influence US anti-communist policy in general was clearly stated by the Foreign Office in February 1948:

> On the whole the Americans seem to be very ham-handed in their anti-Communist and anti-Soviet publicity ... we should hope however by consultation in suitable cases to prevent our getting in each other's way. *We also – perhaps rashly – rather hope to be able to influence them imperceptibly in the direction of greater subtlety.*[27]

The statement, though understated, showed British intentions and foreshadowed the paths that the two countries would take from this point on as the Cold War progressed. The communist coup in Czechoslovakia caused the Americans to radically revise their appreciation of the international situation and challenged their earlier assumptions that the Cold War was highly unlikely to culminate in

---

[24] The National Security Council did consider withdrawing US support for Greece as an alternative to its current actions but it stated that to do so would lead to the loss not only of Greece and "American prestige" but also of the whole Middle East. (NSC 5/2, paragraph 8 a) February 12, 1948, FRUS 1948, Vol. IV, Eastern Europe and the Soviet Union (Multilateral Relations, pp. 1–732), pp. 46–51.

[25] Extract from "Views of the Policy Planning Staff on the Mediterranean Area" (868.00/2-1648), FRUS 1948, Vol. IV, Eastern Europe and the Soviet Union, pp. 53–5.

[26] The United States had no combat troops in Greece during the Greek Civil War, but it sent 300,000 soldiers to Korea and 537,000 to Vietnam.

[27] C. F. A. Warner to Sir John Balfour, February 26, 1948 (FO 953 128). Emphasis added.

a military confrontation. The sense of crisis generated by this event, combined with the Berlin blockade, led the United States to judge the importance of non-communist European states by what they could contribute to Western defense. In this context, notwithstanding the realities of conditions in Greece, the country and its military became even more important for the United States. Even in Britain, the Labour MPs who had been most critical of the foreign policy pursued by Bevin and Attlee since 1945 changed their opinions publicly to oppose the Soviets and to support not only Bevin and Attlee but also Truman.[28]

However, Lord Inverchapel believed that Britain's current stability might encourage the United States to give priority to other nations that were in immediate and obvious danger of falling to communism. He also thought that many Americans were arguing against further aid to Britain because they were convinced that Britain was so far gone economically that it was beyond help. Finally:

> ... in their perhaps excessive zeal for the unity of democracy, Americans are apt to minimize the politics and strategic importance of enabling Britain to maintain her imperial responsibilities. ... Americans have too recently emerged from a happy security of the world policed by the Royal Navy, a world in which the pound sterling seemed impregnable, to fully appreciate the cataclysm which would fall upon it if United Kingdom were no longer able effectively to play her part as a world power.[29]

According to Inverchapel, Britain possessed an advantage in its unique access to the United States government. He felt it should exploit this advantage to the full and prove to those who mattered in the United States that the most critical problem facing them was the possible chaos that would result from any further weakening of Britain's economic and imperial influence.[30]

However, his emphasis on maintaining Britain's place in the world was incompatible with the new realities of Britain's official relations with the United States. Officially at least, the British had to appear to accept the part of a diminished world power in partnership with the United States. To secure their objectives, they continued to try to shift American public and political opinion to maintain the maximum possible leverage. They next proposed forming an Eastern Mediterranean

---

[28] Morgan, *Labour in Power*, pp. 238, 276–7.
[29] Inverchapel to Foreign Office (24), May 13, 1948, BDFA, Series C, Part IV, Vol. 3, pp. 77–82.
[30] Inverchapel to Foreign Office (24), May 13, 1948, BDFA, Series C, Part IV, Vol. 3, pp. 77–82.

bloc, made up of Italy, Greece, Turkey, and the Arab states, to oppose Soviet expansion. The Americans considered the idea "hopeful" but had not yet given it enough thought to endorse it. They did, however, state that such closer economic relations could benefit Greece, while closer political relations between Italy, Greece, and Turkey could be used to "prevent them [the Arabs] from following an unwise foreign policy." It could also lead to Italy, Greece, and Turkey acting as a successful "bridge" between the Arab states and Britain and the United States.[31]

Concerns were also raised by British intelligence estimates that the DSE strength in March 1948 was 26,000 throughout Greece; a month earlier, a British intelligence officer had stated that if Markos Vafeiadis continued to fight a small guerrilla campaign, he could ultimately win.[32] Such reports, combined with the coup in Czechoslovakia on February 25, 1948, put pressure on the Truman administration, both internally and externally, to do even more to oppose communist expansion.

The British believed that the only plan that would simultaneously allow them the time and financial security to restore their power and provide for the successful defense of Western Europe was one in which the United States played a key role. This became one of the main focus points in talks over the Brussels Pact in March 1948. The key British contribution was known as the "commitment clause" in Article IV of the pact, which pledged individual and joint action in response to an aggression against any one of the signatory powers. Though the clause was modified in subsequent months, this significant political shift represented a fundamental change in American foreign policy (guaranteed American military intervention in Europe when the North Atlantic Charter establishing NATO was signed a short time later). It is recognized as one of Bevin's main achievements as Foreign Secretary.[33]

Bevin's success was noteworthy because, in spite of his strong commitment to establishing a system of Western European collective security against the USSR, he was very reluctant, as were many in the British government, to encourage, much

---

[31] Memorandum of Conversation: American views on the Formation of an Eastern Mediterranean Bloc (890.00/2-448), February 4, 1948, FRUS 1948, Vol. IV, Eastern Europe and the Soviet Union (Multilateral Relations, pp. 1–732), pp. 41–3.

[32] NARS 868.00/2-1748, *10th Infantry Brigade's Fortnightly Intelligence Review*; NARS, RG 319, P&O, 091, Greece, TS Entry, 154, Box 13.

[33] Bullock, *Bevin*, p. 645. For the text and analysis of the BTO pact, see: https://www.cvce.eu/collections/unit-content/-/unit/02bb76df-d066-4c08-a58a-d4686a3e68ff/a2ca068b-fa0c-4137-b58f-ce516c25fab0/Resources#3467de5e-9802-4b65-8076-778bc7d164d3_fr&overlay The Pact was modified in 1954, and then became article V: see: https://www.cvce.eu/collections/unit-content/-/unit/02bb76df-d066-4c08-a58a-d4686a3e68ff/9059327f-7f8a-4a74-ac7e-5a0f3247bcd3/Resources#7d182408-0ff6-432e-b793-0d1065ebe695_fr&overlay

less tie himself and his country to, any of the European unification policies. This reluctance was partly due to 600 years of British policy, which advocated never becoming too involved in continental alliances, but it also reflected differences in "folk" memories between Britain and the continent. Bevin saw the British government and its institutions as having held off and then defeated the Nazis, while the continental populations remembered how poorly their governments had fared against the Germans. For Bevin, this came to mean that the British government had a much greater degree of legitimacy than other European governments as a protector not only of the British people but also of Western civilisation.[34] This belief was reinforced by the communist coup in Czechoslovakia in 1948.

When the communists assumed control of Czechoslovakia on February 25, 1948, by deposing the president and assassinating the foreign minister, it sent a shock wave through the West. In the United States, it led to an acceleration in anti-communist economic action. The Senate approved the Marshall Plan by a vote of 69 to 17. The communist coup in Czechoslovakia also shocked the United States into supporting Britain and France entering into a mutual defense treaty known as the Brussels Treaty, which was a European precursor of NATO. The next international threat emerged with the upcoming elections in Italy.

The United States was so worried about possible communist victories in European elections that President Truman broke American law by sending arms covertly to Italy in order to allow government forces to prevent a communist coup.[35] What was known to the British but not to the Americans at the time was that, just as he had done in Greece, Stalin had ordered French and Italian communists to participate in the democratic process and not to engage in violence.[36] British intelligence, being far better adapted, more advanced and more competent than the fledgling CIA, was often hesitant to share information with the United States, especially information that might have reduced American intentions to intervene against Soviet expansion.[37]

---

[34] Ibid, pp. 646–56.
[35] Miller, pp. 48–51.
[36] Ambrose, pp. 92–3.
[37] Bullock, p. 557. To continue to exert influence and relay information to the United States, the Foreign Office-controlled British Information Service (BIS) had a staff of 200 people and a budget of over one million dollars. See: BIS Services, FO 953/116 PG 1451/10. BIS Staff, FO 953/8 and FO 953/454. Its public diplomacy/propaganda efforts greatly resembled those of BSC. The BIS organized staff exchanges to Britain, wrote and distributed pamphlets and (as shown by an examination of the FARA 1938 records for the first nine months of 1948) was capable of large-scale distribution of information. The US Department of Justice recorded that from Jan. to Sept. 1948, the BIS produced: pamphlets—25,000, films—100, magazine articles—500, radio broadcasts—100. Statistics in: "FARA 1938," Department of Justice records, National Archives, Washington D.C.

Instead, Britain pointed to its centuries of worldwide diplomatic experience as justification for why the Americans should just trust what the British were telling them. Though the situation would not last for long, throughout the late 1940s, the Americans were led to believe that their liaisons with the British were particularly valuable.[38] What the CIA could do, however, was place millions of dollars in the hands of anti-communists and democrats in Europe—and in the case of Italy, they ended up winning the election. (This was the beginning of the covert CIA interference in foreign politics that would recur repeatedly in the twentieth century, notably in Iran and then in South America).[39] Shortly thereafter, the United States Congress approved $4 billion for Truman's policy of containment.[40] Additionally, the Americans used the situation to indicate to Greece the fragility of the European political and economic systems and to assure Greece that they would continue to oppose communism and support economic development. Given the possibility of an economic bloc with Italy in the Eastern Mediterranean, the US encouraged Greece to drop its claims against Italy for war reparations.[41]

The British used the crisis in Italy to further encourage continued US intervention on the continent. When Bevin was notified of the communist coup in Prague, he informed the American Ambassador in London, Lewis Douglas, that "Italy might go next." If the Americans were engaged in Greece and could be further engaged in Italy, it was less likely that they would abandon Greece.[42] The British maneuver worked. Though many US officials felt that the relationship between Britain and the US was beneficial and open, some American Embassy staff in London felt that the British exercised control, or at least possessed too much influence, over embassy affairs.[43] However, domestic British issues had come to the forefront. In the House of Commons in March 1948, Prime Minister Attlee issued a declaration banning known members or associates of the British Communist Party (BCP) from working in any post "vital to the security of the

---

[38] Coleman, p. 359.
[39] Lovett to US Embassy in Greece (411), April 3, 1948, FRUS 1948, Vol. IV, Eastern Europe and the Soviet Union (Multilateral Relations, pp. 1–732), pp. 68–70. The State Department also ordered the embassy to inform the Greek government that the US had aided the non-communists in Italy to reassure the Greek government that the US would oppose communism everywhere.
[40] Ambrose, pp. 91–4.
[41] Lovett to US Embassy in Greece (411), April 3, 1948, FRUS 1948, Vol. IV, Eastern Europe and the Soviet Union (Multilateral Relations, pp. 1–732), p. 69.
[42] Dixon (Prague) to Bevin (8), February 25, 1948, BDFA, Series F Europe, Part IV, Vol. 14.
[43] Richard M. Bissell, assistant to the deputy administrator of the Economic Cooperation Administration, quoted in: Moss, pp. 133–4.

state" and had them removed or re-assigned.[44] This represented a climax of sorts for the late 1940s. From 1948 onward, the immediate post-war cooperation (1945–7) between communist parties and the governments of European countries would diminish as US/Soviet antagonism rose.

The British purge of communists, combined with the communist coup in Prague and the Soviet blockade of Berlin, helped the British sell themselves to the Americans as the leader of anti-communism in Europe. The day after the coup in Prague, Bevin met with US Ambassador Lewis Douglas and called for a conference between Britain, the United States, and other Western governments to quickly and strongly counter the communist offensive.[45] Greece became even more important to the British as a symbol because the civil war there could easily be held up as continuing evidence of Soviet plans for world domination. As a result, the British cabinet authorized Bevin to do whatever was necessary to address the "Threat to Western Civilization."[46]

This was a high point for British policy in the late 1940s and was the culmination of the agreement that the British had solicited from the Americans on March 11, 1948, when, after Bevin proposed a scheme to George Marshall to guarantee Atlantic security, the Americans responded promptly and positively that they were prepared to engage at once in discussions on what would become the North Atlantic Treaty Organization.[47]

An interesting symbol of change in Anglo-Greek relations occurred in April 1948 with the Greek celebration of the union of the Dodecanese with Greece. The British Ambassador noted that the Greeks did not single out the British for any public or private praise over their efforts to capture the islands or the British government's contribution to the union. The British Ambassador believed that the possible reason was the Greek government's unease about praising the British contribution to the liberation of the islands in the presence of the Americans, given Britain's declining and America's increasing role in aid to Greece.[48]

---

[44] Childs, pp. 557–8. A similar measure had been taken in the United States the previous year (1947). See: Memorandum by the Secretary of State to the President (611.20), February 7, 1947, FRUS 1947, Vol. I, General, The United Nations, pp. 712–15. However, the height of loyalty tests for government positions occurred in 1950 with McCarthyism. In June 1950, the United States passed legislation requiring non-communist oaths. See Franks to Younger (499), June 20, 1950, BDFA, Part IV, Series C North America, Vol. 4, 1950, pp. 93–8. See Chapter 5 for more information.

[45] Douglas and Bevin, Top secret record of conversation, February 26, 1948; FO 800/460.

[46] "The Threat to Western Civilization," March 3, 1948, (CP(48)72, CAB 129/25). See also Kirby, pp. 408–9.

[47] Marshall to Murphy, Germany (403), March 6, 1948, FRUS, 1948, Vol. III, Western Europe, p. 389.

[48] Norton to Bevin (125), April 9, 1948, BDFA, Series F Europe, Part IV, Vol. 17, p. 119.

Militarily, by mid-April 1948, the Greek government had an army of 180,000 troops. It was finally receiving the new American weaponry, and Tsaldaris paid a visit to Foreign Minister Bevin to discuss the continuing British role in Greece. Tsaldaris asked Bevin whether he believed that the latest developments in Berlin and Vienna were backed by the Soviet Union and whether they were an indication that the Soviets were no longer concentrating their efforts on Greece. Bevin answered that he had no way of knowing but felt that it was possible that the Soviet Union might be reconsidering its general foreign policy.[49]

This international development was complemented by Greek and Turkish talks on issuing a joint declaration with the Arab countries of the Eastern Mediterranean regarding the proposed economic and political bloc. According to US reports, the Greeks and Turks made great progress toward reaching an agreement, but when they approached the US for approval and recognition, they were told to put the initiative on hold.[50] Palestine was about to change everything.

Palestine, Israel, and the Rest of the Eastern Mediterranean

In addition to the issues in south-eastern Europe, the British and the Americans faced challenges in the Middle East. The determination of the British mandate in Palestine and the Israeli declaration of statehood on May 14, 1948 were the occasion for a lengthy report by the British Embassy on US policy in Palestine. The British Embassy was highly critical of American policy in the region, which was not surprising considering Britain's distaste for the UN plan (which Truman favored) that advocated dividing Palestine into two sections: one Jewish and one Palestinian. Britain's primary objection to the American policy was its lack of decisiveness. This was a result of domestic American political conflicts between those such as Secretary of State Marshall, who supported temporary trusteeship following the British withdrawal from Palestine while a longer-term solution was sought, and others such as Truman, who favored partition.[51] There was also an opportunity for the British to solidify their

---

[49] Since November 1947, US strategic interests in Italy had grown, and the US had pressed for the "relaxation of unduly onerous terms of the Italian Peace Treaty" in order to accelerate Italian economic recovery. See: Report by the National Security Council (NSC 1/1), November 14, 1947, FRUS 1948, Vol. III, Western Europe, pp. 724–6.

[50] Lovett to US Embassy in Turkey (203), April 23, 1948, and Lovett to US Embassy in Greece (411), April 3, 1948, FRUS 1948, Vol. IV, Eastern Europe and the Soviet Union, pp. 79–80.

[51] British Embassy to the State Department (G2/-/47), FRUS 1948, Vol. V, Part 2, The Near East, South Asia, and Africa, pp. 533–6.

relations with the Arab states, but US action in regard to Palestine precluded that possibility while simultaneously eliminating the prospect of the Mediterranean bloc. The British firmly believed that the situation developing in the Middle East represented a grave threat, and they were later proved to be correct.[52]

When the UN announced its plan to partition Palestine in November 1947, the Zionists quickly rushed to fill what had been a political vacuum. "In the resulting vacuum, the Jews were able to achieve the de-facto partition of Palestine and to represent that they were doing no more than give effect to the recommendations made by the United Nations .... American policy has followed events rather than directing them"—largely, the British Embassy believed, because of the US desire to avoid having to commit any troops to the region. All in all, it was a "melancholy story of indecision and weakness."[53]

This dispatch is significant in relation to Greece because it illustrates Britain's ongoing lack of faith in American decision-making. The British were convinced of the right course of action and were frustrated by the American inability to use US power, as the British put it, "wisely." The American policy planning staff foresaw a dramatic loss of US prestige in the area and believed that the USSR would gain an advantage through the UN partition plan because of the resulting strife in the area, which would come at the expense of the United States. The report also stated that supporting partition in Palestine could lead to similar proposals in Greece, Turkey, and Iraq and that it had already caused severe damage to the US strategic position in the Middle East. Giving weight to these fears was that, while talks on Palestine were continuing, Tito had increased his aid to the DSE and KKE in terms of both material and propaganda (hard power and soft power, respectively, in the terminology of international relations), partially recognizing the provisional government of northern Greece under Markos Vafiadis and increasing his shipments of war materiel to the DSE.[54] Marshall also claimed that supporting the creation of Israel would damage US relations with the

---

[52] British Embassy to the State Department (G2/-/47), FRUS 1948, Vol. V, Part 2, The Near East, South Asia, and Africa, pp. 533–6.

[53] Balfour to Bevin (848), May 24, 1948, BDFA, Series C North America, Part IV, Vol. 3. Doc. No. 26, May 24, 1948, pp. 97–101. The Arab states were also fearful that a Jewish state would use its position to expand at the expense of the surrounding Arab states. See: Lovett to US Embassy in Pakistan (31), January 28, 1948, FRUS 1948, Vol. V, Part 2, The Near East, South Asia, and Africa, pp. 569–71.

[54] Cannon, Yugoslavia, to Marshall (272), March 22, 1948, FRUS 1948, Vol. IV, Eastern Europe and the Soviet Union (Multilateral Relations, pp. 1–732), pp. 62–3.

British and the Arabs. He was proven half-right.[55] For these reasons, Marshall strenuously opposed the plan, but Truman supported it.

Not surprisingly, most of the European Jews who had survived the Holocaust had no desire to return to their old countries, and many went to Palestine, where a large Jewish population had been growing since the beginning of the twentieth century. Britain had been governing Palestine and had attempted to prevent increased Jewish immigration to the area to safeguard its oil interests in the Middle East. However, much like in Greece, British resources were exhausted in Palestine, and they turned the problem over to the United Nations.

After opposing each other's policies in Western and Eastern Europe, the Soviets and the Americans were nevertheless able to come to an agreement to divide Palestine and create a Jewish state along the Mediterranean. On May 14, 1948, Israel declared its independence in the UN, and the United States, and the Soviet Union were the first countries to recognize the new state.

Shortly thereafter, Egypt, Jordan, Lebanon, Syria, and Iraq formed an alliance intent on wiping it out. The Israelis appealed to the United Nations for aid, and the United States and the Soviet Union forced through a ceasefire that gave the Israeli army time to re-arm. When the fighting resumed, the Israelis ignored the UN-imposed boundaries and continued their conquest of Arab territories.

When the armistice was signed in January 1949, Israel, aside from having much larger borders than originally envisioned, was also home to many thousands of Palestinians. This situation would lay the foundations for the troubles that persist in the area to the present day, and although Truman attempted to persuade the first Israeli Prime Minister, David Ben-Gurion, to grant concessions on both refugee and boundary issues in Palestine, he responded by threatening the US President that the American Jewish community would turn against him if he continued to insist on such concessions.[56] Thus, the creation of a Jewish state not only forever altered relations between the Arab and Anglo-American worlds; it also sealed the doom of the proposed Eastern Mediterranean economic bloc, the potential of which will never be known.

Considering the rich trading history of the Eastern Mediterranean, it is possible that had the Palestinian question been handled differently and the

---

[55] Report by the Policy Planning Staff (PPS/19), January 19, 1948, Kennan to Lovett (PPS 19/1), January 29, 1948, FRUS 1948, Vol. V, Part 2, The Near East, South Asia, and Africa, pp. 546–54, 573. George Kennan analyzed the impact of the American support of the creation of a Jewish state and said that it had severely damaged US prestige in the Arab world, which after the First World War and the disintegration of the Ottoman Empire had seen the US as a liberator and guarantor of freedom without political motivation.
[56] Ambrose, pp. 99–101.

economic and political relations between Italy, Greece, Turkey, and the Arab countries of the Eastern Mediterranean been developed and formalized, many of the problems that have persisted there since 1948 might have been solved or even avoided entirely. Greece lost another potential source of income when it was encouraged to drop its claims for reparations against Italy in exchange for the promise of a regional economic union that would never materialize.

Understandably, the Greek Foreign Minister was concerned with what the international developments would mean, not only for Western aid to Greece but also for continuing economic development. In June, Tsaldaris met with Foreign Secretary Bevin in an attempt to re-start talks on the proposed Greek-Turkish economic pact with the Arab states of the Eastern Mediterranean, but again, the Greeks were told to wait because of the continuing problems in Palestine.[57] The British were again able to take advantage of international developments to draw the United States further into European and international affairs when the USSR blockaded Berlin. The scale of US support given to Berlin during the Soviet blockade was astonishing, and the British were able to use this crisis to increase American support not only for Greece but also for Europe as a whole. The crisis provided the justification for the United States to place bombers in Germany, and the Americans dramatically increased their ability to launch atomic strikes against the Soviet sphere. The event also accelerated the development and ratification of the North Atlantic Treaty Organization the next year.[58]

The blockade also gave the Americans and the British the excuse they needed to allow strategic bombers carrying nuclear weapons to be stationed on English soil and enabled the British to accelerate the Brussels Treaty talks.[59] This period saw Britain's position in the world "transformed" as it was able to rely more on American intervention in Europe, particularly in Greece. The rising fear of Soviet expansion among the general population allowed the Attlee government to justify its defense spending and its continued "leaning" on the US for support.[60] However, paradoxically, this period also

---

[57] Bevin to Norton (225), April 16, 1948, BDFA, Series F Europe, Part IV, Vol. 17, pp. 122–3, June 4, 1948 (no. 313 R 6756/3668/19), p. 132. On June 2, 1948, far less comprehensive agreements were signed separately between the United States and Greece and between the United States and Turkey in which the countries promised only to "respect economic cooperation." See: Editorial note in document (1211), June 30, 1948, FRUS 1948, Vol. IV, Eastern Europe and the Soviet Union (Multilateral Relations, pp. 1–732), p. 114.

[58] Reynolds, p. 176. Furthermore, the departure of British Ambassador Lord Inverchapel from Washington in June 1948 and his replacement by the pro-American Sir Oliver Franks symbolized the close relationship between the two governments at this time.

[59] Reynolds, p. 176.

[60] Reynolds, p. 177.

marked the beginning of greater divergences between American and British policy, not only in Greece but also toward the Soviets. Though Britain had used its influence effectively to have the US assume responsibility for British strategic interests, the disagreement between the two over Palestine and the resulting failure of the plan for an Eastern Mediterranean bloc showed that the United States would increasingly follow its own path. The British could only attempt to continue to "guide" the Americans as much as possible, while also tying Britain's fortunes to America's to avoid being left behind and ignored.[61]

Notwithstanding these diverging priorities, the US Congress approved 200 million dollars of military aid for Greece and Turkey. By this time, the military situation in Greece had also improved, and the US, having been informed of rumors that the DSE was considering surrender, anticipated that the military conflict in Greece would end in 1948.[62] The Americans also believed that strong demonstrations of their support for Greece and public declarations of their optimistic appraisal of the military situation could have a positive effect on the Yugoslav and Bulgarian governments and their decisions on whether to continue to assist the Greek communists.[63] In light of the positive progression of events for Anglo-American intentions in Greece, the US Congress approved 225 million dollars of aid for Greece and Turkey by 1949. However, despite their success on the military front, the Americans realized that the troubles in Greece would persist, particularly economically and politically. They also believed that a center-left government (as the British had proposed) would have the best chance of dealing effectively with the country's economic and social problems, whereas a right-wing government would "carry on a 'blood feud' against all Greeks who do not agree with them politically." The Americans felt that if they did not intervene deeply enough in Greek politics, then the "Greek rightist parties" would continue to keep Greece in "turmoil indefinitely."[64]

---

[61] These special interests included big business such as Pan Am airlines, Zionists, and oil companies.
[62] Marshall to Griswold (Gama 885), June 4, 1948, FRUS 1948, Vol. IV, Eastern Europe and the Soviet Union (Multilateral Relations, pp. 1–732), pp. 102–3.
[63] Rankin to Marshall (1066), June 12, 1948, FRUS 1948, Vol. IV, Eastern Europe and the Soviet Union (Multilateral Relations, pp. 1–732), pp. 105–7.
[64] Marshall to AMAG (Gama 1001), June 23, 1948, Griswold to Henderson (868.00/6-2448), June 24, 1948, and Marshall to US Embassy in Greece (856), June 26, 1948, FRUS 1948, Vol. IV, Eastern Europe and the Soviet Union (Multilateral Relations, pp. 1–732), pp. 108–9, 112–14.

The Effects of the Tito-Stalin Split: July to October 1948

By this time, the growing tensions between Stalin and Tito had reached boiling point. In July, Tsaldaris informed Secretary of State Marshall that the Soviet Ambassador had secretly approached him in June, immediately prior to the Cominform's denunciation of Tito, and proposed to settle the outstanding issues between the USSR and the Greek government, especially the issue of Cyprus. However, demonstrating the continued American reliance on British input when it came to Greek affairs, Marshall ordered the US Embassy in London to inform Bevin and to take no other action until the British Foreign Secretary had expressed his opinion on how to proceed. However, Marshall did venture that, in his opinion, the Greek government should not reject the Soviet proposals outright, in order to create the best chances for the resolution of any outstanding issues.[65]

Bevin replied that although he also supported listening to the Soviet proposals, they should be viewed with skepticism and were likely just an attempt to discredit the Greek government and ministers by approaching individuals secretly rather than liaising with the government as a whole. Furthermore, Bevin stated that Tsaldaris should clearly tell the Soviet representative who had approached him that he was not prepared to discuss Cyprus, which was not surprising since the British intended to hold on to Cyprus as a base of operations, especially given their loss of influence in Egypt and Palestine. Summarizing the US position, Marshall said that unless Tsaldaris was already aware of it, it was better for Ambassador Douglas not to inform him that the US and Britain were coordinating their policy on this issue or to inform him of Bevin's attitude regarding Cyprus.[66]

The doubts of the previous year over whether the US would stay in Greece resurfaced in August 1948. Marshall informed the US Embassy in Athens that the American public increasingly felt that "American ideals" were being compromised by US support of the current Greek government. Though the US supported the Greek government's demand for unconditional surrender of the DSE, it was extremely concerned about how the government would treat surrendering guerrillas, especially since regular executions were still taking place.

---

[65] Marshall to US Embassy in London (2846), July 21, 1948, FRUS 1948, Vol. IV, Eastern Europe and the Soviet Union (Multilateral Relations, pp. 1–732), pp. 115–16.
[66] Marshall to US Embassy in London (1080), August 2, 1948, FRUS 1948, Vol. IV, Eastern Europe and the Soviet Union (Multilateral Relations, pp. 1–732), pp. 117–18.

Despite progress on the military front in Greece, the "right-wing" tendency of the Greek government was making it difficult for the US to justify domestically its continued presence in Greece. Marshall therefore instructed the embassy to inform the Greek government that the American government wished it to "re-examine" its policy regarding court-martial sentences and to "halt the cycle of killing in Greece." This was especially important to the US in light of the upcoming UN General Assembly meetings, in which it anticipated attacks from communist member states on the Greek government and on continuing Anglo-American support of it.[67] The US also wanted the Greek government to take its ongoing problems with Albanian assistance to the DSE to the UN; however, Bevin felt that this would cause unacceptable delays in implementing possible solutions. Tsaldaris met with Bevin, who agreed to consider the Greek request to make a formal diplomatic complaint to the Albanian minister in Belgrade since the British had no direct diplomatic representation in Albania.[68]

By mid-August 1948, the US believed that its efforts since the declaration of the Truman Doctrine had been successful and that at present, unless there was a complete change in tactics (all-out invasion, etc.) from Greece's communist neighbors, it was no longer in danger of falling to them. In the US view, which was mirrored by the British, Greece was no longer a "special case" that required "special consideration and treatment" compared to the nations of Western Europe or the Middle East. Though there was still an internal military threat, the Americans believed that the Greek military could now deal with it. Furthermore, they believed that the Greek economy, though still weak, was no longer in danger of complete collapse and could "at least be held together for the next four years," assuming that the European Recovery Program (better known as the Marshall Plan) continued and that the Greek government cooperated with the US. One of the most interesting sections of the dispatch addressed the eventual size of the Greek military and the prospect of decreasing US military aid to Greece. The long-term reduction of the Greek military was opposed by the majority of Greek political and military leaders: even with victory in sight, these leaders continued to demand new weapons and increase the size of the

---

[67] Marshall to US Embassy in Athens (1124), August 6, 1948, FRUS 1948, Vol. IV, Eastern Europe and the Soviet Union (Multilateral Relations, pp. 1–732), pp.118–19.
[68] Bevin to Reilly (442), Record of Meeting, August 25, 1948, BDFA, Series F Europe, Part IV, Vol. 17, pp. 140. The Greek government also approached the US to ask it to raise the issue with the USSR as to whether the Soviets could persuade the Albanians to disarm the DSE in their territory, but the US refused, saying that it would by "inappropriate" to ask the USSR at this time. See: Memorandum of Conversation, = August 10, 1948, FRUS 1948, Vol. IV, Eastern Europe and the Soviet Union (Multilateral Relations, pp. 1–732), pp.122–4.

military to respond to possible future aggression.⁶⁹ In a dispatch a few days later, Marshall responded that even a dramatically reduced Greek military "would constitute a serious drain" on Greek financial resources, so the US would have to exert the control it had over Greece based on loan agreements they had signed in order to control Greek expenditures as much as possible. The US would also have to consider these facts when calculating the amounts of future aid to Greece.⁷⁰

Regarding the military conflict, by the end of August 1948, the US had "reliable information" that the Soviets were pressing the KKE to pursue a political solution designed, in the opinion of the British and Americans, to preserve at least some communist party presence in Greece.⁷¹

The renewed Soviet focus on conciliation meant that, externally at least, it was fairly clear that the DSE had lost. The policies of the Big Three regarding Greece would now have to focus on how to present the situation internationally, namely, in the UN General Assembly. The British were nervous that given the favorable military conditions in Greece, the US might consider removing AMAG. Through Ambassador Oliver Franks, Bevin informed the State Department that he believed that the continued presence of the British and American military missions in Greece constituted a "steadying influence." This was especially important, he argued, considering that attacks "from within and without" would continue for the foreseeable future, and the Attlee-Bevin administration could hardly justify maintaining a British military presence in Greece should the US remove its forces. Marshall informed Franks that there would be no discussion of reductions until at least December 1948, when the situation in Greece would be re-examined. Off the record, Marshall offered a final "reassurance" to the British:

> ... if we find it necessary to withdraw our military mission from Greece, I fully expect that the US Government will give the British Government more notice of

---

⁶⁹ McGee to Lovett, August 11, 1948, FRUS 1948, Vol. IV, Eastern Europe and the Soviet Union (Multilateral Relations, pp. 1–732), pp. 124–9. To clarify, though talks were held in August 1948 on reducing aid to Greece, the proposed reductions would not take place until 1950. In 1948, American shipments of supplies (money, material, food, and clothing) were still increasing based on estimates from previous years. Though easily recognizing this fallacy in others, the United States would use the same argument to justify increasing the size of its armed forces in peacetime. This trend continues to the present day.
⁷⁰ Marshall to US Embassy in Greece (Gama 1246), August 16, 1948, FRUS 1948, Vol. IV, Eastern Europe and the Soviet Union (Multilateral Relations, pp. 1–732), pp. 135–7.
⁷¹ Grady to Marshall (1640), August 21, 1948, FRUS 1948, Vol. IV, Eastern Europe and the Soviet Union (Multilateral Relations, pp. 1–732), pp. 138–41.

this intention than Mr. Bevin gave me in February 1947 in regard to the necessity of the British Government to discontinue its support to Greece.[72]

Though Britain and the US had worked and would continue to work together in Greece, Marshall's statement was a clear indicator of US opinion. The US would make the decision independently of British objectives, and the State Department was still angry to some degree about the timing of the British declaration from the previous year. The statement reinforces a central point of this book that in February 1947, the State Department was in fact shocked by the British declaration that they would leave Greece.

Some authors have suggested that in February 1947, the Americans were already well aware of British intentions regarding Greece, but Marshall's comment a year and a half later indicates otherwise. The fact that Bevin also needed to justify a continued British military presence in Greece at this time shows, first, that the British had misled the Americans in February 1947 about how weak they actually were and, second, that well into 1948, Bevin was still holding on to the notion that Britain had to maintain a troop presence in Greece to have a say internationally with the Soviets and Americans.

However, in September 1948, American attention in northern Greece became focused on the murder of the American journalist George Polk. Members of the American military, such as General Donovan, strongly criticized the Greek police's handling of the matter, but the Greek Ambassador told British Consul Riley that the Thessaloniki gendarmerie directorate had provided useful assistance to the investigations.[73] What would not be revealed until many years later was that the police had resorted to torture to extract a forced confession of the murder from a Greek in order to placate the Americans.[74] The head of the British police mission in Thessaloniki supposedly provided an account of the Polk murder to British Ambassador Riley. However, interestingly, that report does not appear in the confidential print series.[75] The murder took place at a time

---

[72] Memorandum of Conversation between Franks and Marshall, September 7, 1948, FRUS 1948, Vol. IV, Eastern Europe and the Soviet Union (Multilateral Relations, pp. 1–732), p. 147.

[73] Riley to Foreign Office (301), September 15, 1948, BDFA, Series F Europe, Part IV, Vol. 17, pp. 196–7.

[74] Gerolymatos, pp. 188–92.

[75] Riley to Foreign Office (301), September 15, 1948, BDFA, Series F Europe, Part IV, Vol. 17, p. 197. It seems that whatever is contained in this document is still too sensitive to be released to the general public, and the only hope is that it will be made available in future to reveal what information the British and Americans actually had about the person who committed the Polk murder. The most likely scenario is that Polk was killed either by the Greek government or by a right-wing group for his criticism of the current Greek political climate. The importance of maintaining US aid to Greece was so high that the US and Britain would accept nothing that disrupted the plan of action. They allowed an innocent man to accept the blame for a crime he did not commit in order to placate the public back home.

when the Greek government was again using the threat of the DSE to request additional funding to enlarge the Greek Army. Polk, who had been heavily critical of corruption in the Greek government, was shot in the head. A few days later, on 28 September 1948, Tsaldaris met with Foreign Secretary Bevin and implored him to discuss the Greek military situation with Marshall.[76] He explained that the Greek government wanted to rapidly train another 70,000 soldiers for the planned Peloponnesian campaign in November. The cost would be US$10 million, but the Americans initially denied the request and considered using United Nations peacekeepers instead. The British and American governments had also sent diplomatic notes to the Albanian government protesting Albania's allowing Greek communist military forces to use its territory and freely cross the Albanian border as a tactic against the Greek national army.[77]

Shortly thereafter, Foreign Secretary Bevin met with George Marshall in Paris to discuss the conditions in Greece. Marshall informed Bevin that there was a continuous divide between American military and reconstruction policy, with the heads of the two missions arguing over who should appropriate the necessary funds. Bevin was still under intense pressure from the British government to remove the few British troops that remained in Greece, notably two garrisons in northern Greece in camps just outside Thessaloniki. The British Foreign Secretary was keen to resolve the military situation before the economic situation so that he could finally remove the remaining British troops and thus alleviate domestic political pressure. As a result, Bevin presented the United States with Tsaldaris' request to rapidly mobilize thousands more Greek soldiers to enlarge the forces that were available to confront the communist guerrillas.[78]

On the other side, anxious to begin to reduce the Greek armed forces, at least to some degree, Marshall stated that budgetary, morale-related, and combat considerations had been taken into account by American military personnel in Greece and that the Greek military did not currently need to be increased.[79] Furthermore, in a conversation with Tsaldaris, Marshall explained that he believed that at least for the foreseeable future, the United States and the USSR

---

[76] The timing is interesting, since the request was made such a short time after Mr. Polk was killed.
[77] Record of Meeting between Minister Tsaldaris and Foreign Secretary Bevin (498), September 28, 1948, BDFA, Series F Europe, Part IV, Vol. 17, pp. 198–200.
[78] Record of Meeting between Minister Tsaldaris and Foreign Secretary Bevin (498), September 28, 1948, BDFA, Series F Europe, Part IV, Vol. 17, pp. 198–200.
[79] For reports on US studies related to possible reductions of the Greek armed forces, see: Grady to Marshall (Gama 1282), September 20, 1948, and Grady to Marshall (Amag 1581), September 29, 1948, FRUS 1948, Vol. IV, Eastern Europe and the Soviet Union (Multilateral Relations, pp. 1–732), pp. 151–3.

would not experience a rapprochement. However, he believed that in time, "the truth must prevail" and that "the force of world opinion" would force the Soviets and their satellites to change their policies. Until then, the United States would continue to provide funds and material to others despite the "difficulties involved."[80]

However, in the autumn of 1948, the British noted problems between the various American missions and the Greek government. In particular, the military and economic missions were finding it extremely difficult to work with the various Greek ministries, which continually resisted such American concerns as price control, decentralization, and reducing over-employment by government corporations. The Americans were further frustrated by "fantastic" Greek demands for "thousands of miles of roads, reconditioning of ports to a standard higher than existed in the United States, and so on. They were completely unrealistic."[81] The Americans antagonized the Greeks (making them unwilling to cooperate) by insisting that Greek newspaper printers pay full market price for their paper rather than the government subsidizing half the price, as it had formerly done. Further aggravating American-Greek relations and demonstrating the absence of fear about "biting the hand" that was feeding Greece, the secretary general of the Greek trade union federation sent angry telegrams to the State Department and to trade union organizations in the United States "alleging that the American mission was endeavouring to keep wages down."[82] In short, the picture that emerges from the closing months of 1948 is that the country was perceived as being desperately in need of reform, but neither its own elites nor the Americans were willing to implement such reform.

1948: October to December, Rising Doubts

The diplomatic exchanges regarding Greece at this time highlight the deficiencies of the Greek state as seen by British and American officials, who were continually frustrated by Greek intransigence, incompetence and corruption—to the point that they began threatening the Greek government to secure its cooperation.

---

[80] Memorandum of Conversation between Marshall and Tsaldaris, September 30, 1948, FRUS 1948, Vol. IV, Eastern Europe and the Soviet Union (Multilateral Relations, pp. 1–732), pp. 154–5.
[81] Norton to Bevin (95), September 29, 1948, BDFA, Series F Europe, Part IV, Vol. 17, pp. 200–1.
[82] Norton to Bevin (95), September 29, 1948, BDFA, Series F Europe, Part IV, Vol. 17, pp. 200–1.

They also highlight the tendency of the Greek government to continually refer to the communist threat to justify its actions and claims.

Despite the military successes of the summer, through autumn 1948, military and economic conditions again worsened. Although both the British and the Americans still believed that the country was important to Western interests, they had serious doubts as to whether they could stay in Greece in any capacity. Marshall reported that morale was extremely low, not only in the Greek government but also in the British and American military missions. The Anglo-American missions and the Greek military were extremely frustrated that the DSE was still able to use the Albanian and Yugoslavian borders and that the UN had been unable to take any action to stop them.[83] Therefore, Marshall finally gave in to the Greek government and endorsed its earlier request to increase the Greek military by 15,000 men, if only to improve morale and allow for the rotation out of the most tired and demoralized troops. His justification for reversing his earlier position was that Greece, like Berlin, was a single point in the Soviet strategy, but that all such points were interconnected, and how the US reacted in one area had repercussions in another. In a meeting with Tsaldaris, Marshall stated that although the Greek government did not have to worry for the time being about a reduction in its armed forces, the most important object was to focus on "refreshing" the troops, i.e., allowing them to rest and giving them reasons for optimism. Furthermore, the US noted that despite continuing Albanian and Bulgarian aid to the DSE, Yugoslavian aid had diminished, possibly as a result of the Tito-Stalin split, and although it was too early to tell whether this was a real change in Yugoslavian policy or just limited local developments, it would be important to monitor the situation so that policy could change accordingly.[84]

---

[83] Bevin to Reilly (498), September 28, 1948, BDFA, Series F Europe, Part IV, Vol. 17, pp. 198–9. The British and Greek governments were still uncertain whether the Yugoslavian border was actually closed, but they believed that supplies were still coming to the DSE via Albania. The Greek government requested that the British consider "some kind of control" of the Albanian coast to prevent arms from being shipped there.

[84] Marshall to Lovett, October 20, 1948, Memorandum of Conversation, October 21, 1948, Lovett to US Embassy in Turkey (A-176), October 21, 1948, FRUS 1948, Vol. IV, Eastern Europe and the Soviet Union (Multilateral Relations, pp. 1–732), pp. 162–7. Documents from this time reveal a very confusing picture of various understandings of actual conditions on the Greek-Yugoslav border. The British and Americans were not sure of Tito's intentions. Furthermore, as recent investigation has shown, despite Tito's guarantees to the British, Greeks, and Americans about returning Greek children, there is evidence that he held thousands of children against their will and attempted to make them become Slavs in an attempt to use them in the future for claims against Macedonia. See: Irini Lagani, "To Paidomagoma' kai oi Ellino-Yugoslvikes Skeseis – 1948–52" (Sideri: Athina, 1996). Also, for the Yugoslavian view of the conflict, see: Svetozar Vukomanovic, *How and Why the People's Liberation Struggle of Greece met with Defeat*.

Ambassador Norton described how the military situation had "deteriorated" again in October 1948, when the guerrillas in the Peloponnese succeeded "in producing these conditions of anarchy, economic chaos, lawlessness, misery and uncertainty, which are the ideal breeding ground of communism." Subsequently, the attitude toward Britain and the United States in the Greek media rapidly worsened as the two Western powers were accused of having made past mistakes that had contributed directly to the "present Greek tragedy" and of having:

> ... aggravated the situation by attempts at reconciliation with the Communists in the early days after the world war, and of having finally failed to sanction the increase in size of the Greek army and provided it with the necessary equipment for the overthrow of the Communists.[85]

These comments reveal British indignation at not being praised for the efforts they had made in Greece in the mid- to late 1940s. Numerous dispatches contain ambassadors' and consuls' opinions about public sentiment toward Britain, indicating that it was an extremely important consideration for the British government. The dispatches also frequently noted the status of public opinion and public and army morale, which were understandably low by the end of 1948, as they essentially had been since the German occupation of Greece in 1941. However, these opinions were apparently monitored not only for reasons of pride. In many of the diplomatic reports from embassies all over Europe and the United States, British diplomatic staff members were extremely careful to note public opinion as they perceived it from numerous sources: newspapers, magazines, and other diplomats. The purpose seems to have been not only to keep Whitehall up to date with such currents of feeling but also to identify how best to respond to and, if necessary, counter the opinions being spread.[86] It was not as easy for the British to do this in Greece as in the United States because of the language difference. American diplomats, echoing the British Foreign Secretary's sentiments, repeatedly commented on how much easier and more efficient communication was between the US and Britain than

---

[85] Collard to Norton (74), October 12, 1948, BDFA, Series F Europe, Part IV, Vol. 17, p. 202.

[86] The British government firmly believed in the power of public opinion, not only in its own country but in others, and made sure they were kept apprised of it in order to know how to best deal with those countries' officials. This concept of "defensive realist" action is supported by Ian Hall, who argues that realism rather than liberalism dominated post-war British policy. See: Ian Hall, "Power Politics and appeasement: Political Realism in British International Thought, c. 1935–1955" (*British Journal of Politics and International Relations* (BJPIR), 2006, vol. 8, issue 2).

with other nations because of the ability to converse and consult one another in their mother tongue.[87] It was an advantage that the British would adeptly use to their benefit.

By November 1, 1948, the British in the USA were keenly aware of the shift in their relationship with the Americans, and William Edwards, the head of the British Information Service in the United States, summed up the new power balance as follows:

> Whether we like it or not, we have to admit in this stage of our history, that the United States has assumed such a dominant place in the world, and our affairs are so inextricably linked with hers, that British policy can never totally be effective unless it has the tacit support and backing of the American people – or at least it is not actively opposed by them.[88]

US Ambassador Douglas reported that Britain's government believed that the British decline was temporary and that, in combination with the Dominions and what remained of the Empire, it could regain enough economic strength to deal with the United States on relatively equal terms.[89]

In Greece, by the end of November, the communist army was still making gains in the north and in the Peloponnese, and the progress of the national army, in the words of the Consul General of Athens, W. L. C. Knight, "was nothing short of lamentable." As winter approached, both the Americans and the British believed that the communist forces had regained the initiative in the conflict.[90] As the campaign worsened for the Greek army, the Greek government requested even more men and material, but Ambassador Grady rejected the request. He stated that the national army had already been trained by the Americans and British, and everything from its daily meals to the animals it used to transport supplies was paid for and provided by the United States. He added that it was impossible to understand how such a force, supported by a navy and air force and numbering almost 300,000, could not defeat a force of 25,000 with far less

---

[87] Coleman, p. 356, citing: "Hearings Before the Subcommittee on National Security Staffing," p. 243.
[88] William P.N. Edwards to Ambassador's Staff Meeting (Notes from meeting in the USA), November 1, 1948, FO 953/130 P 9826/151/950.
[89] Douglas to Marshall (3625), August 11, 1948, FRUS 1948, Vol. III, Western Europe, pp. 1113–17. Later, in London in August 1948, American Ambassador Lewis Douglas took note of the distinct anti-American sentiment, which was very strong, and reported it to Washington. This proved to be diplomatically very problematic for the British, who were still trying to reconcile their internal politics with foreign needs. See: Douglas to Marshall (3625), August 11, 1948, FRUS 1948, Vol. III, Western Europe, pp. 1113–17.
[90] WLC Knight to Foreign Office (53 and 37), November 4, 1948, BDFA, Series F Europe, Part IV, Vol. 17, pp. 203–4.

food and supplies. Therefore, in his opinion, the lack of success could not be attributed to insufficient numbers and material but was mostly down to a lack of leadership and "fighting spirit." He commented that the Greeks were far too dependent upon foreign assistance and lacked the will to implement their own solutions. Finally, he stated that while a military threat to Greece continued to exist, the US Congress would likely continue to support Greece, but increasing the military at this time would only hurt Greece's economy without achieving significant gains on the military front.[91] However, unbeknownst to the US or Greece, the DSE was in such a poor state that discussion of a ceasefire had already begun within the KKE.[92]

An explanation for the poor performance of the Greek armed forces may also be found by examining an event in the northern Greek town of Katerini, which was the site of an American military base. A national militia unit was created there to demonstrate a national government presence to the locals. The men were appointed to guard an armory and were given *fustanellas* as uniforms and newly acquired American-made weapons. They received no training whatsoever, and in addition to having no knowledge of how to use their weapons, they slept through their shifts.[93] This was just another example of the incompetence of the Greek military at the time and the misuse of American aid.

After almost five months of waiting, talks about forming a defensive pact between Turkey, Greece, Iran, and Egypt with US backing were renewed. This was part of a wider problem for the United States, as summarized by the Director of Near Eastern and African Affairs (NEA). He stated that the problem of the US tying itself to a Western European defense pact without including weaker nations from elsewhere in the world could be interpreted as the US having less interest in those weaker nations, which in turn would provide the USSR with the opportunity to influence and then dominate those nations. The NEA therefore recommended a comprehensive policy that would include any nations threatened by the USSR.[94] This report not only shows that the US was increasingly and firmly taking hold of the British desire to tie the US to European (and by extension worldwide) anti-communist efforts; it also points to

---

[91] Grady to Marshall (Amag 1613), October 22, 1948, FRUS 1948, Vol. IV, Eastern Europe and the Soviet Union (Multilateral Relations, pp. 1–732), pp.168–70.
[92] Bullock, *Bevin*, p. 630, and Stavrakis, *Moscow and Greek Communism*, pp. 171, 178.
[93] Pichos, "Verbal interview" (2011).
[94] Memorandum (840.20/10-2648), October 26, 1948, FRUS 1948, Vol. IV, Eastern Europe and the Soviet Union (Multilateral Relations, pp. 1–732), pp.172–6.

the development of a US foreign policy that would continue to evolve into ever greater levels of intervention in foreign countries and regional politics.

Despite its generally increasing interventionism, at this time the US was still reluctant to appoint a government in Greece. A political crisis in November 1948 that threatened to destroy the government provided the US with the opportunity to "step in at any moment and attempt to constitute a government," but Ambassador Henry Grady advised that this action would be only temporarily beneficial and would cause more problems in the long term. He added that the US desired a constitutional and non-dictatorial solution and would continue to monitor the situation to ensure that such a solution was achieved. Grady even stated that it was in Greece's best interests to be forced to find its own solution rather than being permitted to "turn to us for direction." In a statement often repeated by British and American officials alike, Grady said that the main problem was that Greece had no capable and selfless statesmen around whom a consensus and a functioning government could be formed.[95]

American projections for Greece up to 1950 were set out in a National Security Council (NSC) report which stated that by then, Turkey would have greater strategic importance to the US than Greece, and that if Turkey was granted greater assistance as a result of its higher degree of strategic value, it would assume a "position more comparable to western countries than Greece."[96]

These assumptions were also based upon the continued poor performance of Greece's large army, and plans again began to circulate about switching tactics and reducing the size of the armed forces. Even though the US was bearing the direct cost of the military, it explained that the indirect costs of so large an army were also "staggering," largely because army members, who should be amongst the most productive members of the Greek economy, "became non-producers when serving in the army." Grady said that according to the US Military Mission officers in Greece, far from helping the military situation, regular increases in the size of the army made Greek soldiers less willing to fight as it persuaded them that the conflict was "America's war rather than Greece's." Grady also wrote that although Greece had been a focal point "on the democratic front" over the previous year, by now it "deserves only secondary consideration." For the US, the democratic defense of Europe now "hinged on England and Turkey." Should hostilities erupt, in his estimation, Greece would be of very little value, but should

---

[95] Grady to Marshall (2246), November 6, 1948, FRUS 1948, Vol. IV, Eastern Europe and the Soviet Union, pp. 180–1.
[96] McGhee to Lovett (868.20/11-1948), November 19, 1948, FRUS 1948, Vol. IV, Eastern Europe and the Soviet Union, pp. 184–6.

the "Cold War" continue, the communists must be prevented from assuming power. He added that the political establishment in Greece was incompetent and incapable of implementing effective measures to deal with either economic or military problems. Therefore, in his opinion, US aid to Greece should be not increased but merely maintained.[97]

The Joint Chiefs of Staff supported Ambassador Grady's statements, saying that not only was Turkey more valuable than Greece strategically, but that in the event of a shooting war, Turkey's "high national spirit and geographical situation makes it possible now for that nation to resist Soviet aggression."[98] These dispatches are very revealing since they illustrate not only the changing geopolitical reality of the Balkans but also how Greece's political situation was viewed from abroad. They also show how the British had achieved their objective of persuading the US to view them as indispensable to European security.

Another bright point for the British was that as a result of the Tito-Stalin split, there was an opening to bring Yugoslavia closer to the Western sphere. At the end of December 1948, Secretary Bevin informed Ambassador Norton of Britain's desire to encourage Greek and Yugoslavian relations to the point that the two governments could reach an agreement and settle some of their outstanding differences to achieve a political solution and an end to Yugoslav support of the Greek communists. This dispatch goes on to reveal a fascinating aspect of British foreign policy designs for Greece.

Bevin informed the Greek Ambassador that the internal situation, in the British view, was "most unsatisfactory." He asked the Greek Ambassador:

> Had the Greek government considered that the Americans, who have now accepted wide commitment throughout the world, might tire of their efforts to achieve a solution in Greece? The Americans have shown that they were quite

---

[97] Grady to Marshall (Amag 1652), November 22, 1948, FRUS 1948, Vol. IV, Eastern Europe and the Soviet Union (Multilateral Relations, pp. 1–732), pp. 187–91. Although his views were accepted as very close to those of the State Department, his recommendation for 150 million dollars in aid was seen as too low, and 200 million dollars in aid was approved for Greece into 1949. See: McGee to Lovett, November 24, 1948, ibid., pp. 192–95. After having observed the Greek national army in action, he commented that the Greek artillery corps was carelessly firing expensive ammunition, "much in the manner of American children setting off firecrackers on July 4th." Grady to Marshall (Amag 1657), December 7, 1948, ibid., pp. 210–12.

[98] Joint Chiefs of Staff to the Secretary of Defense (SANACC 358/8), November 24, 1948, FRUS 1948, Vol. IV, Eastern Europe and the Soviet Union (Multilateral Relations, pp. 1–732), pp. 191–2. For a comprehensive US analysis of the situation in Greece, see: Report by the US Policy Planning Staff on US aid to Greece (PPS 44), November 24, 1948, ibid., pp. 195–203.

prepared to cut their losses. So far as the United Kingdom was concerned, they should realize that the continued presence of British troops in Greece was an embarrassment to his Majesty's Government and I would find it increasingly difficult to defend to the Labour Party their maintenance there for much longer. On the other hand, I certainly wanted to see Greece kept free from communism, and I was there for speaking frankly and as a friend of the Greek people. I have every confidence in the Greek people and their soldiers, but the political leadership of Greece seemed to be in it to the point of your responsibility. The situation must be taken in hand at once and I'll be glad to learn M. Pipenelis' [the Greek Ambassador to Britain] ideas for a possible solution.[99]

The Greek Ambassador replied that he believed that problems had arisen because the recommendations of the Greek general staff had not been followed. The Greek government simultaneously desired a free hand in planning military operations and expected the Americans to give it whatever supplies and funds it required without any accountability on its part. Bevin responded to the Greek Ambassador that President Truman had heavily criticized Greek action, or the lack thereof, and that if his negative reports were to be translated into congressional action, it would be very difficult to subsequently begin to act in Greece's favor again. Bevin then urged the Greek Ambassador on his return to Greece to inform the government of Bevin's personal opinion that there should be "no delay in showing that the Greek leaders really intend to take grip on the situation."[100] Bevin believed that this demonstration was vital for the American State Department to make a strong case to Congress for continuing the aid that Greece still needed. Bevin told the Greek Ambassador that he believed this was a critical time for Greece and that if the Greeks were able to reach an agreement with Yugoslavia and settle the issue of the northern borders, then real progress could be made on the military front. This would improve the government's image, making it seem that it was taking control of the situation in its country and, as a result, justifying continued and further American intervention.[101] However, it is important to note that despite British claims and American discussion of the possibility of withdrawing from Greece, there seemed to be no real possibility

---

[99] Bevin to Norton, Record of Meeting (620), December 29, 1948, BDFA, Series F Europe, Part IV, Vol. 17, pp. 212–13.
[100] Record of Meeting (620), December 29, 1948, BDFA, Series F Europe, Part IV, Vol. 17, p. 213. These statements seem to find resonance today with the EU's statements to the Greek government.
[101] Record of Meeting (620), December 29, 1948, BDFA, Series F Europe, Part IV, Vol. 17, p. 213.

of such a withdrawal. By this point, the United States had simply invested too much in Greece to leave. Bevin's threats and Truman's statements should therefore be seen mainly as expressions of frustration and tools to attempt to motivate the Greek government to follow Anglo-American policy.[102]

Despite the American predominance in Greek affairs, the British still exerted a fair amount of influence up to the end of 1948. Britain's influence in Greece was again revealed when Bevin stated that there were two ways to strengthen the internal political situation. The first way was for the British and the Americans to suggest that a particular individual be made prime minister, and the second was to leave it to the Greeks to form their own government but for the British and Americans to advise the Greek king, who would then relay their recommendations to the constitutional authority of the Greek government. In both cases, Bevin stated that, intentionally or not, the British would continue to exert significant control over Greek decision-making, although Bevin stated that he had no desire for Britain to intervene and "make and break governments." However, he did not understand how, at a time when the very future of Greece was at stake, politicians could not move past their party differences and work together for the benefit of their country and their people. He said that his greatest disappointment was not in the Greek army, the American intervention or the Greek people but in Greece's politicians. He added that it was wrong for the politicians in Athens to believe that whatever actions they took, they could continue to rely on American and British aid without making any sacrifices themselves or subduing their party and personal ambitions in order to provide a strong and effective government for Greece during the crisis. Once again, Bevin told the Greek Ambassador that if worst came to worst, the Americans could be tempted to simply leave and "cut their losses."[103] The frequency with which Bevin described American perceptions of Greek failures and the possibility that the Americans were prepared to abandon their international responsibilities if the costs outweighed the benefits shows how deeply the British believed that their fortunes were intertwined with continued American intervention. This belief was not lost on American politicians.

---

[102] For the US discussion about threatening to suspend aid or leave Greece entirely and why such actions would ultimately be counterproductive to US interests, see: McGee to Executive Secretariat, November 26, 1948, FRUS 1948, Vol. IV, Eastern Europe and the Soviet Union (Multilateral Relations, pp. 1–732), pp. 203–4.

[103] Record of Meeting (620), December 29, 1948, BDFA, Series F Europe, Part IV, Vol. 17, p. 214.

Lewis Douglas, the American Ambassador to the United Kingdom, produced a report in an attempt to identify the sources of the simultaneous feelings of American dependency and anti-Americanism that he was perceiving among both the British government and the British people. He stated:

> Britain accepts our assumption of world leadership in face of Russian aggression, and Anglo-American unity today is more firmly established than ever before in peacetime. But Britain has never before been in a position where her national security and economic fate are so completely dependent on the mercy of another country's decisions. Almost every day brings new evidence of her weakness and dependence on the US. This is a bitter pill for a country accustomed to full control of her national destiny.[104]

Douglas also identified the British desire to understand the current situation and develop a plan to improve it and to restore Britain to its former position of international prominence:

> While they do not expect to regain their former relative supremacy, with help from the US they are confident that in conjunction with the British Commonwealth and Empire they will again become a power to be reckoned with, which, associated with the US, can maintain the balance of power in the world.[105]

At the end of 1948, although the British still clung to those hopes, which had been correctly outlined by Douglas, their ability to achieve them was in doubt. But it was in Greece that their policy objective could at least be partially fulfilled, if not in regard to Greece itself, then at least in regard to US policy on Greece. While the United States was committed to at least maintaining its current level of involvement in Greece, it was also tying itself to the mutual defense agreements that Bevin had envisaged. The Vandenberg Resolution had provided for US participation in regional organizations, such as the Brussels Pact, that affected American national security, and the State Department acknowledged that such steps constituted a "radical departure from past American peacetime policies." Both the Greeks and the Turks had expressed their desire to be included in a possible North Atlantic pact, but at the time, the US said that their participation was unlikely due to their geographical location. However, they were free to

---

[104] Douglas to State Department (3625), August 11, 1948, FRUS 1948, Vol. III, Western Europe, p. 1113.
[105] Douglas to State Department (3625), August 11, 1948, FRUS 1948, Vol. III, Western Europe, p. 1113.

pursue their own mutual defense pact and were informed that when the time was right, the US would examine that proposal.[106]

Therefore, by the end of 1948, although it was disappointed in the Greek political, economic, and military situations and notwithstanding its numerous threats, the United States was just as committed to Greece, if not more so, as it had been the previous year. Though the US estimation of Greece's strategic value had diminished, Greece's value to the British had increased. Involving the US in Greece had led to firm US guarantees for protecting Western security interests in Europe, the Eastern Mediterranean, and the Middle East. While the issue of Palestine had resulted in deep divisions within the US government, between the British and the Americans and between the West and the Arab world, it did not bring about a change of policy over US intervention in Greece. Additionally, from the British perspective, 1948 had to be considered a success, since Britain was seen as the United States' key partner and therefore as crucial to securing Western European security. It had also succeeded in creating a mutual defense pact that would tie Western Europeans together in defense.[107]

In spite of the numerous reversals on the ground in Greece, and resulting statements from the British and Americans that they may have to leave the country, the reality was that these were just statements. Too much had been invested and the Cold War was under way. There was no real possibility that Greece would be left to her own devices. This reality would have consequences for Greece's future, for while at the end of 1948 the Americans still opposed the possibility of a dictatorship in Greece, over the next year, their insistence on democracy would eventually change to an insistence on mere stability.

---

[106] Lovett to US Embassy in Turkey (588), December 15, 1948, FRUS 1948, Vol. IV, Eastern Europe and the Soviet Union (Multilateral Relations, pp. 1–732), pp. 213–15.

[107] The formation of NATO essentially represented the antithesis of the United Nations. The former attempted to preserve peace through the threat of the use of force, while the latter attempted to preserve peace by preventing the use of force. Thus, in 1949, US foreign policy dramatically changed, giving rise to unprecedented levels of foreign intervention.

5

The Tide Turns: The End of the Greek Civil War and the Supremacy of the United States

1949: January to April

Overall, from January to March 1949, the situation of the Greek armed forces improved. The British Consul in Patras, explained that regions in the Peloponnese were being cleared and that the communists who remained in hiding "are slowly being liquidated by the gendarmerie mobile patrols, which are scouring the countryside in the wake of the Army." The communists who were surrendering also informed the government forces of the disintegration of the guerrilla forces.[1] The major contributing factor was the previous year's split between Tito and Stalin, which by January 1949 had led to a purge of all pro-Tito factions from the DSE. Among other allegations, the Titoists were criticized for having lost to the British in December 1944, and the result was an "anti-Tito body" on the border of Yugoslavia.[2]

Ironically, the pro-Stalin movement in the DSE, created within the KKE (although indirectly encouraged by the Tito-Stalin split), added to the British and American perception that the Soviets were still determined to control Greece. Tito was quickly courted by the West; Yugoslavia, officially at least, closed its borders; and the DSE found it much more difficult to receive the supplies it needed to carry on the armed struggle.[3] Had it remained aligned with Tito, it

---

[1] Crosthwaite to Foreign Office (58), March 19, 1949, BDFA, Series F Europe, Part IV, Vol. 22, p. 78.
[2] Nachmani, p. 511.
[3] However, new evidence uncovered in the Czech archives has shown that the DSE received massive amounts of foreign aid from Cominform nations both before and after the Tito-Stalin split. Nikos Marantzidis and Kostas Tsivos, pp. 193–201. Tables of amounts of aid given to the KKE, dated July 31, 1950. Marantzidis and Tsivos argue, in fact, that had the DSE not been so well supported by Cominform nations, the Civil War may not have started at all and certainly would not have continued until 1949.

is possible that his rapprochement with the West could have secured a better peace for the DSE; however, its fanatical devotion to Stalin helped the Greek government maintain Western support. Therefore, although Stavrakis claimed that the Tito-Stalin split had eliminated the DSE's chances for victory,[4] it may be more accurate to say that it was the DSE's *reaction* to the split that resulted in its destruction, not the split itself.

In terms of US-Greek relations, by January 1949, the US was clearly frustrated with the Greek government and politicians. It felt that Greece was focusing its efforts on acquiring even more US aid rather than attempting to make effective use of the aid which it had already received. Additionally, while still committed to Greek political and territorial integrity, the US was not prepared at this time to support the creation of a Mediterranean Pact. The possibility of the US being associated "for reasons of defense with nations outside of the Western Hemisphere" was seen as a "radical departure from traditional American foreign policy" for which the US was not prepared, at least for the time being.[5]

The Americans also informed Deputy Prime Minister Tsaldaris of their displeasure with the Greek government for not making good use of the aid that had already been given, which was currently "higher even than the rate for China." Moreover, the acting secretary of state told the ambassador that the US government was extremely alarmed about the number of refugees in Greece, which had grown from 300,000 to 700,000 over the past year. The Greek government had been unable to deal effectively with either the social or the military situation, despite the aid provided by the United States. This "reprimand" of sorts was followed by the statement that Greece and Turkey would not be invited to sign the North Atlantic Pact, since they "could certainly not be considered in the North Atlantic family of nations."[6]

---

[4] Stavrakis, *Moscow and Greek Communism*, pp. 171–73.
[5] Satterthwaite to Lovett, January 3, 1949, FRUS 1949. The Near East, South Asia, and Africa, Vol. VI, pp. 227–30. The fact that Greece was considered outside the Western Hemisphere also demonstrates US opinion about the country and its place in the new geopolitical order. The US focus was on NATO, which Greece would join in October 1952. However, eventually NATO would begin to involve itself in "out-of-area" operations. See: Spero S. Z. Paravantes, The issue of NATO "out-of-area" operations: from West Africa to the borders of the Near East: www.cvce.eu/en/recherche/unit-content/-/unit/e7c423ed-a376-4a57-a415-f8519344e558/3a02a425-4d6a-419a-b61d-bef706c470d2/Resources#efcb0e9c-5b0a-47bd-8eb3-1b0bae19cf28_en&overlay
[6] Memorandum of Meeting between Greek Ambassador to US and Acting Secretary of State, January 4, 1949, FRUS 1949. The Near East, South Asia, and Africa, Vol. VI, pp. 231–33. The language here is also demonstrative. Using the word "family" to describe the future North Atlantic Pact members indicates again how Greece and Turkey were really viewed: although not in the Soviet sphere, they were not yet in the Anglo-American family either.

The first indication of a change in US policy toward the Greek government occurred when, after more in-fighting and Greek government inaction, the Greek king suggested the appointment of a non-elected joint Papagos-Markezinis coalition. By all accounts, this would have been a quasi-dictatorial solution, with the two party leaders ruling in the name of the king. Although the Americans were reluctant to support any "extra-parliamentary" solution, instead favoring attempts to make the government more efficient by eliminating certain ministries, the US Ambassador to Greece believed that the situation might change in the future and the US may be required to support a non-democratic solution. The State Department agreed with the Ambassador and advised that he meet with his British counterpart to coordinate joint Anglo-American analysis of and recommendations for the situation in Greece.[7] This was the beginning of the US shift from calling for a representative democracy in Greece to calling merely for stability. The fact that the State Department ordered coordination with the British also indicates the importance that the Americans still placed on British expertise in Greece.

The crisis in the Greek government was so serious that the British Ambassador to Greece believed that current efforts to reshuffle and improve the functioning of the government could be the last chance for a parliamentary democracy in Greece. The British and Americans also agreed that the Greeks had to be "shocked into a sense of reality," which they thought could be achieved through an official joint Anglo-American statement, regarding the inability of the Greek government to subdue personal differences and political considerations for the good of the country.[8]

The Americans were further aggravated by a meeting with General Papagos in which he said that he had agreed to assume the post of commander-in-chief only if he was given an army that he considered to be an adequate size. In his view, the current size of 250,000 men was insufficient for the task that Britain and the United States was expecting the army to perform. Henry Grady, US Ambassador to Greece, wrote, "Not only what Papagos said, but the tone in which he said it, deeply disturbed me. In the vernacular, he was telling us off." Papagos' statements angered the US Ambassador so much that he informed the State Department. In turn, the State Department ordered him to convey to the Greek government that not only would the US refuse to finance or allow an increase in the size of the Greek

---

[7] Grady to Lovett (24), January 5, 1949, Lovett to Grady (27), January 7, 1949, FRUS 1949. The Near East, South Asia, and Africa, Vol. VI, pp. 233–6.
[8] Grady to Lovett (74), January 12, 1949, FRUS 1949. The Near East, South Asia, and Africa, Vol. VI, p. 236.

military but the Anglo-American military missions would continue to have a say in the military campaign, despite Papagos' statements to the contrary. Furthermore, while the US had confidence in Papagos' military capabilities, his statements had created an "unfortunate impression" in the United States.[9] Papagos had jeopardized Greece's continuing aid by insulting the very country that was providing it.

As a result, on February 17, 1949, President Truman ordered a reassessment of current US-Yugoslavian and Greek-Yugoslavian economic and political relations. The British and Americans decided to try to use the opportunity to normalize Greece's relations not only with Yugoslavia but also with Bulgaria and Albania, if possible. Greece therefore regained some of its lost importance in Anglo-American planning, since the normalization of its relations with these nations could provide the British and Americans with an opportunity to make diplomatic advances into the Soviet sphere.[10]

Although the full effect of the DSE's purge of pro-Titoists would not be felt until the summer, by March 1949 the British military advisers who were part of the joint British and American training units were finally reporting positive results from the previous year's decision to improve the training and morale of the Greek National Army rather than simply spending more money to increase its size.[11] The Americans noted, that by not denouncing Tito as the Cominform had done, Markos Vafiadis had become "especially reprehensible" to the Soviets and to the majority of the KKE. The Americans speculated (and would later be proven correct) that Vafiadis' omission had led to his dismissal and replacement by Zachariadis. Though they could not be certain of it at the time, they added that any attempt by Moscow to turn the KKE against Tito would only strengthen the American and Greek position and could possibly lead to the normalization of relations between Greece and Yugoslavia. Joint Anglo-American action in response to the political crisis of the previous month was also showing benefits, as the new Greek government was described as the best since the elections of 1946. US Ambassador Grady also stated that agreement with the British was vital for success, even though US policy "was determined independent of

---

[9] Grady to Acheson (228), February 7, 1949, Grady to Deputy Prime Minister Tsaldaris, February 15, 1949, FRUS 1949. The Near East, South Asia, and Africa, Vol. VI, pp. 245–9.

[10] Cannon (Yugoslavia) to Acheson (161), February 16, 1949, Drew, UNSCOB II to Acheson (308), February 19, 1949, FRUS 1949. The Near East, South Asia, and Africa, Vol. VI, pp. 250–6.

[11] Report on Greece by the British Chief of Imperial General Staff (March 1949), FO 371/78348/R3285/G. The Greek government had repeatedly pressed both the British and the Americans for increases in military strength since the end of 1947. However, by September 1948, the Americans were planning reductions of the armed forces. See Chapter 4, Section: 1948, January to May. Record of Conversation (225), April 16, 1948, BDFA, Series F Europe, Part IV, Vol. 17, pp. 122–3.

British views and not influenced by them." Grady also stated that public opinion favored both the new government and the United States because the government had come about through normal parliamentary procedures and was "not an American creation." He commented that Papagos was suitable as head of the Greek armed forces but not as a political leader, and that Greece was an example of America's new role in the "free world." This role, brought about by America's post-war prosperity, required a degree of statesmanship and wisdom that the US had "never before been called on to display."[12]

The new responsibility accepted by the United States coincided with rising Soviet-Yugoslav tensions when the USSR began moving troops into Romania and increased economic pressure on Yugoslavia. The British theorized that these actions could be in support of a possible "Macedonian" state, but both the US and Britain had already guaranteed that they would never recognize a state that laid claim to Greek Macedonia.[13] The Americans received reports that the Yugoslavians were secretly proposing to meet with the Greek government to "discuss the possibility of 'entente' between the two countries." The Americans also received confirmation of a split between the Soviets and Yugoslavs, and began planning how to take full advantage of it.[14]

In the spring of 1949, Ambassador Grady reported that the military situation in Greece was the most encouraging it had been since the inception of the Marshall Plan. Furthermore, he stated that morale was high, the Greek government was "promising" and the United States was "now getting good returns for the money invested." He therefore recommended that the US Congress continue to supply aid to finish the job it had started in Greece.[15] The improving military situation in Greece coincided with the signing of the North Atlantic Treaty on April 4, 1949 by Britain, the United States and Canada, in addition to Belgium, Denmark, France, Iceland, Luxembourg, Italy, Portugal, the Netherlands, and

---

[12] Grady to Acheson (319), February 19, 1949, FRUS 1949, The Near East, South Asia, and Africa, Vol. VI, pp. 256-7. The fact that Grady felt it necessary to state that US policy had been developed independently could be interpreted to mean that the opposite was true, or at least that that perception was in circulation. Grady also cautioned against allowing anyone to use America's power to impose American will "on a people we are trying to make free." It was a remarkably prescient statement in light of how US foreign policy has developed since 1949. Many would argue that US foreign policy since then has focused solely on using US power to impose American will on foreign states.

[13] British Embassy (US) to State Department, March 17, 1949, FRUS 1949. The Near East, South Asia, and Africa, Vol. VI, pp. 265-7. See also: Memorandum of Jernegen, March 10, 1949, ibid., p. 261.

[14] Grady to Acheson (516), March 18, 1949, FRUS 1949. The Near East, South Asia, and Africa, Vol. VI, pp. 267-8.

[15] Grady to Acheson (Amag 36), March 30, 1949, FRUS 1949. The Near East, South Asia, and Africa, Vol. VI, pp. 281-5. The positive political situation would not last—the government was paralyzed by in-fighting until mid-April. For details see: Rankin to Acheson (774), April 16, 1949, ibid., pp. 295-7.

Norway. Additionally, Britain's view that it would benefit from economic union with Western Europe began to change from early 1948. By early 1949, Britain was moving away from the idea of such an economic union, believing that a Western European economic collapse would be disastrous for Britain if it was too closely tied to Western Europe. Instead, Britain had formed the Western Union, a military alliance formally called the Brussels Pact.[16] Furthermore, in January 1949, the non-communist nations withdrew their membership of the World Federation of Trade Unions. This was also representative of the rift not only between the communist and non-communist worlds but also between Britain and Europe, as Britain's economy and organizations moved closer to those of the United States.[17]

A Critical Month: May 1949

After the Berlin blockade was lifted on May 12, 1949, the Soviets altered the outlook for the Balkans by reversing their previous position, proposing an immediate end to the hostilities in Greece and finally volunteering to participate in international committees to solve the Greek issue. The Soviet representative to the UN approached the British and American representatives with a ceasefire proposal for Greece. Although the Soviet stipulation that the KKE be treated as a government was rejected by the British and Americans, they were now at least interested in hearing what else the Soviets proposed. The Soviets recommended new elections with a "higher body" to oversee them, and when asked about Greece's northern frontiers, Soviet representative Gromyko, accepting the current borders, said, "Greece has its boundaries and we are talking about the boundaries of Greece."[18]

American Assistant Secretary of State Dean Rusk indicated that Gromyko's comments seemed to suggest that the USSR would not support a "free Macedonia." Rusk also theorized that with the easing of the situation in Berlin, the USSR was attempting to settle its European political situation in order to

---

[16] Weiler, pp. 116–17. The Brussels Treaty Organization, or Western Union, came into being in 1948 and lasted until 1954, when it was modified by a new treaty and the organization was renamed the Western European Union (WEU). It never represented an alternative to NATO, but rather a prototype of sorts, with the Brussels Pact signatories all joining NATO the following year. WEU continued to exist until 2010, when it ceased operations and had its archives transferred to Luxembourg. Many of its responsibilities were integrated into the EU's Common Security and Defense Policy (CSDP). For most of its existence, WEU served mainly as a forum for consultation between members on issues such as weapon production and coordination with NATO, as well as some broader social, economic, and political matters.

[17] Childs, p. 560.

[18] Memorandum of informal discussion on Greece, May 5, 1949, Editorial note in Austin to Acheson (598), May 14, 1949, FRUS 1949. The Near East, South Asia, and Africa, Vol. VI, pp. 303–9.

focus on developments in Asia. Finally, Rusk stated that perhaps the US could use Greece to discern Soviet intentions toward the West, possibly leading to an eventual reduction in the amount of aid provided by the US.[19] A few days later, Rusk, McNeil, the British representative, and Gromyko met again to discuss the Greek situation, on which progress had stalled in talks in the UN Conciliation Committee. Gromyko presented three proposals to solve the situation that were almost identical to the proposals advanced by the British and Americans two years earlier. He suggested joint Anglo-American and Soviet supervision of elections and patrols of Greece's northern borders, followed by a complete withdrawal of all foreign military assistance from Greece. Though the discussion was non-binding and informal, it supported the Anglo-American belief that the Soviet Union's foreign policy objectives had fundamentally changed.[20]

Immediately prior to the commencement of the Council of Foreign Ministers (CFM) in Paris, the Americans restated their desire to use Greece as a way of discerning Soviet intentions. However, US Secretary of State Acheson also said that while the US would not negotiate with the Soviets without Greece's participation, he hoped that developments within Greece would not be raised at the conference in such a way as would undermine Greek morale or damage the chances for peace in "delicate contacts with the Soviets." For its part, the Greek government informed the State Department that it had no desire for its situation to be discussed "behind closed doors at the CFM, but rather to keep everything in the open in the General Assembly." This position was fully supported by the British and American governments, but these exchanges represented a dramatic shift in the Big Three's policies toward Greece.[21] Whereas over the previous three years it had been Britain and the US that were pressing for a Big Three consensus on Greece in settings such as the Security Council or the Council of Foreign Ministers (i.e., less representative bodies), now it was the Soviet Union that was attempting to achieve a "quick fix" by imposing a superpower-approved solution. Despite the sudden willingness of the USSR to discuss and participate in a resolution of the ongoing struggles in the Balkans, the Big Three still could not reach a consensus on what positions to take to do so. Furthermore,

---

[19] Memorandum of informal discussion on Greece, May 5, 1949, Editorial note in Austin to Acheson (598), May 14, 1949, FRUS 1949. The Near East, South Asia, and Africa, Vol. VI, pp. 303–9, 319–21.
[20] Memorandum of informal discussion on Greece, May 5, 1949, Editorial note in Austin to Acheson (598), May 14, 1949, FRUS 1949. The Near East, South Asia, and Africa, Vol. VI, pp. 303–9, 319–21. For details of UN Conciliation Committee negotiations see ibid.: Document 906, May 7, 1949, pp. 312–14, Document 696, May 10, 1949, pp. 315–16, Document 586, May 12, 1949, pp. 316–17.
[21] Acheson to US Embassy in Greece (749), May 19, 1949, Minor to Acheson (989), May 19, 1949, Memorandum (Rusk), May 19, 1949, FRUS 1949. The Near East, South Asia, and Africa, Vol. VI, pp. 322–5.

as Greece, Albania, Yugoslavia, and Bulgaria argued back and forth over the exact wording and content of various draft resolutions proposed by the UN Conciliation Committee, the local situation in the Balkans remained unsettled. These factors, combined with the ongoing Greek Civil War, meant that at the domestic, regional, and international political levels, there was still some way to go before consistency or stability could be achieved in Greece.

The State Department outlined the US position on Gromyko's suggestions: it believed that the Soviets could greatly improve the situation by exerting their influence on the countries that were supplying aid to the KKE, but maintained that the US did not recognize the DSE as "having any status under international law," nor did it subscribe to the sphere-of-influence notion or consider Greece's northern borders "as a dividing line between two such spheres." In Greece, the DSE was reported to have offered repeated peace proposals, but these were rejected by the Greek government, which maintained that an "unconditional surrender" was the only acceptable solution. Though the Greek government's response was officially accepted as both "legally" and "morally" justified, the US representative to UNSCOB II felt that its demand was unrealistic and could damage the prospect of actually bringing the military struggle to an end.

The State Department also wrote that new elections under foreign observation would be "retrogressive and unwarranted," since fair elections had been held in 1946, when the Soviets had had the opportunity to participate. Additionally, the Yugoslavian-Soviet split had greatly improved the likelihood of achieving US objectives for the Balkans and "projecting Western policy in the area through the intensification of psychological warfare, utilization of economic leverage and political activity." Furthermore, due to current developments, an option now existed for:

> ... some face-saving formulae [which] might be acceptable to the Russians. This possibility should be explored since we would welcome a solution of the Greek problem, which now requires a diversion of our military resources *from more profitable areas*.[22]

---

[22] Preliminary US Reaction to the Gromyko Balkan Proposal, May 20, 1949, FRUS 1949. The Near East, South Asia, and Africa, Vol. VI, pp. 326–30. Emphasis added. The use of the word "profitable" leads to numerous questions regarding the United States' "real" intentions in Greece. The fact that the document was sent as "top secret" to the British Foreign Office and to the Greek Prime Minister could indicate that the US did not intend to give the impression that it saw Greece only as either a money-making or a money-losing situation. However, if it really was in Greece to protect Greek independence and "Western civilisation" by opposing communist expansion, as had been publicly and privately stated many times before, then perhaps the words "vulnerable" or "productive" would have been used instead.

In later discussions with the Greek Ambassador, Assistant Secretary of State Rusk again assured him that no negotiations about Greece would take place without Greece's participation, that the British and American positions had remained essentially unchanged since the first UNSCOB mission and that, likely because of the problems with Tito, it seemed that the USSR recognized Greece's borders as they currently stood. Finally, Rusk suggested that the USSR was presumably trying to preserve some level of communist presence in Greece, which was why it was pressing for conciliation and new elections in which it was now prepared to play a part.[23] The British, however, despite the cautiously optimistic American appraisal of the international situation, were much more suspicious of Soviet intentions.

The Foreign Office believed that there was no evidence that the USSR truly wished to bring an end to the turmoil in the Balkans and that it was now acting only as a result of recent failures in Greece. It argued that any response to the Gromyko proposals should come directly from the Greek government as conditions that would *follow* a ceasefire/surrender, not as conditions *for* a ceasefire. The British also demanded that any proposal be subject to permission for UNSCOB II to investigate in Albanian, Yugoslavian, and Bulgarian territory to determine whether all aid to the Greek communists had in fact ended. Finally, they insisted that all Soviet pressure against Turkey and any Soviet involvement in Cyprus must end.[24] The British were still not fully satisfied that their Eastern Mediterranean interests had been sufficiently guaranteed for them to support any Soviet proposal, even in light of possible tentative Greek and American interest in the proposal.

The Americans were not in favor of Big Three talks on these issues and issued a statement that the British proposal contradicted the US position, that such issues should be worked out in the United Nations. The US also stated that "unrelated questions of Corfu, Turkey and Cyprus should also be dealt with in the UN, rather than in a Great Power forum."[25] Essentially, although the US had

---

[23] Memorandum of Conversation between the Greek Ambassador and the assistant Secretary of State, May 20, 1949, FRUS 1949. The Near East, South Asia, and Africa, Vol. VI, pp. 330–3.

[24] Enclosures A and B in: Miller to Rusk (G.10/49), May 25, 1949, FRUS 1949. The Near East, South Asia, and Africa, Vol. VI, pp. 341–4. Cyprus was still very important to the British as a strategic point in the Eastern Mediterranean. They would not tolerate any threats to their position of influence there, as would later be demonstrated by the issue of Greek-Cypriot unification.

[25] Webb to Acheson (Telac 13), May 25, 1949, FRUS 1949. The Near East, South Asia, and Africa, Vol. VI, pp. 344–5. The US would dramatically reverse this policy in the 1970s, unilaterally encouraging the Turks to invade Cyprus.

already developed and acknowledged its new foreign policy, it was not prepared to publicly contradict itself or to act unilaterally on certain issues. Furthermore, Ambassador Grady recommended a cautious approach, since "time will reveal reasons for altered Russian tactics." He added that Greece was currently a powerful example of the success of US efforts to oppose communist expansion. He reported that the Greek government was in favor of holding elections once the Civil War had ended, and he recommended that they be given international supervision. However, Grady also stated that in his opinion, Greece would remain vulnerable even after the end of the Civil War and that the US should continue its military assistance.[26]

Ambassador Grady approached the Greek government regarding possible international involvement in Greece to supervise elections, amnesty and the outlawing of the KKE. He reported back to the State Department that the Greek government would strongly resist any foreign supervision, especially in a form that included the USSR, but might accept it under joint Anglo-American pressure. Since the KKE had advocated armed insurgency against the Greek government, the State Department supported the Greek decision to outlaw it; however, the US agreed with an earlier British proposal "not to let the situation in Greece drift" and to work with the USSR to find a "face-saving" opportunity to withdraw from Greek affairs and reach a peaceful solution.[27] Whether or not that was achievable remained to be seen.

1949: June to September

By mid-June, the furor created by the Soviet peace initiative in May had begun to die down. The State Department reported that although it was sympathetic to the Greek government's position, it could not refuse any possibility for peace, and it ordered the US Embassy to inform the Greek government that it had to clarify its position regarding amnesty for the DSE in order to mitigate foreign criticism. The State Department also informed Ambassador Grady that the head of the AMM had advised maintaining the same levels of aid to Greece and keeping the Greek army at its current

---

[26] Grady to Webb (1032 and 1046), May 26 and 28, 1949, FRUS 1949. The Near East, South Asia, and Africa, Vol. VI, pp. 345–9.
[27] Acheson to Webb (2204), May 31, 1949, Webb to Acheson (Telac 51), June 3, 1949, FRUS 1949. The Near East, South Asia, and Africa, Vol. VI, pp. 350–3.

strength until at least 1950.[28] But the death of Prime Minister Sophoulis on June 24, 1949 sparked another crisis in the government over who would assume leadership.

Deputy Prime Minister Tsaldaris claimed the position as leader of the largest party in the coalition (the Populists), but he was opposed by Sophocles Venizelos, head of the Liberal Party, whom the Americans ideally wanted to see as deputy prime minister. The State Department was extremely concerned that the prevailing instability could lead to the Populists seizing control, taking advantage of public uncertainty and eliminating competent ministers from other parties in the cabinet. It therefore instructed Ambassador Grady to inform Venizelos that the US was disappointed in his position and would hold him responsible and "place on him personally, full responsibility for consequences related to the prolongation of the crisis." So, contrary to earlier statements about allowing the Greek government to solve problems on its own, here the Americans openly exerted their influence. They offered two "solutions" to Deputy Prime Minister Tsaldaris and Venizelos. Both included the continuance of the cabinet as constituted by Sophoulis and supported by the king, the first option with Deputy Prime Minister Tsaldaris as prime minister and Venizelos as deputy and the second with the roles reversed. On June 30, agreement was eventually reached on the appointment of Alexander Diamedes as prime minister, with Tsaldaris and Venizelos as deputy and second deputy prime minister, respectively.[29] This incident clearly demonstrated not only the weakness of the Greek political system but also the Americans' willingness, despite statements to the contrary, to impose solutions on the Greeks.

Regarding the improving situation with Yugoslavia, the British Embassy in Washington informed the State Department that Tito was anxious to receive aid from the West, and that in return he had already cut off supplies to the DSE and offered to prevent any DSE guerrillas who crossed into Yugoslavia from returning to Greece. This offer was officially made in a speech given by Tito in Poland on July 10, in which he announced the closure of the border between

---

[28] Webb to Grady (A-404), June 18, 1949, Acheson to Grady (941), June 23, 1949, FRUS 1949. The Near East, South Asia, and Africa, Vol. VI, pp. 358–60. At this time there were also discussions about appointing an individual to lead conciliation efforts in the Balkans. The first suggestion was for William Lyon McKenzie King, the former prime minister of Canada, to take the position. See: Memorandum, June 17, 1949, ibid., p. 357. Domestically in the US, anti-communist legislation was passed on June 20. Previously referenced in Chapter 3: Franks to Younger (499), June 20, 1950, BDFA, Part IV, Series C North America, Vol. 4, 1950, pp. 93–8.

[29] Acheson to Grady (976), June 29, 1949, FRUS 1949. The Near East, South Asia, and Africa, Vol. VI, pp. 362–3. This "solution" was remarkably similar to the appointment of Papadimos in November 2011 to deal with the Greek financial crisis, with Papandreaou and Samaras serving as deputies.

Greece and Yugoslavia.[30] Despite Tito's statements, UNSCOB II stated that it had evidence that aid was still making its way into Greece from Yugoslavia, but that this might have been occurring in a "twilight period" in Yugoslavian policy, when the central government had changed its policy but the border areas were still unable or unwilling to enforce it. However, UNSCOB II also reported that KKE radio broadcasts clearly indicated a break in relations between the KKE and Yugoslavia that would only continue to widen.[31]

In mid-July 1949, the Greek government proposed an economic policy to its American overseers that it believed would facilitate the functioning of the Greek government. The proposal contained two elements: first, currency sold to importers would be subjected to a tax, the proceeds of which, perhaps not surprisingly, would be used to meet the promised increase in civil servants' salaries. At a time when millions of Greeks were still suffering from the effects of the Civil War and the German occupation, Greece still had strict food rationing, thousands of Greeks had been forced to leave their homes, thousands of kilometers of road had been destroyed and villages had been obliterated, the Greek government came up with a tax program to increase its own salaries. Understandably, this proposal was not supported by the Americans, and when the Greek deputy prime minister met with British Ambassador Sir Clifford Norton to discuss it, Norton swiftly rejected the policy.[32] This event, while relatively insignificant, is indicative of two underlying principles of this study: first, the frequent unity of British and American policy toward the Greek government, and second, the seemingly unending detachment of Athens from the rest of Greece and the problems that were created as a result.

Militarily, by July 1949, the Greek national army was taking the initiative and aggressively engaging the DSE in the north. However, the DSE continued to employ the tactic of withdrawing into the mountains and then over the border

---

[30] Peake to McNeil (14), Yugoslavia, Annual Review for 1949, January 27, 1950, BDFA, Part IV, Series F Europe, Vol. 27, 1950, pp. 163–9. In the annual review, Ambassador Peake stated that there was a difference between Tito's official statements about closing the border and the practice of Yugoslav soldiers stationed there who had been working with the DSE for many years. He added that the British would likely not see an actual change in attitude between the Greek and Yugoslav governments until 1950. See also: British Embassy to State Department (760.H68/6-3049), June 30, 1949, FRUS 1949. The Near East, South Asia, and Africa, Vol. VI, pp. 363–4. See also: Memorandum of Conversation, August 16, 1949, FRUS 1949, Eastern Europe and the Soviet Union, Vol. V, pp. 924–8.

[31] UNCSCOB II to Acheson (1335), July 12, 1949, FRUS 1949. The Near East, South Asia, and Africa, Vol. VI, pp. 366–7. This break had taken a year to show results, however, and Tito took advantage of the situation to attempt to play off the East and the West against each other.

[32] Norton to Bevin (120), July 13, 1949, BDFA, Series F Europe, Part IV, Vol. 22, 1949, pp. 87–8.

into Albania or Bulgaria, and when it did so, the army asked the British and Americans what to do next. This frustrated both British and American observers:

> It is a great pity that the Greeks should ask advice on this point [of following the communists across the border]. They would have done much better to have simply kept quiet and pursued the rebels into Albanian territory in order to destroy them. It is almost excessively good behaviour on their part to ask our opinion.[33]

However, while the Greek army was finally seeing positive results after years of futility, its success came at a price for Greek society. The lack of external pressure on the government to control the extreme right was resulting in a new wave of the "White Terror." In northern Greece, where the KKE had been so strong, right-wing paramilitary groups were now able to exert their own policies, independently of the central government. For example, in Katerini, Pieria, the right-wing group VEN, which had officially formed as a support group for the Greek army, forced the locals to carry a second identity card.[34] Meanwhile, to explain the DSE's loss of its most consistent backer, the British Embassy in Belgrade quoted Yugoslav Foreign Minister Edvard Kardelj as stating:

> The Greek Communist leaders had forgotten the interests of the democratic movement in Greece and judged participation in the struggle against Yugoslavia more important than the struggle against foreign involvement in Greek affairs.[35]

Though the DSE had lost Yugoslavia's backing, the Greek government, under intense British pressure, had begun to pursue the resumption of diplomatic relations with Tito. However, Albania and Bulgaria were still offering assistance to the DSE. The United States ordered its embassy in Belgrade to praise Tito's decision to cease aiding the DSE, remarking that it also indicated a success in US policy toward Yugoslavia. The embassy also took the opportunity to press Tito to normalize relations with the Greek government and to return the abducted Greek children, a matter on which the Greek government was willing to begin negotiating immediately.[36] However, research into the Yugoslavian treatment of

---

[33] Minutes of the Foreign Office, July 1949, FO 371/78443/R7136.
[34] Pichos, "Verbal interview" (2011).
[35] British Embassy, Belgrade, to Foreign Office, July 25, 1949, (FO 371/78448/R7166).
[36] Acheson to US Embassy in Belgrade (372), July 12, 1949, FRUS 1949. The Near East, South Asia, and Africa, Vol. VI, pp. 369–70. There has been recent scholarship on this issue, which gives a much more nuanced view of it than the traditional Cold War narrative. See: Danforth, Loring and Riki van Boeschoten. *Children of the Greek Civil War: Refugees and the Politics of Memory*.

the abducted Greek children shows that Tito lied to the Greeks, British, and Americans when they urged him to return the children. He kept the children and attempted to prevent them from speaking Greek, intending to use them to create a Slavic population and then introduce it into Greek Macedonia to support his territorial claims there.[37]

While Tito's actions had profound implications for the Macedonian question, in the short term, it did not affect the international settlement of border issues. On August 2, 1949, UNSCOB II presented the General Assembly with its signed report, which was subsequently unanimously accepted. Aside from summarizing its formation and activities since 1947, the report also outlined in detail the aid for the DSE that was still coming into Greece, mainly from Albania.[38] Shortly thereafter, following a discussion with Deputy Prime Minister Tsaldaris, the British chargé d'affaires informed the State Department that both the British and French governments believed that the Greek army was planning an attack on Albania. Contradicting statements by UK Foreign Secretary Ernest Bevin in July, the British advised that the US should move quickly to prevent Greece from attacking Albania and noted that they had informed the Greeks that should a conflict with Albania be initiated, no military or diplomatic support could be guaranteed to them.[39]

In mid-August 1949, Tsaldaris again met with Bevin in Strasbourg to discuss international alternatives to Greek military intervention in Albania that would address the Albanians' continued assistance to Greek communist forces. Bevin said that if the communist forces continued to retreat into Albania and to launch attacks from that country, regardless of whether the Albanian forces were actually taking part, the incident would cease to be a Greek issue and would move into the international sphere of aggression by one state against another. He suggested that the matter be taken up in the United Nations, with Britain and the United States leading the action against Albania. Bevin informed Deputy Prime Minister Tsaldaris that regardless of Yugoslav designs on Albania (which the Americans also believed existed) or Albanian provocations, the best defense for Greece was

---

[37] Lagani, "The Education of Children of the Civil War," pp. 125–46.
[38] Editorial Note #2 in: Minor to Acheson (542), July 29, 1949, FRUS 1949. The Near East, South Asia, and Africa, Vol. VI, pp. 376–80.
[39] Memorandum, August 5, 1949, FRUS 1949. The Near East, South Asia, and Africa, Vol. VI, pp. 381–4.

continued British and American involvement in the area.⁴⁰ He therefore implied, as the British Embassy in Athens had done, that it would be unnecessary and potentially dangerous (in light of Soviet-Albanian mutual defense treaties) for Greece to attack Albania. At the end of August, Tsaldaris met with Assistant Secretary of State Rusk to obtain clarification of the American position on the same issue. Rusk stated that the US could not support the suggestion that Greece meet with UN members to find a solution to the Albanian problem because there was no clear plan of action, and it would be pointless to sit with other nations merely to discuss the issue.⁴¹

However, the Americans believed that persuading Albania to stop supporting the DSE was the key to finally ending the Civil War, and, supported by the British and French, they were willing to approach the Albanian government to negotiate an improved international standing for Albania if it agreed to prevent the DSE from resupplying and regrouping in its territory.⁴² Accordingly, the British and Americans offered Albania the possibility of joining the UN should it take the necessary steps to inhibit the DSE from using its territory. The British stated that if the Albanians provided proof that they were disarming and interning members of the DSE in their territory, it would greatly benefit Albania's chances of being admitted to the UN.⁴³ As negotiations with the Albanian government progressed, there were also indications that the Bulgarian government was ready to cease its "intervention in Greek affairs."⁴⁴ Just before discussions on the situation in Greece were due to be held in the UN General Assembly, conditions on Greece's northern borders finally seemed to be stabilizing.

In preparation for the discussion of the Greek case before the General Assembly, the United States prepared a resolution calling on both Albania and

---

⁴⁰ Bevin to Crosthwaite (214), August 16, 1949, BDFA, Series F Europe, Part IV, Vol. 22, pp. 142–3. The concept of using one state's territory as a staging area to attack another as grounds for charges of aggression under international law is valid but was not made so until the definition of the crime of aggression under international law was agreed upon in the summer of 2010. For greater detail, analysis and explanation of the definition of the crime of aggression, punishment, and enforcement, see: Pichou, (2012). For the American assessment of Yugoslavian plans for Albania and a report of French assessments, see: Memorandum, August 5, 1949, FRUS 1949. The Near East, South Asia, and Africa, Vol. VI, pp. 382–4. In November 1949, the British Ambassador to Yugoslavia met with Tito, who claimed that the Albanians were attempting to provoke the Yugoslavians at the border. Peake to Bevin (1035), November 2, 1949, BDFA, Series F Europe, Part IV, Vol. 22, 1949, p. 279.

⁴¹ Memorandum of Conversation, August 29, 1949, Memorandum, August 5, 1949, FRUS 1949. The Near East, South Asia, and Africa, Vol. VI, pp. 389–92.

⁴² Acheson to US Embassy in London (3099), August 29, 1949, FRUS 1949. The Near East, South Asia, and Africa, Vol. VI, pp. 392–3.

⁴³ Holmes to Acheson (3598), September 3, 1949, FRUS 1949. The Near East, South Asia, and Africa, Vol. VI, pp. 398–9.

⁴⁴ Memorandum of Conversation, September 8, 1949, FRUS 1949. The Near East, South Asia, and Africa, Vol. VI, pp. 401–4.

Bulgaria to cease all aid to the DSE. Coinciding with what the State Department called the "outstanding progress" of the Greek Army in destroying the few remaining DSE units and with the Yugoslavia-Cominform split, the United States felt that its policy in Greece had been successful. Greece was no longer faced with a "solid bloc of equally hostile states at her northern frontiers." Then, in a comment that clearly expressed American priorities and reflected the post-Second World War style of US foreign policy, the State Department said that its objective was to bring about a settlement of the Balkans dispute that the General Assembly could endorse "on terms satisfactory to the United States and to the Greeks." The State Department also ordered that attempts be made to further implicate the USSR in "the plot against Greece" to ensure support for the US resolution in the General Assembly.[45] While the United States was prepared for the General Assembly to consider a resolution that dealt with both internal and external factors to settle the Greek problem, the Greek government officially requested that the General Assembly consider only the issue of continuing Albanian and Bulgarian interference in Greek affairs. The US refused the Greek request and made numerous "suggestions" to the Greek government in preparation for the UN General Assembly (GA):

> ... prior to the meeting of the GA, Greek Government (GG) should announce, on its own initiative, policy it will follow in treating guerrillas after main fighting has ceased. This should be as lenient as possible .... GG might announce program for political rehabilitation and economic reestablishment [of] former guerrillas ... statement by GG that it would welcome observation and advisory assistance of UN rehabilitation program ... GG should announce intentions to hold new elections within specified period ... would be excellent political move if elections be accompanied by plebiscite on question (of) whether or not KKE should be re-legalized ... Greeks be prepared to accept this (international supervision of elections) ....[46]

The point is not whether the Greek government was ethically or legally correct in its desire to prevent a foreign ruling on its domestic affairs or whether the American "proposals" were justified. What is significant about the above statement is the United States' disregard for the expressed interests of the Greek government and the emphasis on US interests. The fact that this priority was

---

[45] State Department to the US United Nations Delegation (SD/A/C.1/272), September 9, 1949, FRUS 1949. The Near East, South Asia, and Africa, Vol. VI, pp. 404–9.
[46] Acheson to US Embassy in Athens (1503), September 10, 1949, FRUS 1949. The Near East, South Asia, and Africa, Vol. VI, pp. 409–12.

clearly expressed by the State Department gives us a clearer understanding of the position the Americans would increasingly adopt toward Greece. The US was not prepared to allow Greek political goals to impede its wider-reaching political and strategic objectives, and it had no qualms about ordering the Greek government to follow a specific course of action. Though generally supportive of the US position, Britain was not in favor of allowing Soviet participation in any supervisory body because of the trouble that the USSR could cause. The Foreign Office was more concerned with the opinion of the Greek government than were the Americans, its position being that that no resolution should be put forward in the GA without consulting the Greeks and obtaining their approval.[47]

On September 14, 1949, the British Ambassador to the United States, Sir Oliver Franks, reported a conversation with US Secretary of State Dean Acheson in Washington. The two men had discussed possible reconciliation between the Greek, Albanian, and Bulgarian governments. Acheson believed that a possible way to settle the frontier concerns of the Greek government was to hold a meeting under the auspices of United Nations officials, to be attended by the Soviet, British, French, and American governments, together with the Albanian, Bulgarian, and Greek governments. Bevin and Acheson agreed that if the opportunity arose, they should try to "bring down" the Albanian government, but they would have to proceed cautiously and wait to see how affairs in Greece and Yugoslavia played out.[48]

A week later, Greek officials met with the US Secretary of State and Ernest Bevin at the Astoria Hotel in New York. Deputy Prime Minister Tsaldaris informed Acheson that the Greek government was very anxious to prevent the 10,000 or so estimated bandits who had escaped into Albania from re-forming to launch another attack on Greece. He added that there was some sentiment within Greece that the Greek army should simply pursue the bandits into Albanian territory. Bevin questioned whether there was actual evidence that preparations for a new attack from Albanian soil were being made, and the Greek Ambassador admitted that there was none. Bevin then stated that he had seen reports that the Albanians were attempting to inhibit the rebels from using

---

[47] Memorandum of Conversation, September 13, 1949, FRUS 1949. The Near East, South Asia, and Africa, Vol. VI, pp. 412–14.
[48] Memorandum of Conversation, September 14, 1949, FRUS 1949. The Near East, South Asia, and Africa, Vol. VI, pp. 414–16. For the British perspective of these talks see: Franks to Bevin (4412), September 14, 1949, and, Record of Conversation between Acheson and Deputy Prime Minister Tsaldaris (14), September 20, 1949, BDFA, Part IV, Series F Europe, Vol. 22, 1949, pp. 145–7.

their territory. The Greek Ambassador replied that if this was true then it was satisfactory, but there had to be solid proof; the Greek government could not "believe Albanian statements to the effect that they would disarm the rebels" and therefore argued for some sort of United Nations control. Bevin did not support the Greek proposals and stated his opposition by saying that he could not proceed "without consulting my colleagues in the cabinet." This statement is significant, since Bevin had previously had no difficulty in forcing his policies through the cabinet and even on the prime minister. The fact that in this case he claimed that he could not proceed without consulting others may also indicate his opposition to the Greek proposal. Furthermore, Bevin told Tsaldaris that at the recent London ambassadors' meeting, "Greek affairs had not been considered," which indicated that other events had superseded Greece in importance for the British.[49]

In the same vein as the Albanian statements, the Bulgarian government also stated that it was disarming any rebels that crossed into its territory. Bevin stressed that the Greek government should proceed with the utmost caution, "and above all they must not embark on any ventures themselves," because doing so could threaten British interests in the region. It is revealing that Bevin did not say that the Greek government had no right to present a resolution to the United Nations; he simply tried to stress to the Greek Ambassador that he did not believe the Americans would support the draft as prepared.[50] Under international law, every nation has the right to present a resolution to the General Assembly and to the Security Council. Bevin stated that his main problem with the resolution that the Greeks had prepared concerning possible action against Albania for not disarming the Greek rebels using its territory was that it seemed "to contemplate enforcement measures and these are a matter for the Security Council rather than the assembly. The first step must be before the United Nations to establish if the threat to peace existed. After that, they could proceed to consider what steps should be taken."[51] However, once again, international developments and the nuclear race between the USA and the USSR overshadowed events in Greece, even though the Greek National Army

---

[49] Bevin to Crosthwaite (214), August 16,1949, BDFA, Series F Europe, Part IV, Vol. 22, pp. 142–3, and, Memorandum of Conversation, September 14, 1949, FRUS 1949. The Near East, South Asia, and Africa, Vol. VI, pp. 414–16.

[50] Record of Conversation between Acheson and Deputy Prime Minister Tsaldaris (14), September 20, 1949, BDFA, Series F Europe, Part IV, Vol. 22, 1949, pp. 146–147.

[51] Record of Conversation between Acheson and Deputy Prime Minister Tsaldaris (14), 20 September, 1949, BDFA, Series F Europe, Part IV, Vol. 22, 1949, pp. 146–7.

had already won a significant victory (which turned out to be decisive) against the Greek communist forces a month earlier in August 1949.

The United States had based its defense against possible Soviet aggression on use of the atomic bomb, or rather the *threat* of use of the atomic bomb. Great Britain had hoped that NATO might counterbalance the Soviet numeric advantage (in terms of soldiers and tanks) in Europe, but the Americans intended to rely mainly on an expanded air force and increased production of atomic bombs. Many US officials believed so strongly in the advantage of the nuclear bomb that they encouraged Congress to deny President Truman's request to fund NATO to the extent he desired. However, on September 22, 1949, the Soviet Union exploded its first atomic bomb, thereby negating the American nuclear advantage. Six days later, Congress approved the funds that the president had requested for NATO.[52]

Meanwhile, in Greece, the American Embassy was instructed to inform the Greek government not to attack Albania. President Truman endorsed the State Department's position, saying that Greece "was like any other dog who has been down in a fight and then gets on top," and the US should therefore do anything necessary to restrain the Greek government, both from possible military actions and from the mistreatment of DSE prisoners, who the Americans feared would all be "slaughtered."[53] However, the Greek government often ignored continued instructions from the British and Americans regarding the fair treatment of prisoners. The Greek government felt, with some justification, that Greece was too important a symbol in the fight against communism for the British and Americans to abandon the country over the mistreatment, execution and deportation of political and military prisoners. This is perhaps one of the first examples of the "pragmatic hypocrisy"[54] employed by the British and Americans after the Second World War. They declared their support for Greece as a defense of democracy, while tolerating high levels of arbitrariness and retribution and the denial of basic rights and freedoms to those it captured and/or arrested.

By the end of September 1949, although the British and the Americans had seen their significant investments in opposing communist expansion pay off in Greece, at international level they were faced with the problem of Soviet

---

[52] Ambrose, pp. 105–6.
[53] Memorandum of meeting with President Truman, October 1, 1949, FRUS 1949. The Near East, South Asia, and Africa, Vol. VI, pp. 427–8.
[54] Term used to describe the contrast between Anglo-American policy objectives for Greece as they were stated, and the way that the Greek government took advantage of their support to deny basic rights and freedoms to prisoners.

superiority in numbers and equity in atomic weaponry. Given their apparent failure in Eastern Europe and China and a new atomic parity with the USSR, Greece maintained its position as an important anti-communist symbol.

1949: October to December

The end of the military conflict in Greece was tentatively announced by Ambassador Grady in October 1949, who also reported that promising economic conditions had finally been achieved, mainly due to continuing international economic aid, the end of the military conflict and the devaluation of the drachma. However, he also predicted strong Greek opposition to American military aid cutbacks because the Greeks reasoned that "a large army will force [the Americans] to give large aid." He therefore recommended not only reducing military aid to Greece but also reducing the size of the Greek army by 50,000 men by January 1950. Confirming Grady's communication, the KKE broadcast a statement ending the armed struggle on October 16, 1949. On October 19, Dean Acheson said that he believed the conflict in Greece was over, and the next logical step was to gradually reduce US military expenditure there.[55]

As a result of the end of the armed conflict in Greece and the need to reinforce British garrisons in the Middle East and Asia, especially Hong Kong, the British announced that they would finally be withdrawing their remaining troops from Greece.[56] In light of the current situation in Greece, Ambassador Grady felt that the withdrawal of British troops was not only convenient but would be beneficial in terms of international public opinion since it would coincide with American military reductions in Greece. Furthermore, Grady recommended to Ambassador Norton that the British Embassy announce the withdrawal of the whole British battalion, not a gradual reduction.[57] In spite of Grady's statements, the US Joint Chiefs of Staff were not pleased about the British withdrawal.

---

[55] Grady to Acting Secretary of State (3084), October 3, 1949, Acheson to Grady (1789), October 20, 1949, FRUS 1949. The Near East, South Asia, and Africa, Vol. VI, pp. 431–6.
[56] Memorandum of Conversation, October 20, 1949, FRUS 1949. The Near East, South Asia, and Africa, Vol. VI, pp. 435–6.
[57] Grady to Acheson (2144), October 21, 1949, FRUS 1949. The Near East, South Asia, and Africa, Vol. VI, p. 437.

Unbeknownst to Grady, the Joint Chiefs had requested that the British notify them in advance whether they would withdraw in stages or all at once. But less than twenty-four hours after that request was sent to the British, they simply presented the US with a fait accompli similar to the one that they had presented in 1947. However, owing to political considerations and the fact that it would still take some months to withdraw all British forces from Greece, the Joint Chiefs said that they would communicate their displeasure only "through military channels."[58]

In light of the British withdrawal and pending US military reductions in Greece, the Greek government approached the US regarding its desire to adhere to the North Atlantic Treaty. Acheson repeated that the US could not support Greece's petition for membership at that time, but he reassured the Greeks that the US would not permit its investments to be jeopardized by external threats and would come to Greece's aid should such a threat arise.[59] Reflecting the success of Churchill's and then Bevin's efforts to tie the United States and Britain together based not only on their shared strategic interests but on their shared culture, the US military planning committee for Greece sent a top-secret message to the Department of the Army stating that

> ... the English-speaking world must stand solidly together in support of these strategic concepts. Specifically, the US and British Commonwealth must be solidly unified militarily and must pursue this common objective on a combined basis. However, the US is financing the program necessary to mould this belt of nations into a unified whole. Thus, the US must hold the predominant position on all fronts in the establishment of policy ....[60]

These words echo statements by Bevin and Churchill from the mid-1940s and show how successful the British were in shaping US policy toward communism, not only with regard to Greece and the Eastern Mediterranean but for the entire world. Though the United States had clearly eclipsed Britain as the West's leading power, there can be little doubt that the British played a key role in how that transition occurred.

---

[58] Memorandum of Conversation, October 27, 1949, FRUS 1949. The Near East, South Asia, and Africa, Vol. VI, pp. 445–7.
[59] Memorandum of Conversation, October 29, 1949, FRUS 1949. The Near East, South Asia, and Africa, Vol. VI, pp. 447–9.
[60] Head, JUSMAPG to Department of the Army (L 4192), November 7, 1949, FRUS 1949. The Near East, South Asia, and Africa, Vol. VI, pp. 453–7.

In November, the General Assembly accepted the proposed resolutions calling both for peace in the Balkans and for the return of the abducted Greek children.[61] On November 22, 1949, the official celebration of the departure of British troops from Greece took place. Ambassador Norton spoke of "poignant memories of the campaign in 1941" and the "salvation of Greece from the Communists in December 1944," and described how "in Salonika British troops had stood on guard during the past long period of internal trouble and anxiety."[62] He continued:

> The event was a great success and a marked tribute to the consistently good conduct of British troops in a foreign country. It was a glorious sunny Athenian day; very large crowds gathered in the streets and warmly applauded the smart bearing and drilled the troops .... This time they showed their sincere appreciation of what the British army had meant for Greece by the applause and cheering which could be heard from the distant streets through which the troops marched. I have learned from many quarters, both high and low, and the fact is evident from the sympathetic articles in the newspapers, that the withdrawal of British troops is a matter of keen regret .... It was felt that this was the end of the chapter, and though the immediate future of Greece looks fairly rosy so long as American help continues on its present scale, the solemn, memorable celebration has caused the view of hard searching, coinciding as it does with the approaching day for elections and a new confrontation of economic and social problems, to say nothing of the clouds in the northern horizon.[63]

Though the military situation had been resolved, there were still daunting threats to Greece, especially in the economic field, that coincided with communist expansion in the Far East. With the British and Americans fearing that internal problems could once again lead to communist gains, the Americans began to consider that it would be better to continue to aid the Greek Army so that it would be well positioned to respond to "internal" threats to the country. This meant that "on the level of Greek external security, Washington felt that not much could be done."[64] Even after the end of the Civil War and the strengthening of Greece's army, at the end of 1949, the American Joint Chiefs of Staff stated

---

[61] For full text of the General Assembly Resolutions of 17 and 18 November, see: Official Records of the General Assembly, Fourth Session, resolutions, pp. 9–10.
[62] Norton to Foreign Office (221), November 22, 1949, BDFA, Series F Europe, Part IV, Vol. 22, p. 150.
[63] Norton to Foreign Office (856), December 3, 1949, BDFA, Series F Europe, Part IV, Vol. 22, pp. 150-1.
[64] Hatzivassiliou, p. 11.

that they believed that Greece's borders were indefensible.[65] Such a statement could only be made in secret and only once the Civil War was over. Greece's security would be maintained through agreements with its northern neighbors and through the army, so that internal threats could be tackled if and when they should arise.[66]

The last issue to be faced by the British in Greece in 1949 was the unification of Greece and Cyprus, and the British response clearly showed how much influence they still exercised, not only on the Greek government but also on the Americans and other foreign governments. The British were angered by some unauthorized and unauthenticated newspaper articles reporting that *enosis* between Greece and Cyprus was fast approaching. Ambassador Norton stated that the Greek government would be well advised to announce that all Greeks, either in Greece or Cyprus, who were pushing for immediate action for the unification of Cyprus and Greece were doing a disservice to their country. However, when Tsaldaris stated that a joint British and Greek declaration regarding the matter could ease tensions, Ambassador Norton objected, saying that to issue a joint statement "would look like commitment on the part of his Majesty's Government." The British wanted to preserve their interest in the Mediterranean but at the same time to appear not to be directing any events from abroad. The British Embassy staff communicated with the United States Embassy and the South African Embassy to obtain statements of support to pressure the Greek government to issue a statement against the unification of Greece and Cyprus and to recommend to the Greek government that "this was no time to seek to weaken British influence there [in the eastern Mediterranean]."[67] These actions were indicative of Britain's policy of being very active behind the scenes while on the surface maintaining an image of impartiality and non-intervention. The Cyprus issue was important for British interests in the Eastern Mediterranean since by maintaining Cyprus as a protectorate, Britain had a strategic base for monitoring shipping routes and was able to protect its access to the Suez Canal.

While the "victory" in Greece was significant to the British and Americans (as Pyrrhic as that victory was for the Greeks), it was dwarfed by the catastrophic American anti-communist policy in the Far East. In 1949, in December, Chiang

---

[65] Stefanidis, pp. 29–30, 39, quoted in: Hatzivassiliou, p. 11. For US notification to the Greek government and plans for the Greek national army, see: Grady to Diomedes, October 23, 1949, Grady to Acheson (2164), October 14, 1949, Webb to Grady (gamma 59), November 22, 1949, FRUS 1949. The Near East, South Asia, and Africa, Vol. VI, pp. 440–5.

[66] The coup d'état of April 1967 was only eighteen years away.

[67] British Embassy (Athens) to Foreign Office (856), December 3, 1949, BDFA, Series F Europe, Part IV, Vol. 22, pp. 151–2.

Kai-shek was forced to flee to Formosa. The loss of China to the communists was an almost unimaginable tragedy for those in the US congress opposing Truman, and the effects of the "loss of China" were felt all over the world.[68] Suddenly, the communists were on the move again. Within a period of six months, the West had lost their atomic superiority and the fourth largest country on earth. The feelings were summed up in 1973 by American writer William Manchester:

> The China they knew – Pearl Buck's peasants, rejoicing in the good earth – had been dependable, democratic, warm and above all pro-American. Throughout the great war the United Nations Big Four had been Churchill, Roosevelt, Stalin and Chiang. Stalin's later treachery had been deplorable but unsurprising. But Chiang Kai-shek! Acheson's strategy to contain Red aggression seemed to burst wide open … Everything American diplomats had achieved in Europe – the Truman Doctrine, the Marshall Plan, NATO – *momentarily seemed annulled by this disaster in Asia.*[69]

This dramatic reversal of fortunes internationally had profound implications for Greece. Paradoxically, the communist victory in China made the communist defeat in Greece both less and more significant for the West. Because of China's size and strategic value, it was far more important in practical terms than Greece. However, the communist defeat in Greece increased the country's symbolic value to the West. There was no way that Greece could be allowed to permit any communist influence whatsoever, let alone fall into the communist sphere. The result was that the Right was given carte blanche, and Greece's shift from democracy to "stability" began to gain momentum.

---

[68] Stephen Kotkin considers the loss of China as the single greatest blunder on the part of the US since the end of the Second World War. See his interview at the Hoover Institution: https://youtu.be/1fgDu57N-Qw

[69] Manchester, p. 215. Emphasis added.

6

Détente and the Revelation of the New World Order

1950: January to June

Back in 1946, the British had struggled to convince the United States of the danger presented by communist expansion in the immediate aftermath of the Second World War, but by 1950 they were struggling to restrain American anti-communism.[1] In Greece in early January 1950, the main problem was not a military but a social one. With the end of the Civil War, the Greek government was finally forced to deal with the daunting social problems that had remained unresolved since the German occupation. Ten percent of the Greek population still lived as internal refugees, and international aid and Greek government programs were barely sufficient to clothe, feed, and provide shelter to these Greeks while they waited to be repatriated. Though the American ambassador stated that finding a solution to the refugee problem in Greece was a top priority for the American mission, no further American funds were considered "necessary in view of the generous contributions from the Economic Cooperation Administration (ECA)."[2]

---

[1] Bullock, pp. 790–5. Though the British would use the crises in China and Korea to demonstrate to the United States that they were still its most reliable ally, what is notable about this period, aside from the massive reversal in Anglo-American roles, is communist motives and objectives. Stalin refused to allow Soviet representatives to participate in the UN Security Council hearings on North Korea since they could involve China. As a result of the recently signed Sino-Soviet pact, a conflict in Korea could draw the USSR into a war with the West, a situation which Stalin had demonstrated his desire to avoid on numerous occasions. See: Pechatnov, pp. 90–111.

[2] Norton to Attlee (1E), January 4, 1950, BDFA, Series F Europe, Part IV, Vol. 27, pp. 49–50. Ambassador Norton continued his dispatch by estimating the property damage caused by the communist forces at 90 million British pounds. He also stated, however, that the average Greek peasant "does not expect much from the Greek government, and most of those already repatriated appear to be accepting the inevitable hardships of this first winter fairly cheerfully" (Paragraph 8).

Behind closed doors, the Americans informed the British that they had misgivings about the Greek Minister of the Economy. The UNRRA embassy then secretly told the British that Minister of Labor Constantinos Karamanlis (who would become prime minister after the Junta in 1974), opposed the repatriation of Greek refugees because he believed that if the winter was overly difficult, the repatriated peasants might vote for opposition parties because they felt that the government had not done enough for them. Sir Clifford Norton, British ambassador to Greece, concluded this dispatch by stating that at the end of the previous year (1949), Greece had only just reached the recovery point that Western European nations had reached in 1946, and it would be many years before Greece could dispense with international assistance.[3]

Indicating the relative decline in Greece's importance to the British, Yugoslavia was described by the British ambassador to the country, Sir Charles Peake, as "today the most important pillar of peace in this part of Europe. The Yugoslav government's actions would fail to please only those who did not want peace in the Balkans," i.e., the Cominform, which had been attacking the Yugoslav-Greek peace initiative. The British ambassador continued, stating that the Greek Civil War had been a direct consequence of Cominform policy and that peace had been made possible by the Greek and Yugoslav people, who had traditionally lived in friendship. The Yugoslav government pledged to assist Greeks demanding the return of their children who were still being held in Yugoslavia and informed the British Ambassador in Belgrade that good relations with neighboring countries would greatly improve the chances for peace and security in Yugoslavia.[4]

By the end of January, the demobilization of the Greek armed forces was also proceeding as scheduled, but the Greek government was not diverting the extra funds to its economic recovery programs. Furthermore, the Greek government refused to commit to the cuts desired by the United States. Henry Grady, who was serving simultaneously as both ambassador to Greece and administrator of the US aid program in the country, stated that almost one-third of Greece's budget was being spent on the military—a proportion that the economy simply could not support. He was also continually frustrated by the unwillingness of the Greek government to make any concessions for the good of the Greek people. He strongly recommended that the United States reduce military aid to support an army of only 70,000–90,000 troops, which would be able to maintain internal

---

[3] Norton to Attlee (1E), January 4, 1950, BDFA, Series F Europe, Part IV, Vol. 27, pp. 50–2.
[4] Peake to Foreign Office (383), BDFA, Series F Europe, Part IV, Vol. 27, May 17, **1951** (1951 is likely a typographic error since all of the other documents in this section are dated 1950), pp. 67–8.

security and deal with guerrilla attacks but little more. This reflected his belief (shared by the Joint Chiefs of Staff) that should Greece be invaded, no Greek army of any size could withstand it. The assistant secretary of state supported this view since the evidence available at the time indicated that the USSR had diminished interests in Greece. Even though American and Greek relations with Bulgaria were still tense, overall, the situation in the Balkans seemed to have been settled.[5]

In terms of the state of Anglo-American relations, an appraisal by the State Department rated Britain as "our strongest and most reliable ally." Furthermore, in February 1950, the United States guaranteed the protection of the British Isles:

> We are fully committed to the protection of the British Isles, in the event of an attack. Even without commitments, the British Isles are an essential base for a successful counter-attack on the continent and their control of areas all over the world which are necessary to us in a global war, makes it a primary objective to protect them.[6]

The British had managed not only to ensure that Britain was viewed as the "best and most reliable ally" of the US but also to achieve US guarantees of military intervention in Britain and Western Europe and US recognition of the parts of the British Empire/Commonwealth that were still under British control and/or administration. This was a huge success for British policy, since just three years earlier the British had still been struggling to combat negative views in the United States government of Britain's importance as a strategic partner.[7] Greece had played a key part in that achievement.

Coinciding with the improved regional situation in the Balkans and after the Greek elections of 5 March, 1950 had been held in relative calm, the United States forecast reduced amounts of aid for Greece heading into the summer of 1950.[8] The British did not share the Americans' assessment of the election results. In

---

[5] Grady to Greek Prime Minister Theotokis, January 17, 1950, Grady to Acheson (213), January 30, 1950, Memorandum of Conversation, February 3, 1950, FRUS 1950, Vol. V, The Near East, South Asia, and Africa, pp. 335–40.

[6] Satterthwaite to Thompson (740.5), February 8, 1950, FRUS 1950, Vol. I, National Security Affairs; Foreign Economic Policy, pp. 143–4.

[7] Cross-reference with Chapter 3 (1947): Balfour to Bevin (2037), August 23, 1947, BDFA, Part IV, Series C North America, Vol. 2, 1947, p. 222. Balfour stated, "Our critics and detractors in the United States are constantly on the watch for the opportunity to assert that American confidence in Britain is misplaced … we should be at peculiar pains to comport ourselves in such a manner as to make ourselves proof against such slander."

[8] See editorial note, FRUS 1950, Vol. V, The Near East, South Asia and Africa, p. 341. King Paul had dissolved the government on January 7, 1950 and had the head of the caretaker government declare elections for forty-five days later.

the words of Ambassador Norton, "the results have indeed disappointed those who wish to see a strong and stable Greek government tackling economic and social problems of the country; one may well ask how any such government could have emerged from the existing parties."[9]

In spite of British predictions, the US nonetheless forecast that by 1951, military aid to Greece could be halved and economic reconstruction could be stepped up. The Americans also believed that Greece would continue to require substantial amounts of economic aid into 1952 but decided not to inform the Greek government of that estimate because they did not want it to feel that it could rely indefinitely on international aid.[10]

Regarding the internal situation in Greece, the National Security Council stated that although the US had been somewhat successful in decentralizing the Greek government and reforming taxation and the civil service, the Greek government would continue to be problematic and to "remain below Western standards." In terms of the Tito-Cominform split, US Under-Secretary of State Webb stated that perhaps this event had "tipped the scales in our favour." The split, combined with a strong US stand on Greece (which Webb also credited as a crucial factor leading to the split), had made US policy in Greece "successful beyond expectations."[11]

However, at the end of March, renewed political intrigues in Greece frustrated American expectations and desires. A plan had been in place to form a coalition government under General Plastiras, with the leaders of the other major parties serving in the cabinet. This plan was welcomed by the US as representative of the will of the Greek people after the elections. However, after pledging to support the government, Minister Sophocles Venizelos, the leader of the Liberal Party, suddenly withdrew his support and, with the king's approval, stated that he intended to form a government that would constitute only approximately 20 percent of the popular vote. Prior to Venizelos' decision, Ambassador Grady

---

[9] Norton to Bevin (74), March 16, 1950, BDFA, Series F Europe, Part IV, Vol. 27, p. 58. For British and American preferences on the best type of government for Greece, see: Norton to Bevin (120), April 28, 1950, BDFA, Series F Europe, Part IV, Vol. 27, p. 66. They "formed the impression that a coalition ... was the right answer for both internal and external reasons," but whether that was an actual possibility is open for debate. Norton's statement from the previous month certainly indicates that he felt it was unlikely.

[10] Memorandum of US policy in Greece, March 6, 1950, FRUS 1950, Vol. V, The Near East, South Asia and Africa, pp. 342–5.

[11] Memorandum of US policy in Greece, March 6, 1950, FRUS 1950, Vol. V, The Near East, South Asia and Africa, pp. 342–5. The impression of success in Greece (at least from the perspective of keeping the country out of the Soviet sphere of influence) was a leading factor in the development of NSC 68, which would be given to President Truman in April 1950. See also: Lagani, "US Forces in Greece," p. 310.

had clearly expressed the United States' views on how the new government should be formed, and the move by Venizelos and the king seemed designed to exclude prominent centrist and left-wing leaders from the government. However, again clearly indicating the US shift in emphasis from democracy to stability, the State Department said that the US would work with any Greek government "which enjoys the support of the Greek people expressed through their duly elected parliament and which is desirous and capable of carrying out the objectives of US aid program."[12]

It was a carefully worded response that, while not explicitly supporting or condemning the new Greek government, made it clear that the main condition for continued US support was the government's adherence to US objectives for Greece. A few days later, Ambassador Grady informed Venizelos that while the US was still concerned that the government he proposed to form was not the "*natural result of the elections*," the most important factor for the US was the "*stability and effectiveness* of any Greek cabinet."[13] However, the ongoing corruption of the Greek government continued to frustrate the United States to such a degree that it threatened to withhold funds earmarked for the construction of four hydroelectric dams until the Greek government could ensure that the funds would be used for their intended purpose. Both Ambassador Grady and Paul Porter,[14] who had come to Greece to head the economic recovery program, were extremely frustrated by the "irresponsible politicians and stubborn monarchs" who in their opinion were delaying Greece's economic recovery so that the king could implement a plan to install General Papagos as prime minister. However, despite American concerns and frustrations, the US did not plan to end all aid to Greece. Instead, it decided that no new plans would be approved until the current political situation was resolved.[15]

In the United States, opposition pressure against Truman had been steadily growing for months. There was a widespread assumption among Americans that through its policies and strength of will, the United States could control

---

[12] Minor to Acheson (639), March 23, 1950, Acheson to US Embassy in Greece, March 24, 1950, FRUS 1950, Vol. V, The Near East, South Asia and Africa, pp. 351–3.

[13] Grady to Acheson (666, March 27, 1950), (703, March 31, 1950), (776, April 5, 1950), (852, April 17, 1950), FRUS 1950 Vol. V, The Near East, South Asia and Africa, pp. 354–7, 361–2. Emphasis added.

[14] Not the same Paul Porter who had compiled the first reports on Greece in 1945–6 but a colleague of his.

[15] Grady to Acheson (666, March 27, 1950), (703, March 31, 1950), (776, April 5, 1950), (852, April 17, 1950), FRUS 1950 Vol. V, The Near East, South Asia and Africa, pp. 354–7, 361–2, 364–5. Emphasis added. The crisis was largely initiated by the king's objection to Plastiras becoming prime minister because in 1923, he had abolished the monarchy and exiled the king's family. NOTE: The Venizelos government proved unable to last the month and resigned on April 17.

developments anywhere in the world. This was partly because of American success in the First and Second World Wars and partly because of Americans' perception of power owing to the US nuclear monopoly.[16] However, after the loss of China to the communists and the Soviet demonstration of its atomic capability, the explanation for the failure of American policy that resonated with many Americans was that the United States had been betrayed by communist sympathizers. McCarthyism found support in the Republican Party, which believed that it now had an issue that could bring it back to power.[17] In response, the federal government stepped up loyalty investigations. According to numerous accounts, the Truman administration was "bewildered" by Republican accusations that it was soft on communism.[18] On 30 January, 1950, Truman authorized the Defense and State Departments to review and reassess America's foreign and defense policies since the loss of China and the Soviet acquisition of nuclear power. The result was a report in early April 1950 from the US National Security Council that became known as NSC-68. This document advocated an immediate and large-scale build-up of the United States' military and general strength, as well as that of its allies, with the intention of altering the balance of power and, through means *other* than all-out war, changing the nature of the Soviet system.[19]

It was not totally clear how the desired change to the Soviet system was to be achieved, but the authors of NSC-68 theorized that the United States could rearm itself and Western Europe and wait for the USSR to weaken, thereby ensuring that the Soviets and their influence would not spread beyond their current borders. In essence, it represented the next step in the expansion of the Truman Doctrine, which until this point had been limited to Europe in its application.[20] The Republicans were satisfied with the objectives laid out in NSC-68, but they were not prepared officially to allow the Truman government to abandon Eastern Europe, Russia, and China to communism. However, they

---

[16] Ambrose, pp. 108–10.
[17] The term "McCarthyism" refers to US senator Joseph McCarthy (Republican-Wisconsin), who led a movement which originated in the United States, during the period known as the Second Red Scare (the late 1940s through the 1950s). It was characterized by rising political repression, and was based on the fear of increased communist influence on US institutions, culture, education, and of Soviet espionage.
[18] Ambrose, pp. 111–12.
[19] NSC 68, April 14, 1950, FRUS Vol. I, 1950, National security affairs; foreign economic policy, pp. 234–92. NSC-68 also clearly identified the potential of the US and Western European economies to be converted to war economies (ibid., pp. 256, 262, 282 specifically). It may be argued that the significant increases in military spending in the West were initiated and have continued as a result of the conclusions of NSC-68.
[20] Ambrose, pp. 111–12.

presented no clear idea of how to liberate these countries. NSC-68 forecast that it would cost at least $35 billion per year to implement the program to arm NATO and the United States but also stated that more could potentially be spent since it was assumed that the United States was rich enough to use up to 20 percent of its gross national product for weapons without causing bankruptcy.[21]

Truman recognized the implications of the document; he wrote that it represented a great military effort in peacetime and would therefore require a dramatic increase to the budget and taxes and the imposition of strict economic controls—a drastic change for Americans in peacetime. With only two and a half years left of his term, Truman was uncertain as to whether he could persuade the US Congress to commit to implementing the plans detailed in NSC-68. The document was therefore set aside until the crisis in Korea subsequently brought it to the forefront of US anti-communist policy.[22]

In Greece, the Venizelos government collapsed, not surprisingly since it represented only about 20% of the popular vote, so the State Department endorsed Ambassador Grady's recommendations for the reconstitution of the Greek government. Although the State Department was concerned that US actions could be construed as interference, it stated that this was simply a modified version of the previously agreed plan, but with the republican Plastiras as prime minister. Despite protests from the king and the right, the proposal was approved, and the State Department decided to fully support Grady and to "ignore criticisms and direct appeals from the monarchy or rightist elements to force Ambassador Grady to alter his present policy line."[23] This dispatch is important not only because it shows the rare occurrence of an ambassador making and implementing foreign policy decisions but also because it indicates another step in the direction that US foreign policy was taking; namely, it was beginning to dictate policy in other countries. The aim here is to demonstrate the circumstances and the resulting decisions that were indicative of this dramatic change in US foreign policy, and to pinpoint what

---

[21] Ambrose, p. 112.
[22] Ambrose, pp. 112–13.
[23] Memorandum Re: Grady and re-formation of Greek Government, April 18, 1950, FRUS 1950, Vol. V, The Near East, South Asia and Africa, pp. 365-7. The Plastiras government was "well received" in the United States, and the prime minister immediately set to work to implement economic reforms in Greece, which he felt would be the "best defense against communism" and allow Greece to be a strong positive example for the West. See: Memorandum, April 21, 1950, ibid., pp. 367–9. Later, the State Department sent official letters to the king and Venizelos to thank them for their "support" of Plastiras, thereby contributing to a "presumably more *stable* coalition." Webb to US Embassy in Greece (838), May 8, 1950, ibid., pp. 369–71. Emphasis added.

led the US to embark on this new course. By April 1950, American pressure had dictated the composition that a foreign government would take.

Shortly after the "restructured" Greek government took power, events in Western Europe also pointed to significant changes on the horizon. In May 1950, the chief of France's National Planning Board, Jean Monnet, urged French Foreign Minister Robert Schuman to place all German and French coal and steel production under a common high authority within the framework of an organization that would encourage the future participation of other European nations.[24] This agreement was the first formal step toward the European Union. US Secretary of State Dean Acheson had urged the French government to encourage the integration of the Federal Republic of Germany (i.e., West Germany) into Western Europe, so the plan was welcomed by the Americans. The West German Chancellor also supported what became known as the Schuman Plan; however, the British were much less enthusiastic about the idea.[25]

The upper echelons of the British government did not conceal their resentment that France, which they had long "held in contempt for lacking a spine," had taken the initiative in a significant economic plan that they felt should be reserved for a country (Britain) that had the right to refer to itself as a leading power of Europe.[26] The British were insulted that, unlike the Americans and the Germans, they had not been informed by the French prior to the declaration of this plan. The French explained that they had taken this step precisely to deprive the British government of the opportunity to modify or defeat the French initiative.[27] As Cold War tension increased, both the British and the Americans became more inclined to loosen their control over the Federal Republic of Germany in order to facilitate German reconstruction and to procure material and human resources

---

[24] Vaughan, pp. 51–6. Reprinted memorandum, sent by Jean Monnet to Robert Schuman and Georges Bidault, May 4, 1950.

[25] Rene Leboutte, *The Economic and Social History of the Construction of Europe*, Brussels: Peter Lang, 2008, pp. 107–30.

[26] Gillingham, p. 238.

[27] Record of a meeting at No. 1 Carlton Gardens on May 10, 1950, Doc. 3, D.B.P.O., series II, Vol. I, p. 6. At the same time, the leader of the Liberal Party in Greece, Venizelos, had still refused to join the government because, he stated, he could not work with Deputy Prime Minister Papandreou. The US Ambassador then approached the king and queen and asked them to press Venizelos to join the government, which they agreed to do. The US had serious doubts about Venizelos, calling him "capricious" and lamenting his "manifest incompetence," but although they were fairly certain that he would harm the Greek government personally, they felt that his party had to participate. For details, see: Grady to Acheson (852), April 17, 1950, FRUS 1950, Vol. V, The Near East, South Asia and Africa, p. 364, Minor to Acheson (1081, May 11, 1950) and (1098, May 13, 1950), Acheson to US Embassy in Greece (901), May 18, 1950, FRUS 1950, Vol. V, The Near East, South Asia and Africa, pp. 371–3, 375–6. Ironically, Venizelos, who in April and May was seen as incompetent and self-interested, would four months later be supported by the British and Americans simply because he stated that he was staunchly anti-communist.

for Western defense.[28] It was in this context that the French felt that they could propose their plan, which had the added benefit for them of controlling the Ruhr and limiting the chance of Germany using it for aggression against them once again. The main priority for the British now was their post-war national strategy of focusing on the Commonwealth and transatlantic obligations, which for the time being ranked above their continental European commitments. The French policy was starkly opposed to that approach, setting the stage for ongoing conflicts between Britain and France over EEC membership.[29] In this context, the British focus on Greece shifted north. Until the end of May 1950, the British continued to work on improving Greek and Yugoslav relations in an effort to widen the gap between the USSR and Yugoslavia, thereby bringing the Yugoslavians ever closer to the Western sphere.

Britain encouraged the resumption of numerous lines of communication between Greece and Yugoslavia, including a rail service and a postal, telegraph, and telephone service, and a possible free trade zone in Thessaloniki. However, the British stressed the priority of the return of the abducted Greek children as a "moral and humanitarian question" and were assured by Tito that the Yugoslavian government felt the same way.[30] But Yugoslavia reasserted its demands for the official recognition of the "Macedonian" Slavic minorities in northern Greece. The British immediately reassured the Greek government and made known their opposition to the Yugoslavian demand, saying that "this subject did not exist and that the reference which had been made to it was contrary to the spirit of the relations which were being inaugurated."[31] This was a significant statement for the British to make. It meant that under no circumstances, even the possibility of bringing Yugoslavia closer to the West, were the British prepared to recognize any action that would threaten Greece's territorial or political integrity at the edge of the Iron Curtain.

---

[28] Hitchcock, pp. 119–20 and 124–5.
[29] Minute from Strang to Younger, June 2, 1950, DBPO, Series II, Vol. I, pp. 133–4.
[30] Later in the summer, on August 17, 1950, Bevin intervened with the Bulgarian Ambassador in London on behalf of the Greek government. Bevin questioned the ambassador about the status of the Greek children who were still being held in Bulgaria and when the Bulgarian government intended to repatriate them to Greece. After initial denials, the Bulgarian Ambassador finally admitted that there were still some Greek children in Bulgaria but said he did not know when they would be returned to Greece. The Foreign Secretary urged the Bulgarian Ambassador to pressure the Bulgarian government to expedite the process, since the political benefits of such an action "might be considerable." See: Bevin to Mason (103), August 17, 1950, BDFA, Series F Europe, Part IV, Vol. 27, 1950, p. 89.
[31] Record of Meeting (58), BDFA, Series F Europe, Part IV, Vol. 27, May 27, **1951** (1951 is likely a typographic error since all of the other documents in this section are dated 1950), pp. 69–70.

The Implications of the Crises in Cyprus, China, and Korea

In June 1950, the Greek Cypriots sent a delegation to Athens to speak with the Greek government and to lobby for support from Great Britain, the United States, France, and other nations to encourage the unification of Cyprus and Greece. Ambassador Norton stated that he had made it clear that the British government opposed such a union and that "intelligent Greeks may realize that the agitation is untimely, unwise, and liable to create a rift between their country and Great Britain."[32] The British felt that their continued support amongst the Greeks was a direct result of their "unremitting defense" of the Greek cause in the international sphere and the long-term presence of British troops and missions in support of the reconstruction and protection of Greece during the chaotic years following the end of the Second World War, which were not diminished by Greece's dependency on American military and economic aid.[33] This telegram is quite revealing of British intentions. Copies of it were sent to the British Governor of Cyprus and to the head of the British Middle East Office in Cairo. The ambassador's comments illustrate that Britain was vigorously maintaining any strategic positions that it still possessed, and one of the most significant for it in the Mediterranean was Cyprus.

Meanwhile, in the United States, Truman was still receiving much criticism for being soft on communism. Though he had initially "shelved" NSC-68 as too expensive to implement, by June 1950, international conditions had changed. He needed an incident to spur Congress into action, and one duly occurred on June 25, 1950, when the North Korean army crossed the 38th parallel and invaded South Korea.

The crises in Greece had helped President Truman secure the funds from the United States Congress to implement the first stage of the Truman Doctrine, and the North Korean invasion of South Korea gave him the leverage to persuade Congress to approve the funds for NSC-68. Truman also had the opportunity

---

[32] Norton to Foreign Office (158), June 29, 1950, BDFA, Series F Europe, Part IV, Vol. 27, pp.72–3.
[33] Norton to Foreign Office (158), June 29, 1950, BDFA, Series F Europe, Part IV, Vol. 27, pp. 72–3. The situation in Cyprus would not stay calm for long in 1955, and the Governor of Cyprus, Sir John Harding, ordered the arrest and deportation of Archbishop Makarios, the spiritual leader of the Greek Cypriot nationalist movement. This caused widespread violence in Cyprus, resulting in hundreds of deaths before the Zurich Agreement of 1959 made Cyprus an independent state within the British Commonwealth. Special arrangements were made to placate the Turkish minority, such as maintaining the British naval bases on Cyprus. However, the British would have their hands full with the Cyprus issue over the ensuing decades, and their failure to settle the issue earlier set the stage for the Turkish invasion of Cyprus in 1972. For a more detailed analysis, see: Childs, *Britain Since 1945: A Political History*, pp. 98–9.

to finally secure funds to aid Chiang Kai-shek, who was tenuously holding on to his position in Formosa. Though both Secretary of State Dean Acheson and Chairman of the Senate Foreign Relations Committee Tom Connolly stated in May 1950 that the South Korean elections might force the United States to abandon South Korea, these statements were contrary to the program outlined in NSC-68. Given the continued rise of anti-communist sentiment in both the government and the general population, it would have been political suicide to sacrifice South Korea and Formosa to the communists.[34] On June 25,1950, when the North Korean Army invaded South Korea, the American president moved quickly.

Truman forced a resolution in the United Nations Security Council and the General Assembly condemning the attack and branding the North Koreans as aggressors. He demanded a ceasefire and the immediate return of North Korean forces across the 38th parallel. On June 26, 1950, he released a statement formally extending the Truman Doctrine to the Pacific and pledging that the United States military would intervene against any further communist expansion in Asia.[35]

As a result of more pressing concerns in Asia, the State Department instructed the Greek government to cease and discourage any talks of unification with Cyprus. While the department said that it could understand Greek frustration with the British position on Cyprus and continuing Yugoslavian references to "Greek Slavophones," Acheson believed that neither constituted an immediate threat to Greece. In his view, Greek nationalism would only play into the hands of the USSR, and Greece should refrain from engaging in any policy that might "alienate actual and potential allies." Acheson also criticized the Greek government for not exercising its "undoubted influence over Cypriot '*ethnarchy*' to stop *enosis* [unification] agitation at its source." He concluded that the US was struggling to keep Greece afloat and could not continue to do so "if Greeks continue to exhaust themselves and embarrass us by heading for such distant shores as Cyprus."[36] The British (aided by developments in Korea) had thus managed to secure US support for another of their Eastern Mediterranean objectives. Moreover, Acheson had ordered another foreign state—Greece— to alter its policy, control its population, and exert its influence over a third

---

[34] Ambrose, p. 116.
[35] Ambrose, p. 117.
[36] Acheson to US Embassy in Greece (1292), June 27, 1950, FRUS 1950 Vol. V, The Near East, South Asia and Africa, pp. 378–9.

state—Cyprus—so as to achieve Anglo-American objectives there, threatening alienation and loss of future support if Greece failed to follow US instructions.

Although it had got off to a positive start, the Plastiras government was also now attacked for being infiltrated by communists. This charge was often levelled against it by the king and his supporters on the right and was echoed by the former head of the American Military Mission in Greece, Lieutenant General Van Fleet. Van Fleet sent a message directly to the State Department that greatly alarmed the Secretary of State, who immediately sent a dispatch to the US Embassy in Greece asking for verification. Van Fleet wrote that "communists and fellow travellers" had gradually regained their positions under Plastiras, and after meeting with General Papagos, Van Fleet was convinced that the current government was "dangerous." In response, the US Embassy sent a somewhat contradictory dispatch to the State Department.

First, seeming to support the Plastiras government, it stated that the embassy had no idea how Van Fleet, after having been absent from Greece, could possess more accurate information than the State Department did. Chargé d'affaires Minor also expressed his concern that Van Fleet had not discussed any of these issues with him at the American Embassy, though he had been "uninterruptedly on spot" since the inception of the Plastiras government and had closely watched all developments. Minor added that both he and Porter had closely observed the current Greek government and were much more qualified to comment on it than Van Fleet. Regarding the comment about "communists and fellow travellers," Minor stated that there was no evidence that this was true and that he had discovered that the "Greek Rightists" tended to use these terms very loosely in connection with anyone who disagreed with them. Though Minor acknowledged that in a few cases, especially in labor-related positions, "dubious persons" had been appointed, the US Embassy had successfully lobbied against their appointment and had succeeded in having them removed. Finally, Minor said that in general, the Plastiras government had followed the US policy to attempt "reconciliation and pacification to a degree compatible with national security," ultimately leading to peace.[37] However, despite these supportive statements, Minor went on to report that there was, nonetheless, a danger of renewed communist influence in Greece.

He said that while the Plastiras government might have taken the best path to meet Greece's internal needs, the international situation had again changed

---

[37] Minor to Acheson (222), July 19, 1950, FRUS 1950, Vol. V, The Near East, South Asia and Africa, pp. 380–2.

so much (with regard to Korea) that Greece had to pay more attention to external needs, "like every other nation," and re-focus on the "Communist menace." Minor therefore concluded that in light of the international communist threat, the Plastiras government "may not be the best instrument to carry out this policy."[38]

In a revealing expression of its position on the Greek government, the US Embassy advised the State Department that although the current Greek government was following the correct path for internal Greek policy (peace and reconciliation), in light of international US anti-communist concerns, domestic Greek interests might be superseded, and a change in Greek leadership might be necessary, even if that change would be to the detriment of the Greek people.[39] This dispatch shows not only the beginning of the US trend of sacrificing the domestic good of foreign nations to satisfy its foreign policy objectives but also something much more basic: national self-interest. Though at first seeming to defend the Plastiras government, Minor's comments ultimately appear designed to defend his actions in relation to the Greek government. He expressed offence not at Van Fleet's conclusions but at the fact that he had not been consulted before Van Fleet sent those opinions to the State Department. He then justified his course of action in relation to the Plastiras government rather than justifying the actions of the government itself. Finally, he stated that international concerns had to take precedence over domestic Greek concerns, thus protecting himself from being labelled as soft on communism, a charge that was used frequently in Washington at that time.

British assessments of the latest Greek political crisis differed from those of the US. They revolved around what they described as the "uncertain attitude of M. Venizelos," whose actions were largely dictated by his dislike of Papandreou. However, though the British also acknowledged that Plastiras was no communist despite "having fought ... against the Right" throughout his political career, he had "old friends" who were suspected communist sympathizers. Ambassador Norton also said that because Plastiras was "not an intelligent man," there was a risk that he might follow the advice of these old friends and act too leniently toward known communists.[40] A few days later, Plastiras issued a press release stating that owing to international developments, leniency measures would not

---

[38] Acheson to Minor (167), quoting Van Fleet (L576), July 17, 1950, Minor to Acheson (222), July 19, 1950, FRUS 1950, Vol. V, The Near East, South Asia and Africa, pp. 380–2.
[39] Ibid.
[40] Norton to Younger (169), July 7, 1950, BDFA, Series F Europe, Part IV, Vol. 27, 1950, pp. 73–4.

be extended. Despite this statement, Minor commented that he felt that "the Prime Minister's views on both economic and security questions indicated a lamentable amount of realism."[41] On July 30, former Ambassador Grady was described as reacting "violently" to Van Fleet's letter, saying that Van Fleet had allowed himself to be used to discredit the Plastiras government, probably by Queen Frederica. Grady stated that although Plastiras was sometimes "fuzzy-minded … in his traditional liberalism," he was a patriotic, non-communist Greek. However, the State Department felt that while Van Fleet's conclusions suggested that the situation was more urgent than it really was, the US should be prepared to support a "stronger type of government," possibly under Marshal Papagos, should the Plastiras government disintegrate.[42] Only a few months earlier, the United States had exercised its influence over Greece to help bring Plastiras to power, and now it seemed as though it was preparing to remove him. The Greek army and executive branch of government they had built with the British, permitted such intervention, if not directly, then through the king, who could (and would) dissolve the government. Moreover, adding to an already difficult state of political affairs in Greece, the Cyprus issue would not subside.

There was significant public support in Greece for the Greek Cypriot majority to be reunited with Greece. A massive public demonstration was held on July 21, 1950. Numerous newspapers urged people to attend this event. There are differing reports of the number of people who attended, with the British reporting that the crowd was generally "somewhat apathetic" but nevertheless that "very large crowds were certainly present." On July 24, when the Archbishop of Athens, Spyridon, asked to see the assistant to Ambassador Norton, Mr Crosthwaite, with the leader of the Cypriot delegation, the British diplomatic officer refused to meet with them officially. The archbishop presented a separate resolution stating that Cyprus should be unified with Greece. As the archbishop turned to leave, the diplomatic officer stopped him, "explaining that I was sure that he would not expect me to enter into a discussion on the whole question of Cyprus, but I wish to make one observation to him in my personal capacity." The diplomatic officer stated that he regretted that the archbishop had felt compelled to support the Cypriot initiative for union with Greece at the present time. He told the archbishop that the international situation at present was very dangerous (referring to the war in Korea) and that it was wrong to divert the attention of the

---

[41] Minor to Acheson (147), July 26, 1950, FRUS 1950, Vol. V, The Near East, South Asia and Africa, pp. 386–7.
[42] Memorandum, July 31, 1950, FRUS 1950, Vol. V, The Near East, South Asia and Africa, pp. 395–6.

Greek people from the far more important issue of Greece's economic recovery to the issue of union with Cyprus. The diplomatic officer noted that Archbishop Spyridon had made similar visits to the American and French Embassies.[43]

The American Ambassador, following instructions from Washington (which was following British requests), informed the Greek government that officially, United States policy expected Greece to "concentrate all her energies on essentials rather than to follow a course from which no one would benefit except the Russians." With that, the British and the Americans firmly opposed furthering the cause of Greek nationalism, ensuring that it would become an issue for future governments to deal with. In August, another Cypriot delegation made its way to Greece to lobby for union. Under pressure from the British, the Americans, and the South Africans, the Greek government refused to endorse the demands of the Cypriot delegation, much to the latter's anger and embarrassment.[44]

On the economic front, in August 1950, industrial production in Greece finally passed its 1939 levels. It had been a long process, but the British and Americans were finally seeing some positive results from their reconstruction of the Greek economy.[45] However, these gains, still over ten years behind those of Western Europe, were threatened by plans to dramatically expand the Greek army because of fears that a renewed communist threat such as that in Korea might emerge in the Balkans. The US decided to increase the size of the Greek army so that it would be able to deal with internal and external threats.

Though the State Department had fully supported Grady's assessments and policies, it decided that because of the situation in Korea, it now had "serious reservations about the Plastiras government" and was "presently considering alternative solutions." Greece's new value to US strategic interests was not as a democratic example of anti-communism but rather as a country capable of providing armed forces that, when combined with those of Yugoslavia, could result in over a million anti-Soviet troops in the Balkans. So in addition to abandoning the previously planned troop reductions that had been seen as vital to Greece's economic rehabilitation, the United States was planning to divert

---

[43] Crosthwaite to Bevin (193), August 4, 1950, BDFA, Series F Europe, Part IV, Vol. 27, pp. 83–4.

[44] Crosthwaite to Bevin (193), August 4, 1950, BDFA, Series F Europe, Part IV, Vol. 27, pp. 83–4. The result of the Anglo-American decision to ignore the Cyprus issue at this time without addressing any of the underlying conditions virtually guaranteed that the situation would worsen there over the next quarter of a century, culminating in the Turkish invasion of the island in July 1974.

[45] Crosthwaite to Bevin (190), August 4, 1950, BDFA, Series F Europe, Part IV, Vol. 27, p. 79. Indicative of Anglo-American priorities, Germany and Italy had passed their pre-war economic output almost three years earlier.

funds and supplies to immediately increase the Greek army to 200,000 men, with the possibility of another increase to 400,000.[46]

Politically, the crisis that the US had anticipated and hoped for arrived on August 17, 1950, when Venizelos and the Liberal Party withdrew their support for the government, reportedly because of its leniency "toward former communists and their supporters." Venizelos, whose government had been previously described by Ambassador Grady as "weak and irresponsible" in April 1950,[47] was now named as the United States' choice to replace Plastiras, along with other "palace choices." Plastiras resigned on August 18, 1950, and almost immediately, King Paul gave Minister Venizelos "the mandate to form a new government 'of national unity.'"[48]

In response to Minor's notification of this development, the State Department replied that it supported a government that was not headed by Plastiras, and that although it supported the constitutional process for re-forming the government under Venizelos, it would also support new elections should Venizelos be unable to form a government. The State Department also ordered the embassy to "use the strongest possible influence (to) secure a majority system," thereby avoiding the broad right-versus-left polarization that could result from maintaining the proportional electoral system.[49] Though the same dispatch stated that the US was still not prepared to accept Papagos as premier (unless he was later elected), the Americans were now prepared not only to accept a politician they had previously described as incompetent because they favored his political stance, but also to force a change in the Greek government to achieve the composition they desired.

To make up for the funds that would be lost to reconstruction as a result of again increasing the size of the Greek army, the US Embassy in Greece suggested that it make clear to the Greeks that the crisis had to be met with "better collection of taxes and an increase in direct taxation." The embassy argued that this course of action was reasonable in times of emergency, and since it was being pursued in the United States, there was no reason that it should not be attempted in Greece.

---

[46] Memorandum, August 4, 1950, Memorandum, August 10, 1950, FRUS 1950 Vol. V, The Near East, South Asia and Africa, pp. 397–9. In these memoranda, Van Fleet is quoted as saying that Venizelos might be the best choice to head a new government, despite his known weaknesses, because of his outspoken anti-communism.

[47] Grady to Acheson (852), April 17, 1950, FRUS 1950, Vol. V, The Near East, South Asia and Africa, p. 364.

[48] Crosthwaite to Bevin (89), August 23, 1950, BDFA, Series F Europe, Part IV, Vol. 27, 1950, p. 89. "Palace Choices" refers to ministers preferred and proposed by the monarchy.

[49] Minor to Acheson (549), August 18, 1950, Acheson to Minor (513), August 19, 1950, FRUS 1950, Vol. V, The Near East, South Asia and Africa, pp. 399–403.

It was also suggested that such a plan be presented as a patriotic decision, i.e., in support of the army, rather than focusing on increasing taxation as a means of helping reconstruction.[50] Proportionally, only the Soviet Union had been more economically devastated by the Second World War than Greece, and the Greek people had very little extra, if any, to give in taxes. However, the dispatch clearly stated that military spending would take precedence over reconstruction, that taxes should be collected in support of military spending, and that support of the program should be generated though a focus on patriotism.[51]

Although by now the United States had clearly assumed a predominant position in Greek affairs, the British still exerted considerable influence. Because of the Tito-Stalin split, the British government (moving to solidify its relations with possible adversaries of Stalin who were not yet associated with the United States) continued to pressure the Greek government to improve relations with Yugoslavia. In September 1950, British Foreign Secretary Ernest Bevin summoned the Greek Ambassador for a meeting with the British Parliamentary Under-Secretary and the US Secretary of State.[52] Bevin took the opportunity to "impress upon" the Greek Ambassador how important it was for the British that relations between Yugoslavia and Greece should be normalized. Bevin stated that in his view, it was the duty of the Greek government, in light of current world events, to reconsider the state of its relations with the Yugoslavian government. Bevin suggested that if during the next "4 to 5 weeks the Yugoslav and Greek governments could restore diplomatic relations this would make the most favourable impact on the development of our common affairs." Bevin further stressed that if Yugoslavia "could be firmly aligned in our camp, it would be a triumph for the democracies." In addition to the political benefit, Bevin stated that he was anxious to see an increase in tourist traffic between the two countries and that he wanted "ordinary British people to be able to travel freely throughout the Eastern Mediterranean." He reiterated that he believed that the Greek government would have a greater chance of retrieving the children who were still being held in communist countries if it improved its relations with Yugoslavia and stressed again that if the Greeks were to move rapidly to normalize relations with Yugoslavia, they would be making a major

---

[50] Minor to Acheson (637), August 26, 1950, FRUS 1950, Vol. V, The Near East, South Asia and Africa, pp. 403–4.
[51] There are numerous similarities between the programs implemented and the language used by the US diplomats in Greece at this time and those that were used by the "troika" during the various phases of the Greek crises of the 2010s. Though beyond the scope of this book, this is worth mentioning and will be the focus of a forthcoming publication.
[52] Bevin to Norton (244), September 6, 1950, BDFA, Series F Europe, Part IV, Vol. 27, pp. 92–3.

contribution "to the common cause," which for Bevin was British interests in the Balkans.[53] It appeared to be quite a leap of faith to expect the Greek government to accomplish such a huge task in a short time while still dealing with rebuilding the Greek economy, which had only recently surpassed its 1939 levels of industrial production.[54]

The Greek Ambassador responded to Bevin that the Greek government had been trying for quite some time to normalize relations, but that its attempts had been hampered by the Yugoslavians "putting forward unacceptable claims in relation to Macedonia which, in the opinion of the Greek government, constituted a menace to [Greek] security."[55] Bevin responded that he expected the Greek government, rather than looking to the past, to look to the future and consider the larger issue of the West's common security requirements. Bevin then directed the Greek Ambassador to accompany the British Parliamentary Under-Secretary, Mr. Davies, into another room so that Davies could convey to the Greek Ambassador the assurances that the British had received from the Yugoslavians regarding their intentions toward Greece. Davies assured the Greek Ambassador that he was personally satisfied that the Yugoslavian leaders were sincere in asserting their desire to restore relations with Greece. He also stated that he believed that Marshal Tito had offered personal guarantees to the British regarding the status of the territorial claims they were making in Macedonia. In addition, the Yugoslavians had requested that the British Parliamentary Under-Secretary convey these guarantees to the Greeks directly. Davies concluded that the assurances were valid and that he saw no reason why the Yugoslavians should communicate them directly to the Greek government. The Greek Ambassador asked Mr. Davies why the Yugoslavians were unwilling to reassure the Greeks directly and said that he found this suspicious, particularly considering that "the Yugoslavs were notoriously untrustworthy."[56] Davies replied that if the Greek government were to continue to base its official policy on the view that the Yugoslavian government was untrustworthy, then regardless of any assurances given to the Greeks by the British and by whatever means they were conveyed, no measures would be sufficient to convince the Greeks of their validity. Davies

---

[53] Record of Meeting (244), September 6, 1950, BDFA, Series F Europe, Part IV, Vol. 27, pp. 92–3.
[54] Crosthwaite to Bevin (190E), August 4, 1950, BDFA, Series F Europe, Part IV, Vol. 27, pp. 79–82.
[55] This issue would remain unresolved between Greece and one of the former republics of Yugoslavia, the recently renamed North Macedonia. The 2019 ratification of the Treaty of Prespa (on January 25, 2019; the treaty came into force on February 12, 2019), while triggering protests and backlash against the signing governments of Greece and North Macedonia, settled the dispute between Greece and its northern neighbor after almost seventy years of tensions.
[56] Bevin to Norton (244), September 6, 1950, BDFA, Series F Europe, Part IV, Vol. 27, p. 93.

continued that he simply believed that the Yugoslavians were reluctant to repeat their guarantees directly to the Greek government because it would "touch their pride to do so." Davies concluded that the "touchiness" of the Yugoslavians had to be tolerated, and he urged the Greek Ambassador to recommend that the Greek government take the Yugoslavians at their word.[57] The British were forcing an ally to humble itself diplomatically to appease a country that until very recently had been considered an enemy, simply because immediate British interests were now better served by courting the Yugoslavians rather than supporting the Greeks.

On September 12, the Venizelos government fell and was replaced by a new three-party cabinet, although Venizelos remained as prime minister. The United States also informed Greece that American aid would be reduced from 274 million to 218 million dollars because successive Greek governments had been unable to fully utilize it.[58] As a result, the Greek people would suffer the consequences of continuing foreign interference in Greek affairs that ironically only made Greece more dependent on foreign aid. Additionally, they would be represented by a government headed by an individual who was externally viewed as incompetent but was supported from abroad because of his outspoken anti-communist views.

On September 20, 1950 in New York City, after a meeting of the UN General Assembly, Bevin spoke with the new Greek Foreign Minister, Panagiotis Kannellopoulos, and said that he was more convinced than ever that Greece had to come together and resume its diplomatic relations with Yugoslavia because "the Russians were endeavoring to lull us into a false sense of security and that this might well mean trouble either for the Greeks or the Yugoslavs." He claimed that he believed it was vital for the security of Europe that the borders of the Mediterranean be strengthened from Italy to Turkey.[59] In private discussions with the United States in London, Foreign Office officials also stated that they would attempt to prevent the Cyprus issue from being raised in the General Assembly,

---

[57] Record of Meeting (244), September 6, 1950, BDFA, Series F Europe, Part IV, Vol. 27, pp. 92–3.
[58] Minor to Acheson (859, 899), September 14 and 16, 1950, FRUS 1950, Vol. V, The Near East, South Asia and Africa, pp. 405, 406–7. From January to September 1950, the Greek government was re-formed six times. In light of such domestic instability, it is not surprising that the Greeks were unable to fully/properly utilize the aid that was coming into the country. British sources say that the Venizelos government fell on September 9, 1950. Norton to Bevin (101), September 11, 1950, BDFA, Series F Europe, Part IV, Vol. 27, p. 93. For British reports on the reduction of American aid to Greece and the Greek public's reaction to it, see: Norton to Bevin (281), November 29, 1950, BDFA, Series F Europe, Part IV, Vol. 27, pp. 108–9.
[59] Record of Meeting (no. 27, RG 10392/101), September 27, 1950, BDFA, Series F Europe, Part IV, Vol. 27, pp. 99–100.

not only because of Turkish interests, but also because Cyprus "had considerable value" as a military base. With regard to the military situation in the Balkans, the Foreign Office agreed that in the event of an attack on Greece, a UN action similar to that taking place in Korea was probably the best solution, although it believed that such an attack was unlikely at the time. Additionally, although both Britain and the United States were in favor of strengthening economic and diplomatic relations between Greece and Yugoslavia, Tito was making a rapprochement more difficult because, despite his previous assurances, he was continuing to make territorial claims against Greek Macedonia and to offer no answer regarding the 10,000 to 20,000 Greek children who were still missing.[60]

On September 27, 1950, the Greek Ambassador informed Bevin that Tito was making use of the Greek minority in Yugoslavia to organize anti-Greek-government newspapers. He also said that the Yugoslavians were actively unsettling the Macedonian minority in northern Greece and that, as a result, no Greek political party would be able to survive an election if it were to support the resumption of Yugoslavian and Greek diplomatic relations without first resolving the issue of Yugoslavian intentions toward northern Greece. In New York, Greek Ambassador Nicolaos Politis stated that he believed the Yugoslavians would provide assurances of their intentions as knew that they would only receive Western aid if they did so. However, these assurances had no relation to actual alterations in their behavior. The ambassador concluded that as long as the Yugoslavians continued to act in this manner, no government would be able to explain to the Greek Parliament and Greek public why it was prepared to resume diplomatic relations. He also stated that it was not in Greece's interest to settle these issues when the Yugoslavians would benefit most.[61] With uncharacteristic nonchalance, Bevin responded that if the Yugoslavians were indeed behaving in such an aggressive manner, then it appeared that the resumption of diplomatic relations between the two Balkan nations would be impossible at that time; he would report the developments to the British government.[62]

Ambassador Politis met Bevin in New York to discuss Greece's admittance to NATO, but Bevin stated that it was not the right time for Greece to enter the North Atlantic Pact. He explained that Greece was "already in a very special

---

[60] Memorandum, September 16–23, 1950, FRUS 1950, Vol. V, The Near East, South Asia and Africa, pp. 407–9.
[61] Record of Meeting (no. 27, RG 10392/101), September 27, 1950, BDFA, Series F Europe, Part IV, Vol. 27, p. 99.
[62] Record of Meeting (27), September 27, 1950, BDFA, Series F Europe, Part IV, Vol. 27, p. 100.

position" vis-à-vis the United States because it had President Truman's security guarantee and a special vote in Congress had led to it being given equipment and economic assistance. Bevin concluded that Greece could therefore not receive preferential treatment and would have to wait and take its place in the line-up with other European countries.[63]

Unlike the British, the US was prepared to consider Greece's entry into NATO, but it first wanted Greece and Turkey to come to some sort of military understanding. It approved Greek initiatives to approach the Turkish General Staff, and the US Ambassador in Ankara reported that the Turks were "friendly" to the idea, but for them, an agreement was contingent upon US participation. Though the US was initially reluctant to promise such participation, by the end of October 1950 both Greece and Turkey had been invited by the United States to join NATO and to coordinate Eastern Mediterranean defense.[64] The year 1950 was clearly a period of transition in American policy toward Greece. Prior to 1950, the Americans had favored "moderate" and representative governments. But the arrival of the new US Ambassador, John Peurifoy, on September 22, 1950 clearly demonstrated the State Department's shift from pursuing democracy in Greece to desiring only stability. The prospect of Greece's entry into NATO reflected this ongoing shift.[65]

Anglo-American actions had prevented Greece from falling into the Soviet sphere of influence, but this had involved sacrificing the recovery and cohesion of Greece's government, economy and society. A meeting between King Paul and Peurifoy on November 3, 1950 not only clearly illustrated the American focus on stability over democracy but also foreshadowed the steps that would lead Greece to the crisis over Cyprus and the dictatorship of the 1960s.

The king informed the ambassador that although he had instructed Venizelos to form a government (again), he did not expect it to last very long. If and when it fell, the king would ask George Ventiris to head a caretaker government that would govern until elections could be held 45 days later. In these elections, he would ask Marshal Papagos to form and lead an opposition Nationalist Party,

---

[63] Attlee to Norton (266), October 4, 1950, BDFA, Series F Europe, Part IV, Vol. 27, p. 104.
[64] Webb to Peurifoy (1088), October 4, 1950, Peurifoy to Acheson (1182), October 5, 1950, FRUS 1950 Vol. V, The Near East, South Asia and Africa, pp. 424–6. Turkey was invited on September 19, 1950 and Greece on October 16, 1950.
[65] Peurifoy remains a controversial figure in Greece today because of his direct involvement in Greek politics. His name is used today as an adjective for a foreigner who intervenes in Greek politics. See the article: Bitsika, Panagiota (26 April 1998). "Οι αμερικανοί πρεσβευτές στην Αθήνα" [The American ambassadors in Athens]. To Vima (in Greek). www.tovima.gr/2008/11/24/culture/oi-amerikanoi-presbeytes-stin-athina/

and the king was certain that "the majority of Greece's best men would flock to the Field Marshal's banner." Peurifoy told King Paul that he believed the king had arrived at the best decision for Greece and that he could count on the US Embassy's full support.[66]

With the State Department supporting Peurifoy's declaration, the United States paved the way for the Greek right to dominate politics again. Despite concerns over steps that Papagos had already taken to control the gendarmerie, in addition to his control of the army, the US State Department said that as long as he entered politics freely (i.e., without interference from the king and having resigned as head of the military) and was democratically elected, they would support any strong and stable Greek government.[67] The shift in US foreign policy was virtually complete. Not only had military spending again taken precedence over economic rebuilding, but the nature of the democratic process in Greece had been subjected to international political and military concerns. The British assessed this new Venizelos government as weak and needing American and British guidance to help it deal with the "tangle of internal Greek politics."[68]

One of the strongest indications of British influence over US policy in Greece was that by November 1950, the United States was supporting the Greek monarchy; not only its continued existence, but also its playing a role in government affairs. This was a significant shift in US policy toward Greece; back in 1945, it had disagreed with the British over their support of King George. Perhaps the most significant result of America's "advice" to King Paul and its support of his initiative was that the possibility for military officers to enter Greek politics was maintained. Papagos resigned from the military and became a minority prime minister in May 1951. By November 1952, he would lead a majority government in the Greek Parliament.

In September 1951, as Papagos was realizing his political ambitions, the peace treaty between the United States and Japan dismissed British, Australian, and Chinese demands against Japan for war reparations—just as the Americans had previously dismissed Greek claims against Italy and Germany for reparations.[69]

---

[66] Peurifoy to Acheson (1503), November 4, 1950, FRUS 1950, Vol. V, The Near East, South Asia and Africa, pp. 432–3.
[67] Acheson to Peurifoy (1547), November 9, 1950, FRUS 1950, Vol. V, The Near East, South Asia and Africa, pp. 433–5.
[68] Norton to Bevin (281), November 29, 1950, BDFA, Series F Europe, Part IV, Vol. 27, p. 110.
[69] Ambrose, p. 123.

America was convinced of the value of Germany and Japan as barriers against communism that were vital to US national security interests, and this easily superseded not only the legal rights and economic needs of Allied/occupied nations for reparations but also the basic need and moral right of their people to receive justice. The shift to the "new" American foreign policy of the second half of the twentieth century had taken place, and its effects would be felt for decades to come.

Conclusion

When Harry Truman became US president in 1945, he led a country that expected to return to traditional military and civil relations, and to the historical American foreign policy of non-intervention and isolation. He began and completed the most rapid demobilization of armed forces in modern history, yet when he left the White House, there was an American military presence on every continent on earth and an enormously expanded weapons industry. Truman gave the United States nuclear bombs and rearmed Germany. He forced through a peace treaty with Japan, and dismissed Greek, Chinese, Canadian, Australian, and British demands for reparations from Germany and Japan. By placing American military bases all over the world, he successfully hemmed in Russia and China. Though Korea taught the Americans not to push into communist territory, Truman also showed the communists that any expansion would not go unchallenged and would be met by force. The measure of the success of his policy is that every subsequent American administration throughout the Cold War followed in his footsteps. It may never be possible to put an exact figure on the countless billions of dollars spent on the military for Cold War objectives. Dwight D. Eisenhower's farewell address, which stated "in the councils of government, we must guard against the acquisition of unwarranted influence, whether sought or unsought by the military-industrial complex," was quickly forgotten and replaced by Kennedy's inaugural address: "Let every nation know, whether it wishes us well or ill, that we shall pay any price, bear any burden, meet any hardship, support any friend, oppose any foe, in order to assure the survival and success of liberty. This much we pledge – and more."[1] Four years

---

[1] Truman, Eisenhower, Kennedy, quoted in: Ambrose, pp. 122–6, 151, 171.

later, these words would ring hollow to Greeks as they watched their own tanks roll down the streets of central Athens.

By the end of Truman's administration in 1953, Greece had begun to recover economically, but the end of the Civil War did not bring an end to divisions in Greek society. The dismissal of the republican Plastiras and his replacement with Papagos symbolized the course the Greek state would take over the next decades. If the political system and elections remained more or less independent of government interference, with CIA training and support, the military and police came to be filled with *parakratoi*, shadow governments, designed to take control of institutions in the event of communist infiltration. Behind the shift in US policy, internationally and in Greece, lay British influence.

That is not to say that either they or the Americans wished to set Greece on a path that would lead to dictatorship, regardless of communist action and intention. At least through the late 1940s, both the British and the Americans wished for Greece to have a stable democracy, but certainly for the US, from Truman's second term to Lyndon Johnson's support of the colonels, the emphasis would be increasingly on "stable" rather than "democracy." This was made possible because the memories of the conflicts of the 1940s were built into the institutions created in their wake— which, sadly, seemed destined to carry them on. To quote a fictional military commander, "There's a reason you separate military and the police. One fights the enemies of the state, and the other serves and protects the people. When the military becomes both, then the enemies of the state tend to become the people."[2]

With these words ringing in my ears, the image of the scene at the church in Litochoro with which I opened this book is still clear in my mind as I finish it. The picture, not only of Greeks throwing Greeks to their death in the past but also of the competing narratives of those events in the present, with myself as a silent witness to the description of the disputed history, reinforces how disconnected I sometimes feel there. It also reinforces the realization that Greece is a country of many contrasts; if one is to begin to understand its history and place in the West, one must be able to reconcile contradictory "stories" about the past.

It is here that the "story" of Anglo-American relations in Greece until 1952 has something very important to offer. It demonstrates the importance of keeping such "contradictions" in mind and hints at how to view the interaction

---

[2] Commander William Adama, dialogue written by Ronald D. Moore (*Battlestar Galactica* [2004], Season 1 Episode 2, "Water"). For a policy paper on the separation of military and police, see: George Withers, Lucila Santos, and Adam Isacson, "Preach What You Practice: The Separation of Military and Police Roles in the Americas." (Washington Office on Latin America, November 2010.) ISBN 978-0-9844873-4-9.

between international and domestic developments. If readers can come to terms with the contrasts and contradictions revealed in the study of British-American and Greek relations at this time then they may be able to understand politics elsewhere when confronted with similar contradictions. They will be better equipped to keep them in mind without discarding the whole endeavor. Doing so may also have an ancillary benefit in revealing how democracies involve themselves in the affairs of other nations, how leaders in democracies develop strategies and implement policies to achieve them, and how they reconcile international objectives with domestic politics. This is why Greece matters; in many ways after the Second World War, Greece was the "canary in the coalmine" and a "laboratory" of politics for the West. By 1950, the US shift from being the "arsenal of democracy" to an arsenal of containment was virtually complete, and the success of British influence over American policy in the late 1940s can be seen in the fact that throughout the Cold War, every US president after Truman maintained the policies that the latter implemented with British "assistance."

For Great Britain, the success of its policies was tied to the United States financially and militarily. The war had bankrupted Albion and *Pax Britannica* was replaced by *Pax Americana*. The British never realized their objective of regaining their pre-eminent status on the world stage. They found themselves in a world balanced between the United States on one side and communist Russia (and later China) on the other. In the middle were Europe and the "Third World," which would be used as testing grounds for a new method of warfare that was experimented with time and time again. For a clear idea of Britain's degree of influence over American policy and the degree of consistency in British policy throughout the 1940s, consider Table 1.

Table 1 "Visualization of British and American policy changes toward Greece."

Country	Years	Party	Desired/supported regime type in Greece	Desired/supported international policy
United Kingdom	1940–5	Conservative	Monarchy	Empire//Alliances
	1945–8	Labour	Monarchy	Empire/Alliances
	1948–52	Labour	Monarchy	Empire/Alliances/Cold War
United States	1940–5	Democrats	No interest/democracy	Isolationism//Winning the war
	1945–8	Democrats	Republic/democracy	Internationalism (UN), Containment
	1948–52	Democrats	Monarchy	Alliances/Empire

Considering how far apart British and American policy were in 1945–6, both with regard to Greece and internationally, the shift in US policy to support British objectives was impressive. Aside from the international ramifications of the Cold War, the effects on the people of Greece were equally dramatic.

Despite the promise of American aid, the British continued to play a significant role in Greece beyond October 1947, when the American aid program began. The United States had no intelligence service similar to that possessed by Great Britain, and as a result it was initially dependent upon Britain for intelligence concerning not only Greece but also Europe as a whole. As the Soviet threat continued to grow in 1947, the Americans finally decided that it was time to take action, and they did so in an overwhelming manner, sending millions of dollars in aid and military supplies to the Greek government in its struggle with the DSE.

As happened with the Axis powers in the Second World War, once the Americans became involved in the Greek Civil War, it was only a matter of time before the DSE was defeated. With little international aid, the DSE was unable to last the decade and was defeated in November 1949. The cost paid for the domestic iteration of the Cold War was all too apparent in Greece, with almost a million casualties out of a population of only eight million.

Of the three Great Powers involved in Greece, only the Soviet Union experienced the total failure of its foreign policy. Stalin was extremely cautious in dealing with Greece because he did not wish to encourage more Western intervention in the Balkans. However, he was so cautious that events in Greece overtook his policy decisions. The outbreak of the Civil War at the end of 1946 convinced the United States of the USSR's militaristic intentions, whether real or perceived, and as a result the US pledged its "strategic commitment" to Greece—the very thing that Stalin had hoped to avoid.[3] Though the Soviet Union officially maintained its "hands-off" policy toward Greece from 1944 until the end of the Civil War in 1949, the Greek communists received aid from neighboring communist countries. However, the aid was not substantial enough to compete with the American financial and military aid that was guaranteed to the Greek government.

The British maintained their role as advisers in Greece, and they observed, reported on, and recommended courses of action to deal with the worsening conditions of the escalating Civil War. Underscoring these developments was

---

[3] Stavrakis, "Soviet Policy in Areas of Limited Control," pp. 228–9.

the British and American fear of the USSR and its rapid expansion. Greece was a problem for the West, and both the Americans and the British experienced their share of successes and setbacks in their policies there. Of course Greece was important for the British strategically, as a waypoint between Europe and the Middle East and India. Numerous works have elaborated this point. However, what has often been missed is the symbolic and political value of Greece, not only in the fight against communism but also in demonstrating, both domestically and abroad, how the United States and the United Kingdom would act in the post-Second World War world.

As for the question of whether the Americans were influenced by the British to change their policy toward Greece and, as a result, their policy toward Europe and the Mediterranean, the answer is based on interpreting thousands of documents produced during this period and tracking the often-subtle changes in US policy after British action. The degree to which British foreign policy in Greece from the beginning of the Second World War until the beginning of the Cold War was adopted/copied and implemented by the United States varies depending on the criteria used in the analysis of these events. From the outset, the Foreign Office was determined to reinstall King George, and that objective was accomplished. In addition, the British were determined to prevent Greece from falling under the Soviet sphere of influence, and whether that occurred because of the percentages agreement and the resulting British action in Greece, because of US involvement in Greece, or as a result of a combination of the two, they were successful in this objective as well. Additionally, while Britain may have failed to exclusively retain Greece in its sphere of influence in the long term, the latter at least remained in the Western sphere of influence, and whether or not the Americans were manipulated or felt that they had been manipulated, they did ultimately assume Britain's responsibilities in Greece.[4] American involvement in Greece also represented a change in the global balance of power as the pre-war powers of Britain, France, and Germany were replaced by the Soviet Union and the United States.

In terms of the strongest evidence supporting the main argument presented in this book, the official British memorandum to the state department indicating that the UK was unable to aid Greece any further was the first concrete evidence of the British plan to manipulate the United States into assuming responsibility for British strategic interests.[5] Furthermore, the fact that in the spring of 1948, the

[4] Frasier, pp. 145–54.
[5] Frasier, pp. 179–81.

British informed the Americans that they would keep British troops in Greece for an indefinite period also indicates that they deceived the United States by implying that the British situation was more desperate than it actually was.[6]

The case of Greece highlights the competing wartime and post-war visions that the leaders of the great powers had for both the war and the post-war order. Roosevelt and Churchill certainly wielded power in their governments, but in contrast with the Soviet Union, where Stalin exercised unimaginable power from his dacha, theirs was much more limited. Roosevelt wanted to create a world in which liberal democracies could survive, Churchill a world in which Britain was still relevant, and Stalin a world where he could play Western powers against each other, securing Soviet influence in areas under their control and taking advantage of developments elsewhere to expand Soviet power. While Stalin's objectives remained more or less constant, Truman, Attlee, and Bevin had their own realities to confront. Truman had to fend off domestic attacks that he was "soft" on communism. A self-styled historian, he also regarded any concession to the Soviets as "Munich all over again" (he used the reference numerous times during the Korean War) as he set the US on its path of intervention. In contrast, Prime Minister Attlee was faced with a Great Britain that could no longer play the role of a superpower. For him, domestic British concerns dominated the way in which he viewed Britain's international commitments. Bevin saw things differently: while he was aware of Britain's weakness after the Second World War, for him it was a temporary state of affairs that could be reversed though careful management of the Americans and successful interventions abroad. In Greece, all of these competing strategic objectives and interpretations played out, with the results described in the book coming to fruition.

Examining the history of Anglo-American policy in Greece from 1946 to 1952 and the associated developments worldwide during this period, it may also be possible to re-evaluate Churchill's classification of the relationship between Britain and the United States as "a special relationship." Based on the preceding analysis, together with knowledge of Anglo-American relations over the second half of the twentieth century, it seems much more accurate to classify theirs as "*the*" special relationship of the latter half of the 1900s. If one considers "special" to also include influence, not only on events but also on methods of intervention, interaction, and diplomacy, and considering the ways in which

---

[6] Jones, p. 154.

other powers have followed Anglo-American examples in their foreign policy, then the appropriateness of the above classification becomes clear.

The events that occurred between December 1946 and November 1952 constituted a "perfect storm" for the British to secure American financial and military support against the USSR. Numerous forces and agendas coincided with British interests in order to achieve this support. There were domestic interests in Britain that were more willing to accept American aid than to reduce foreign expenditure. Many parts of the American business sector were dependent upon US government aid to foreign governments who could in turn purchase their products. Then there were events like the Czechoslovakian coup and the Berlin airlift, which convinced even the most ardent critics of Attlee and Bevin that the Soviet Union was expanding its influence. Greece was caught in the middle of the game played between the superpowers, and the brief period in early 1948 when the Americans considered pulling out of Greece quickly receded in the new era of Cold War international politics. Though diplomatic records show that the British diplomats working in and reporting on Greece were focused on securing a democratic future for Greece, they also tried to ensure that British interests were met. If the former conflicted with the latter, than British interests would certainly take precedence, but improving political and economic stability in Greece was also a priority for the British. The fact that they fell short is an indication not of desire but of effect and circumstances. There is, however, an interesting comparison to be made with the Americans. While Roosevelt sought to make the world safe for democracies, neither his administration nor the subsequent administration of Harry Truman made Greece a fully functioning liberal democracy. In this regard there is an interesting parallel to be drawn with Soviet policy for Greece.

If Greece were to be a full liberal democracy that would be a bonus, but in 1950, the priority was simply to achieve stability and security. With internal communist subversion seen as the greatest threat to Greece at the time, simply being avowed non-communists was enough to secure US support. The Soviets had similarly structured (but inverted) designs for Greece: if Greece became a Socialist Republic that would be a bonus, but their main objective was simply to keep the KKE involved in government. Although the Soviet objectives for Greece were not met, the Americans succeeded, and they continued to supply the Greek military with weapons and equipment. British consuls, chargés d'affaires, and ambassadors consistently warned their own government and the Americans about the dangers of failing to curb right-wing excesses in Greece. There is, however, a certain irony to be noted about these British observations.

While the British correctly observed the risks associated with allowing the Greek Right its excesses, they were also responsible for them. In trying to show the United States how opposed they were to communism, the British fell into the trap laid by the communists themselves: viewing opposition collectively, rather than individually. By seeing all internal opponents to the government, or at least the most vocal opponents—often republicans—as communists, they blinded themselves by also adopting a collectivist viewpoint. Rather than accepting the nuance that dissention entails, they passed this "collectivist" view of all Greek internal opposition to the Americans after the *Dekemvriana*.[7] They thus transmitted a view of Greece in which nuance was lost, in which the army could and should be used as the police.

In Greece, American military aid virtually guaranteed that political and social development would be held back. The entire machinery of government, from taxation to the military, could function as it wished, even if it was to the detriment of Greek democracy, because as long as Greece was not communist, the US would continue to supply money and equipment to the military. Though the fear of communism was used both publicly and privately by the British and American governments to both design and justify their foreign policy, there seemed to be another factor involved. An examination of British and American documents from 1949 and 1952 (once the Civil War had ended) indicates that neither government believed that a communist invasion of Greece was imminent, yet they continued to use the threat of such an invasion to motivate their own governments and populations to action. This is contrasted by their dealings with the Greek government until June 1950.

In late 1949, the Americans cancelled a substantial amount of aid that had been promised to Greece because the Greek government had not been efficient enough in implementing the measures of the aid agreement. The cut-off was intended as a warning to the Greek government that the United States government was not prepared to waste money in Greece.[8] If Greece wanted to continue to receive aid, then its government would have to agree to numerous concessions. This period proved to be a watershed, however. On June 25, 1950, the communist threat reasserted itself with the outbreak of hostilities in Korea, and such concessions would not be demanded again.

---

[7] "December Events" referring to the Battle of Athens (December 1944 to January 1945). See Chapter 2.
[8] See Chapter 5.

Conclusion

The Greek government was not forced to embark on sweeping reforms to enable it to become self-sufficient or to generate a widespread sense of legitimacy amongst the general public. By late 1950, Greek politicians, previously blamed by the British and Americans for their lack of ability to accomplish the most basic reforms, found themselves supported by those who had previously strongly criticized them. This occurred in two main ways. First, allowing King Paul, in theory a constitutional monarch, to intervene in the functioning of government (for example dismissing the prime minister) triggering numerous political crises and governmental paralysis. Second, the British and Americans maintained the size and strength of a Greek army that ironically, while well trained and equipped, was also widely believed to have no chance of stopping a communist invasion of Greece should one occur. Greece's external security would be guaranteed by the US and soon by NATO. The role of the military (clearly stated by US policy-makers) was therefore one of national prestige and response to internal threats. This was arguably the most significant effect of Anglo-American policy in Greece during the early Cold War, and one which set Greece on a path to dictatorship. Thus, though Thanasis Sfikas correctly argues the following, there is nonetheless a gap. He writes:

> The KKE's belief that the Civil War was imposed by the British and the Greek Right in 1945 is correct only in part. The exploits of the Right no doubt enabled the Left to take up arms in 1946. Britain however, did not plot a Civil War in which she could hardly afford to get actively involved.[9]

What a close reading of the US and British documents about this time reveals (as Chapters 4 and 5 show) is that, as the US and Britain were discussing the size and composition of Greece's military, they repeatedly stated that Greece's borders were basically indefensible. As a result, the British and the Americans assigned the Greek military the primary responsibility of maintaining internal security. This is a role normally reserved for the police forces in a liberal democracy. The British and Americans did not impose a Civil War, nor did they desire one, but the effects of British and American policy extended far beyond the 1940s. When the colonels seized power in 1967, they followed a path that, if not laid out, had at the very least been cleared by the British and Americans.

It was in Greece that Britain's objective of regaining its Great Power status was attempted and ultimately replaced by an acceptance of the role of significant but junior partner to the United States. With this acceptance came a transformation,

---

[9] Sfikas, *The British Labour Government and the Greek Civil War*, p. 278.

not only of the special relationship but also of Greece. That is why this book focuses on the period 1946 to 1952 in the country, for it was here, confronted with so many changes and crises worldwide, that the British felt maintaining their say could delay and perhaps eventually reverse their post-war decline. However, it was also in Greece that these hopes were dashed and replaced by a new objective: to remain relevant. The United States, adding to mounting pressure for Britain to relinquish its presence in countries like Greece, Palestine, and later India, accelerated British decline and American ascent. This decline also had profound effects on the course of Greek history.

As their power and influence waned, both Greece and the United States were less and less inclined to follow British advice. Tracing the decline of British influence through the late 1940s reveals a direct correlation with tendencies within Greek institutions that increasingly looked to the United States for guidance and support. In the years immediately following the occupation, the British supported and created Greek institutions that were supposed to be as inclusive as possible, including cooperation with the KKE. However, as their power waned, these institutions increasingly viewed any opposition to the government as being driven solely by the extreme left. Purges and persecutions were common, and the army, rather than having the purpose of defending Greece against external threats, was encouraged to act as a national police force to deal with internal opponents who were seen as threats to security and stability. Therefore when the Greek military seized power in 1967, far from being a surprise, it seemed almost a foregone conclusion.

Greece was the first country after the Second World War where the effects of policies implemented in service of the special relationship were felt. Evaluating the success of these policies depends upon the criteria used. If success is defined as anti-communism, as per the British and American view, then the story of Greece is a success. However, if success is defined differently, for example as the ability to effectively and rapidly rebuild economic and social stability, then British and American foreign policy was a failure. By the mid-1950s Greece was still ten years behind the rest of Western Europe in its recovery. There were still almost a million refugees in Greece, and 28,000 children were still missing at the end of 1949.[10] The right's increasing dominance of the government, armed forces and other institutions was filling Greece's prisons with political dissidents,

---

[10] See: *The Greek Tragedy* by Constantine Tsoucalas.

and the British and Americans had the opportunity in the summer of 1949 to help the Greeks build a representative, modern, and functioning government and economy. They could have done more, and as a result, British and American initiatives in Greece in the early years of the Cold War repeatedly failed to create a stable democracy.

They turned their attention to the other "hot spots" in the world, allowing the Greek monarchy to influence the Greek government and Greece's economy and society to languish in uncertainty and instability. Compounding Greece's economic difficulties were American denials of Greek claims for reparations from Germany and Italy. Anglo-American policy placed greater importance on the reconstruction efforts of wartime enemies than those of their wartime ally, and it can be argued that Greece is still paying the price of that decision today.[11]

The great tragedy and irony of Anglo-American policy in Greece is that in trying to build a free and democratic Greek society, the British and Americans supported institutions (namely a Greek constitutional monarchy that allowed the king to dissolve parliament, and a military focused primarily on internal threats) that would hinder those objectives. Speaking in a 2015 interview about the Russian Revolution, Stephen Kotkin said that the problem with a revolution is that the institutions formed to implement the objectives of the revolution are often in opposition to the objectives which launched the revolution in the first place. In his words, "the institutions were in conflict with the goals."[12] The same could be said of the Greek army and executive built by the British and Americans in Greece in the wake of the occupation and Civil War. These institutions certainly did not do away with democracy as a communist state would have, but they weakened it, and by weakening Greek democracy, allowed for the possibility that these institutions could assume full power, should—in their eyes—democracy fail. Perhaps Britain's Ambassador, Sir Clifford Norton, not seeming to write as a detached foreigner but as an observer strongly invested in the future of Greece, delivered the most appropriate summary of this dark chapter in Greek history:

> The sufferings caused by the war and occupation, the growth of the Greek *maquis*, its demolitions and the inevitable German reprisals, the final outbreak

---

[11] Paravantes, "In for a Penny."
[12] Zizek & Kotkin (2015).

of civil war and its suppression by British troops have left, besides material destruction, *black memories, vendettas, fears and hatreds* which will not die out in our time. (emphasis added)[13]

Unfortunately, he was right. Perhaps it is here that an answer to the initial question of the book lies: why reconciliation and recovery has remained so elusive in Greece. Reconciliation requires trust: trust in one's neighbor, trust in one's country, trust in the state, and in the institutions supposed to carry out its obligations. Understanding that which the British and Americans built and supported in Greece from 1946 to 1952 sheds a great deal of light on that which followed, and on that which remains.

---

[13] BDFA, Series F Europe, Part IV, Vol. 5, Doc R 8332/1/19, p. 327. It has taken until the Covid-19 pandemic for Greeks to rally, rather uniformly, around each other, their prime minister, and their government, and for intra-party bickering to be sublimated to the national interests. As of May 2020, Greece has weathered the Covid-19 storm better than most, if not all, of its European partners, and many other countries on Earth, due in no small part to the government's decisive and early interventions and the Greek people largely following their government's instructions. Let us hope, regardless of the path the pandemic takes or the revelations future historians uncover about the pandemic and reactions to it, that for Greece at least, the unity exposed / created by the crisis may help Greeks and their government overcome together the legacy of the events examined in this book.

Epilogue

The mountains look on Marathon,
And Marathon looks on the sea;
And musing there an hour alone,
I dream'd that Greece might still be free[1]

In the early morning hours of Friday, April 21, 1967, M48A3 Patton tanks rolled into central Athens, twenty-three years after Sherman tanks had been used in the *Dekemvriana*. They were not there to protect or restore democracy, but to crush it. The Junta ushered in by the tanks would last until 1974, when an external crisis exposed the weakness and incompetence of its leaders.

One of the ringleaders, Georgios Papadopoulos, had served in the Italian campaign in the Second World War, but joined the collaborationist Security Battalions during the German occupation to hunt down members of Greek resistance groups. Trained by the CIA in the 1950s, he returned to Greece as part of a covert cell within the Greek army, placed there to seize control should a communist infiltration occur. Papadopoulos was ideally suited to the role. He was an inward-facing military man, preferring to prepare for communist subversion from within rather than invasion from abroad.

When that subversion did not materialize, he and a cohort of like-minded middle-ranked officers seized power and imposed a military dictatorship. The coup did not arise out of nowhere. It did not occur because the average Greek's political view had shifted too far to the extremes of the political spectrum. The democratically elected prime minister, George Papandreou, of the Centre Union Party, had been dismissed by the king, triggering a constitutional crisis. The

---

[1] Lord Byron, "The Isles of Greece," 1819 (line 15).

resulting public opposition to the king's decision raised the threat that a "radical" prime minister might take his place: his son, Andreas Papandreou. Papadopoulos and company would not let that happen. Their tanks seized control of key parts of Athens and they used pre-prepared lists to arrest 10,000 people by the end of the day. Greece withdrew from the Council of Europe to avoid being expelled, and at the height of the Cold War, the only democracy left in the Balkans after the Second World War, descended into dictatorship.

While communist states elsewhere have left all the proof one needs to know what a communist Greece would have looked like, the scars left by the Junta on Greek society are nonetheless easily visible today. The tragedy of Greece lies not in the duration of its dictatorship but in its very existence. It lies in the fact that the country that so influenced the West with its ideas of democracy, liberty, and the importance of the individual, was not trusted with these ideals by the British and Americans—who themselves had articulated and championed these values during the Second World War and its aftermath.

Roosevelt's objective of making the world safe for democracy—but not necessarily democratic—took on an ominous meaning in the early Cold War. The role of the United States in supporting the coup in Greece is well known. As the war in Vietnam was raging, declassified CIA reports make it clear that the priority of the US was to ensure that no non-communist countries would be swayed by operatives of the Soviet Union. All other considerations were secondary. It was not until 1990 that US President Bill Clinton apologized for the role of the US in the coup and for US support of the dictatorship. However, the roots that led to April 1967, encouraged by the war in Vietnam, the Suez Crisis, and the Korean War, were laid by the experience of the 1940s. By attempting to accomplish multiple objectives at once, Anglo-American policy in Greece from 1946 to 1952 failed to achieve those most crucial to promote recovery and healing. The failures were not immediately apparent, however, and took fifteen years to materialize.

When the British and Americans came after the Second World War, the records show that until 1948, it was with benign intentions that they began the work of rebuilding the government and army of this small country. However, while their intentions may have been superficially benign, the institutions they created, supported, and trained, robbed the country of that for which it had strived throughout its history: freedom.

They created institutions that allowed men like King Paul, King Constantine II, and Papadopoulos to do away with democracy, to usurp it from within—exactly what they had feared the communists would do. In so doing, they became what they beheld. There is a lesson in this for all of us.

Appendix: Chronology

GREECE	EUROPE / WORLD
1936 Metaxas takes power and outlaws the KKE.	**1936** German troops reoccupy the Rhineland.
1940 28 October: Italy invades Greece.	**1939** 1 September: Germany invades Poland. 3 September: France and Britain declare war on Germany.
1941 January: Metaxas refuses British offer of aid. 29 January: Metaxas dies. Fifty-eight thousand British troops are sent to Greece. 20 April: Greece surrenders to Germany. 27 April: Germans occupy Athens. 30 May: Germans capture Crete. September: EAM formed by the KKE.	**1940** 12 August: Germany launches Operation Sea Lion. 25 August: Britain begins to bomb Berlin. August to September: British win the Battle of Britain.
1942 Spring: King George II and PM Tsouderos visit the Middle East. Summer: First ELAS battalions take to the field in Mt Olympus region. August: Zervas begins to organize EDES. September: Gorgopotamos railway bridge destroyed in first and only joint Greek resistance action.	**1941** 6 April: Germany invades Greece through Yugoslavia. 22 June: Germany invades the USSR. 3 September: Germans reach Leningrad. 7 December: Japan attacks US Navy at Pearl Harbor. 8 December: Britain and USA declare war on Japan. 11 December: Germany and Italy declare war on USA, which reciprocates.
1943 July: National Bands Agreement brokered by BLOs to coordinate resistance between right- and left-wing *andartes*. August: First armed clashes occur between ELAS and EDES. October: After the Italian government's surrender, Italian forces in Greece are disarmed and in some cases executed.	**1942** 23 August: Germans launch attack on Stalingrad. 23 October: Axis withdraws across North Africa to Tunisia following the Battle of El Alamein. 8 November: Allies launch Operation Torch and land in North Africa. 19 November: Red Army launches a winter offensive that surrounds the German troops at Stalingrad.
1944 17 to 21 May: Lebanon Conference attempts to reconcile differing parties and form Government of National Unity. 26 September: Caserta Agreement defines the areas in which the resistance groups can assert themselves and places them under the command of General Scobie. September: Germans withdraw from the Peloponnese. 18 October: Government of National Unity lands in Piraeus just as the last German troops are leaving Greece.	**1943** 31 January: General Paulus surrenders the German forces at Stalingrad. February–May: RAF begins a massive bombing campaign on German cities. 2 May: USSR announces the dissolution of the Comintern.

GREECE	EUROPE / WORLD
3 December: Demonstration in Athens leads to the outbreak of hostilities between EAM/ELAS and the British.	12 May: Axis armies in North Africa surrender.
10 July: Allies launch Operation Husky and land in Sicily.
5 to 10 July: German army launches an attack at Kursk in the largest tank battle of the war.
13 October: Italian government surrenders.
28 November to 1 December: Tehran Conference takes place in Iran.
1945
1 January: Archbishop Damaskinos is appointed as regent.
8 January: ELAS leaders agree to end hostilities by midnight on 15 January.
10 January: Former EAM/ELAS members Stratis and Tsirimokos defect and form their own parties.
12 February: Varkiza accord signed, outlining the program of the new government.
May: Nikos Zachariadis, pre-war leader of the KKE, returns to Greece.
June: Aris Velouchiotis killed near Arta fighting the National Guard.	**1944**
4 June: Allies enter Rome.
6 June: Operation Overlord begins with the D-Day landings in Normandy.
22 August: Allies enter Paris.
29 September: Red Army invades Yugoslavia.
October: Red Army invades Hungary.
16 December: Germans launch an offensive that becomes known as the Battle of the Bulge.
1946
21 January: Greek government declares martial law in the southern Peloponnese.
24 January: Anglo-Greek pact gives Greece £10.5 million loan.
31 March: Greek general election held on recommendation of the British despite KKE boycott.
18 April: Tsaldaris becomes Greek prime minister.
1 September: Greek plebiscite paves the way for the return of the Greek monarchy. Coincides with intensified fighting between right and left.
28 September: King George II returns to Athens.	**1945**
4 to 11 February: Yalta Conference takes place.
15 February: Allies reach the Rhine.
20 April: Red Army enters Berlin.
30 April: Hitler commits suicide in Berlin.
2 May: Berlin surrenders.
7 May: Germany surrenders unconditionally.
5 June: Allies finalize the division of Germany into US, British, French, and Soviet zones of occupation.
17 July to 2 August: Potsdam Conference takes place. Coincides with the election of Attlee as British prime minister.
6 and 9 August: Atomic bombs dropped on Hiroshima and Nagasaki.
2 September: Japan surrenders.
20 November: Nuremberg trials begin.
1947
19 February: Britain informs US state department that it can offer no further assistance to Greece whatsoever.
14 April: Markos Vafiadis, leader of the DSE, ordered to switch from guerrilla tactics to conventional warfare.
November: United Nations Special Committee on the Balkans I (UNSCOB) established and sent to Greece to investigate border violations.	**1946**
1 January: Soviet-Polish pact confirms the Curzon Line.
5 March: In a speech in the USA, Churchill calls on Western democracies to oppose the USSR.
15 July: Truman signs a bill of credit for $3.75 billion for Britain.
1948
The United States, in consultation with the British, decides to support a Greek army whose primary duty is to maintain internal security rather than defend the state against external threats.	

GREECE	EUROPE / WORLD
1949 2 August: UNSCOB II presents its findings to the UN General Assembly. **1950** January: UNRRA Embassy in Athens informs the British that Minister of Labour Karamanlis is opposing resettlement efforts of the nearly 1 million internal Greek refugees. **1951** December: UNSCOB II dissolved. Findings archived. May: Papagos resigns as head of the Greek armed forces **1952** 16 November: General Papagos elected as prime minister.	2 December: Byrnes (USA) and Bevin (Britain) agree to the economic fusion of the US and British zones of occupation in Germany. **1947** 12 March: Truman Doctrine declared. **1948** 17 March: Brussels Treaty signed by Belgium, France, Luxembourg, the Netherlands, and the United Kingdom. **1949** 4 April: North Atlantic Treaty signed. **1950** 9 May: Schuman Declaration: statement made by French Foreign Minister Robert Schuman, to pool French and German Coal and Steel production. **1951** 18 April: Treaty of Paris signed, establishing the ECSC. **1952** 28 April: Treaty of San Francisco officially ends the state of war between the Allies and Japan. 28 April: Treaty of Taipei officially ends war between Japan and the Republic of China (Taiwan).

Bibliography

Unpublished Primary Sources

a) The National Archives (TNA) Kew, England
b) National Archives in Washington
c) The Truman Library
d) North Carolina University

(All Reference numbers are those used in the indexing systems at the above-mentioned archives, unless otherwise stated.)

American Sources

American Consulate in Thessaloniki to the US Secretary of State, "British 10th Infantry Brigade fortnightly Intelligence Report from February 4, 1948" US National Archives, Washington DC, 868.00/2-448.

Foreign Agents Registration Act (FARA) 1938, Department of Justice records, National Archives, Washington D.C.

NARS 868.00/2-1748, *10th Infantry Brigade's Fortnightly Intelligence Review.* NARS, RG 319, P&O, 091, Greece, TS Entry, 154, Box 13.

Porter, Paul A., To the US Department of State, February 17, 1947, University of North Carolina Library, Chapel Hill, Ethridge Papers Number 3842.

Porter, Paul A.,"Our Chances in Greece," August 7, 1947, University of North Carolina Library, Chapel Hill, Ethridge Papers Number 3842.

Porter to Clayton, Feb 14, 1947 and Porter to Truman, March 3, 1947, Porter Papers, Truman Library, pp. 2–5.

Taylor to Truman, June 11, 1946, WHCF Box 44, Truman Papers.

British Sources

(Alphabetical, then chronological order)

437 House of Commons debates, May 16, 1947 (fifth series, collection, 1965)

Balfour, J. Dispatch to the Foreign Office, August 5, 1947, FO 371/61002 AN 2661/1/45.

Bevin, Cabinet Paper, August 11, 1945, CAB 093 3645.
Bevin to the Cabinet. "The First Aim of British Foreign Policy," January 4, 1948, (CP(48)6, CAB 129/23).
Bevin/Foreign Office to Athens Embassy, November 8, 1948, FO 371/72249/R12662.
Bevin to Foreign Office, December 6, 1946, no. 17677, FO 371/58891.
Bevin to Foreign Office, December 7, 1946, no. 17689, FO371/58891.
Bevin, Ernest. "The Effects of our External Financial Position on our Foreign Policy," February 12, 1947. FO 371/62420 UE 678/176/53.
Brimelow, minute, September 9, 1946, FO 371 56835.
British Embassy, Belgrade, to Foreign Office, July 25, 1949, FO 371/78448/R7166.
British Information Service (BIS) Activities, FO 953/116 PG 1451/10.
British Information Service (BIS) Staff, FO 953/8 and FO 953/454.
Cabinet Papers, "Foreign Policy Debate," London, August 1945.
C.F.A. Warner to Sir John Balfour, "Secret", February 16, 1948, FO 953 128.
Clutter (Geneva) to Williams, May 8, 1947, no. 6644, FO 371/67068.
Donnelly, J.C., To the Foreign Office, December 29, 1944, FO 371/38560 AN 4614/34/45.
Donnelly, J.C to Patrick Gordon Walker, May 14, 1946, FO 371/51639 AN 1413/15/45.
Douglas and Bevin, Top Secret record of conversation, February 26, 1948; FO 800/460.
Draft Recommendations of U S Delegation, May 2, 1947, no. 6129, FO 371/67066.
Earl of Halifax to the Foreign Office, June 15, 1945, FO 371/44599 AN 1961/84/85.
Edwards, William P.N., To Ambassador's Staff Meeting (Notes from meeting in the USA) November 1, 1948, FO 953/130 P 9826/151/950.
Foreign Office to Norton, January 8, 1947, no. 113, FO 371/67049.
Foreign Office to Norton, January 19, 1947, no. 715, FO 371/66996.
Foreign Office to Norton, May 13, 1947, no. 6345, FO 371/67067.
Future Foreign Publicity Policy, January 4, 1948; CAB 129 23, CP (48) 8.
Interview between Bevin and Tsaldaris, December 6, 1946, no. 18531, FO 371/58892.
Interview between Harvey and Aghnidis, December 28, 1946, no. 33, FO 371/66994.
Inverchapel to Foreign Office, August 31, 1946, no. 2657, FO 371/51609.
Inverchapel to Foreign Office, January 1, 1947, no. 77, FO 371/66994.
Inverchapel to FO, March 13, 1947, Foreign Office Records, FO371/67035/R3482.
Inverchapel to Foreign Office, April 29, 1947, no. 5742, FO 371/67066.
Inverchapel to Foreign Office, May 10, 1947, no. 6368, FO 371/67003.
Inverchapel to Foreign Office, May 13, 1947, no. 6749, FO 371/67067.
Inverchapel to FO, August 23, 1947, Foreign Office Records, 61056/AN2982.
Inverchapel to British Consuls in the United States, September 13, 1947, FO 371/62416 EU 8789/168/53.
Lascelles to Foreign Office, January 25, 1947, no. 1138, FO 371/66997.

Letter from the Acting Chairman of the Delegation of Greece to the Secretary-General, December 3, 1946, and Enclosed Memorandum', (18181, FO 371/5889).

Memorandum by Bevin, "Policy towards Greece and Turkey," January 25, 1947, no. 34, CAB 129/16/CP (47), also CAB 128/9/CM 14 (47), January 30, 1947.

Minutes by Selby and Williams, February 17–19, 1947, no. 1975, FO 371/67000.

Minutes of the Foreign Office, July 1949, FO 371/78443/R7136.

NARS 868.00/2-1748, *10th Infantry Brigade's Fortnightly Intelligence Review*. NARS, RG 319, P&O, 091, Greece, TS Entry, 154, Box 13, Rawlins, "A military Review of the situation in Greece."

Norton to Bevin, December 28, 1946, no. 143, FO 371/66994.

Norton to Tsaldaris, January 3, 1947, no. 520, FO 371/67049.

Norton to Bevin, February 5, 1947, Doc no. 1809, F O 371/66999.

Norton to Foreign Office, February 5, 1947, no. 1809, FO 371/66999.

Norton to Foreign Office, February 6, 1947, no. 1753,FO 371/66999.

Norton to Foreign Office, February 10, 1947, no. 1869, FO 371/66999.

Norton to Foreign Office, February 10, 1947, no. 1801, FO 371/66999.

Norton to Foreign Office, February 10, 1947, no. 1850, FO 371/66999.

Norton to Foreign Office, May 10, 1947, no. 6345, FO 371/67067.

Norton to Bevin, February 18, 1948, Annual Report (1947), no. 2576, FO 371/72240.

Peck (Thessaloniki) to Athens, February 5, 1947, no. 2096, FO 371/67062.

Peck to Chancery (Athens), February 5, 1947, (no. 2096, FO 371/67062).

Permanent UK Delegation to UNO (New York) to Foreign Office, February 9, 1947, no. 1791, FO 371/66999.

Record of Conversation between Bevin and Molotov, December 9, 1946, minutes of a Conference between Bevin and Byrnes, December 9, 1946, note by Dixon, December 10, 1946, minute by McCarthy, December 19, 1946, no. 18129, FO 371/58891.

Report on Greece by the British Chief of Imperial General Staff, March 1949, FO 371/78348/R3285/G.

Rundell, F.B.A. Minutes of meeting, February 14, 1947, FO 371/61053 AN 635/40/45.

"The First Aim of British Foreign Policy", January 4, 1948, CP(48)6, CAB 129/23.

"The Threat to Western Civilisation," March 3, 1948, CP(48)72, CAB 129/25.

The Report of the U N O Commission in no. 7244, FO 371/67069 and UNO/S C *Official Records,* Second Year, Special Supplement no. 2.

Tsaldaris to Norton, January 10, 1947, no. 832, FO 371/67049.

Warner to Williams, December 11, 1946, no. 18129, FO 371/58891.

Washington Embassy to Foreign Office, "Weekly Political Summary," September 4, 1947; FO 371/61056 AN 3069/40/45.

William P.N Edwards to Ambassador's Staff Meeting (Notes from meeting in the USA) November 1, 1948, FO 953/130 P 9826/151/950.

Windel (Geneva) to Foreign Office, April 18th 1947, Foreign Office to Windel, April 23, 1947, no. 5291, FO 371/67065.

Published Primary Sources

Charter of the United Nations.
Department of State. *American Foreign Policy: Basic Documents, 1941–1949*. Vol. I. New York: Arno Press, 1971.
Department of State. *American Foreign Policy: Basic Documents, 1950–1955*. Vol. II. New York: Arno Press, 1971.
EAM (National Liberation Front). *The White Book: Documents From May 1944 to March 1945*. New York: Greek American Council, 1945.
Foreign Office, Public Record Office, London.
FO 800 (Private Collections – Including Attlee, Bevin, and Inverchapel).
Foreign Relations of the United States (henceforth *FRUS*), Department of State publications, Washington DC. Available at: http://digicoll.library.wisc.edu/cgi-bin/FRUS/FRUS-idx?type=browse&scope=FRUS.FRUS1
  1942, Vol. II, Europe
  1943, Vol. IV, The Near East and Africa
  1944, Vol. V, The Near East, South Asia, and Africa, the Far East
  1945, Vol. VIII, The Near East and Africa
  1946, Vol. I, General: The United Nations
  1946, Vol. II, Council of Foreign Ministers
  1946, Vol. IV, Paris Peace Conference: Documents
  1946, Vol. VI, Eastern Europe and the Soviet Union
  1946, Vol. VII, The Near East and Africa
  1947, Vol. I, General, The United Nations
  1947, Vol. II, Council of Foreign Ministers; Germany and Austria
  1947, Vol. V, The Near East and Africa
  1948, Vol. III, Western Europe
  1948, Vol. IV, Eastern Europe and The Soviet Union
  1948, Vol. V, Part 2, The Near East, South Asia, and Africa
  1949, Vol. I, National security affairs, foreign economic policy
  1949, Vol. V, Eastern Europe and the Soviet Union
  1949, Vol. VI, The Near East, South Asia, and Africa
  1950, Vol. I, National security affairs; foreign economic policy
  1950, Vol. V, The Near East, South Asia, and Africa
Kimball, W. F. ed. *Churchill and Roosevelt: The Complete Correspondence*, 3 Vols. Princeton, NJ, 1984.
MacKenzie, William. *The Secret History of Special Operations Executive, 1940 To 1945*. London: St. Ermin's Press, 2002.
National Archives and Record Administration (NARA II), College Park MD, Record Group (RG) 59, Records of the Office of British Commonwealth and Northern European Affairs, 1941–1953, Lot 54D224, Box 22, "Information for the Survey Group Proceeding to London," February 24, 1945.

Official Records of the General Assembly, Fourth Session, Resolutions.
Preston, Paul and Michael Partridge, eds., *British Documents on Foreign Affairs: (Henceforth referred to as BDFA) Reports and Papers from the Foreign Office Confidential Print* (From 1940 through 1950) MacGregor Knox, ed., University Publications of America, 1998.

    Series F, Europe
    Part III, 1940 through 1945
    Vol. 22, South-Eastern Europe, 1941
    Vol. 24, South-Eastern Europe, 1944
    Vol. 25, South-Eastern Europe, 1945
    Part IV, 1946 through 1950
    Vol. 5, South-Eastern Europe, January 1946 to June 1946
    Vol. 6, South-Eastern Europe, July 1946 to December 1946
    Vol. 10, France, 1947
    Vol. 12, Bulgaria, Greece, and Romania, 1947
    Vol. 14, Poland, Czechoslovakia, Hungary, and Eastern Europe, 1948
    Vol. 17, Bulgaria, Greece, Romania, Yugoslavia, and Albania, 1948
    Vol. 22, Bulgaria, Greece, Romania, Yugoslavia, and Albania, 1949
    Vol. 27, Bulgaria, Greece, Romania, Yugoslavia, and Albania, 1950

    Series C, North America
    Part III, 1940 through 1945
    Vol. 2, North America, January 1942 – March 1943
    Vol. 3, United States, April 1943 to December 1943
    Part IV, 1946 through 1950
    Vol. 1, 1946
    Vol. 2, United States, January 1947 to December 1947
    Vol. 3, United States, January 1948 to December 1949
    Vol. 4, United States, January 1950 to December 1950

Franklin Delano Roosevelt, *Radio Broadcast*.
Stephenson, William. *British Security Coordination: The Secret History of British Intelligence in the Americas, 1940–45*. London: St. Ermin's Press, 1998.
Woodward, Sir LLewellyn. *British Foreign Policy in the Second World War*. Vols. II–IV. London: Her Majesty's Stationery Office, 1970.
Yasamee, H. J. and K. A. Hamilton, eds., *Documents on British Policy Overseas, (DBPO) 1946–1950*. Series I, Volume VII and Series II, Vol. 1. London: Her Majesty's Stationery Office, 1995.

Diaries and Memoirs

Churchill, Winston S. *Before the Storm*. Vol. 2 of *The Second World War*. London: Houghton Mifflin Company, 1951.

Churchill, Winston S. *Triumph and Tragedy*. Vol. 6 of *The Second World War*. London: Houghton Mifflin Company, 1953.

Clive, Nigel. *A Greek Experience: 1943–1948*. Salisbury: Michael Russel Publishing Ltd., 1985.

Hammond, Nicholas. *Venture into Greece: With The Guerrillas, 1943–44*. London: William Kimber, 1983.

Pichos, Vagelis Athanasios, Verbal Interview regarding the Greek Civil War and Foreign Powers in Greece: 1941–1949. Interviewed, Saturday, July 23, 2011, 10:30 to 12:00 PM, Katerini, Pieria, Greece. (unpublished)

Biographies

Bullock, Alan. *Ernest Bevin, Foreign Secretary, 1945–1951*. London: Heinmann, 1983.

Gilbert, Martin. *The Road to Victory: Winston Churchill 1939–1941*. Vol. 7 Toronto: Stoddard, 1986.

Harris, Kenneth. *Attlee*. London: Weidenfeld and Nicolson, 1982.

Kennedy, David, Andrew Roberts and Stephen Kotkin discuss: "The Big Three of the 20th Century" (Stanford University, Hoover Institution, published on August 8, 2019, recorded on July 18, 2019). https://youtu.be/1fgDu57N-Qw

Kotkin, Stephen. *Stalin: Volume I: Paradoxes of Power, 1878–1928*. London: Penguin Press, 2015.

Kotkin, Stephen. *Stalin: Volume II: Waiting for Hitler, 1929–1941*. London: Penguin Press, 2017.

Kotkin, Stephen. *Stalin: Volume III: Stalin at War, 1941 to 1945*. London: Penguin Press, 2019–2020 (forthcoming).

Murphy, J.T. *Labour's Big Three: A Biographical Study of Clement Attlee, Herbert Morrison and Ernest Bevin*. London: the Bodley Head, 1948.

Pelling, Henry. *Winston Churchill*. London: Macmillan ltd., 1974.

Ponting, Clive. *Churchill*. London: Sinclaire-Stevenson, 1994.

Roberts, Andrew. *Churchill: Walking with Destiny*. London: Viking Press; 5th printing edition (November 6, 2018)

Ulam, Adam B., *Stalin: The Man and His Era*. New York: Viking Press, 1973.

Weiler, Peter. *Ernest Bevin*. Manchester: Manchester University Press, 1993.

Secondary Sources, Books, and Articles

Alexander, G. M. *The Prelude to the Truman Doctrine: British Policy in Greece: 1944–1947* (Oxford: Clarendon Press, 1982).

Aldrich, Richard James, ed. *British Intelligence, Strategy, and the Cold War, 1945–51* (London: Routledge, 1992).

Ambrose, Stephen E. and Douglas G. Brinkley. *Rise to Globalism: American Foreign Policy since 1938* (New York: Penguin Books, 1997).

Anderson, Sheldon. *Condemned to Repeat It: Lessons of History and the Making of US Cold War Containment Policy* (New York: Lexington, 2008).

Anstey, Caroline. "The Projection of British Socialism: Foreign Office Publicity and American Opinion, 1945–50," *Journal of Contemporary History* 19, no.3 (July 1984): 417–52.

Banac, Ivo. "The Tito-Stalin Split and the Greek Civil War," in *Greece at the Crossroads: The Civil War and its Legacy*, eds. John Iatrides and Linda Wrigley (Pennsylvania: Penn State University Press, 1995).

Bearentzen, Lars. "British Strategy Towards Greece in 1944," in *British Political and Military Strategy in Central, Eastern and Southern Europe in 1944*, eds. William Deakin, Elisabeth Barker, and Jonathan Chadwick (New York: St. Martin's Press, 1988), 130–150.

Berger, Helge and Albrecht Ritschl (1995) "Germany and the political economy of the Marshall Plan, 1947–52: a revisionist view," in *Europe's Postwar Recovery*. Studies in Macroeconomic History, ed. Barry Eichengreen (Cambridge: Cambridge University Press), 199–245.

Bitsika, Panagiota (April 26, 1998). "Οι αμερικανοί πρεσβευτές στην Αθήνα" [The American ambassadors in Athens]. To Vima (in Greek). www.tovima.gr/2008/11/24/culture/oi-amerikanoi-presbeytes-stin-athina/.

Brown, Seyom. *Causes and Prevention of War*. 2nd Edition (New York: St. Martin's Press, 1994).

Butler, Susan, ed. *My Dear Mr. Stalin: The Complete Correspondences of Franklin D. Roosevelt and Joseph V. Stalin* (New Haven: Yale University Press, 2005).

Casey, Steven. "Selling NSC-68: The Truman Administration, Public Opinion, and the Politics of Mobilization, 1950–51," *Diplomatic History* 4, no. 29 (2005): 655–90.

Childs, David. *Britain Since 1945: A Political History*. 3rd edition (London: Routledge, 1997).

Childs, David. "The Cold War and the British Road, 1946–53," *Journal of Contemporary History* 23, no. 4 (October 1988): 551–71.

Claudin, Fernando. *The Communist Movement: From Comintern to Cominform* (Farmsworth: Middlesex, 1975).

Clogg, Richard. "The Special Operations Executive in Greece," in *Greece at the Crossroads: the Civil War and Its Legacy*, eds. John O. Iatrides and Linda Wrigley (University Park: The Pennsylvania State University Press, 1995).

Close, David H. *Greece Since 1945: Politics, Economy and Society* (London: Pearson Education, 2002).

Close, David H. and Thanos Veremis. "The Military Struggle, 1945–9," in *The Greek Civil War: Studies in Polarization*, ed. David H. Close (New York: Routledge, 1993).

Close, David H. "The Changing Structure of the Right, 1945–1950," in *Greece at the Crossroads: The Civil War and Its Legacy*, eds. John O. Iatrides and Linda Wrigley (Pennsylvania: Penn State University Press, 1995).

Coleman, Jonathan. "Portrait of an Institution: The US Embassy in London, 1945–1953," *The Hague Journal of Diplomacy* 4 (2009): 339, 360.

Conant, Jennet. *The Irregulars: Roald Dahl and the British Spy Ring in Wartime Washington* (New York: Simon and Schuster, 2008).

Creswell, Michael. *A Question of Balance: How France and the United States Created Cold War Europe* (Cambridge, MA: Harvard University Press, 2006).

Creswell, Michael. "How France Secured an Anglo-American Continental Commitment, 1945–54," *Cold War History* 1, no. 3 (October 2002): 1–28.

Danforth, Loring and Riki van Boeschoten. *Children of the Greek Civil War: Refugees and the Politics of Memory* (Chicago: University of Chicago Press, 2011).

Davidson, Eugene. *The Trial of the Germans: Nuremburg 1945–1946* (New York: MacMillan, 1967).

Dietrich, John. *The Morgenthau Plan: Soviet Influence on American Postwar Policy* (New York: Algora Publishing, 2002).

Dilks, David. "British Political Aims in Central, Eastern and Southern Europe, 1944," in *British Political and Military Strategy in Central, Eastern and Southern Europe in 1944*, eds. William Deakin, Elisabeth Barker, and Jonathan Chadwick (New York: St. Martin's Press, 1988): 21–39.

Djilas, Milovan. *Conversations with Stalin* (London: Rupert Hart-Davis, 1962).

Dobson, Alan P. *Anglo-American Relations in the Twentieth Century: Of Friendship, Conflict and the Rise and Decline of Superpowers* (London: Routledge, 1995).

Dorn, Walter L. "The Debate Over American Occupation Policy in Germany in 1944–1945," *Political Science Quarterly* 72, no. 4. (December, 1957): 481–501.

Folly, Martin H. *Churchill, Whitehall and the Soviet Union, 1940–45*. Series: Cold War History (New York: St. Martin's Press, 2000).

Frazier, Robert. *Anglo American Relations with Greece: The Coming of the Cold War, 1942–47* (New York: St. Martin's Press, 1991).

Gardner, Lloyd C. *Spheres of Influence: The Great Powers Partition Europe, From Munich to Yalta* (Chicago: Elephant Paperbacks, 1993).

Gerolymatos, Andre. *Red Acropolis Black Terror: The Greek Civil War And the Origins of Soviet-American Rivalry, 1943–1949* (New York: Basic Books, 2004).

Gillingham, John. *Coal, Steel and the Rebirth of Europe* (Cambridge: Cambridge University Press, 1991).

Glantz, Mary E. *FDR and the Soviet Union: The President's Battles Over Foreign Affairs* (Lawrence: University Press of Kansas, 2005).

Hall, Ian. "Power Politics and Appeasement: Political Realism in British International Thought, c. 1935–1955," *British Journal of Politics and International Relations (BJPIR)* 8, no. 2 (2006).

Hammond, Paul Y. "Directives for the Occupation of Germany: The Washington Controversy," in *American Civil-Military Decisions*, ed. Harold Stein (University of Alabama: University of Alabama Press, for the 20th Century Fund and the Inter-University Case Program, 1963), 705.

Hatzivassiliou, Evanthis. *Greece and the Cold War: Frontline State, 1952-1967* (London: Routledge, 2006).

Hitchcock, William I. *France Restored: Cold War Diplomacy and the Quest for Leadership in Europe, 1944-1954* (University of North Carolina Press, 1998).

Hitchens, Christopher. *Blood, Class and Empire: The Enduring Anglo-American Relationship* (London: Nation Books, 2004).

Hondros, John Louis. *Occupation and Resistance: The Greek Agony, 1941-1944* (New York: Pella, 1983).

Iatrides, John O. *Revolt in Athens: The Greek Communist "Second Round," 1944-45* (New Jersey: Princeton University Press, 1972).

Iatrides, John O. "Revolution or Self Defence? Communist Goals, Strategy, and Tactics in the Greek Civil War," *The Journal Of Cold War Studies* 7, no. 3 (Summer 2005): 3-33.

Iatrides, John O. "Britain, the United States and Greece, 1945-9," in *The Greek Civil War: Studies in Polarization*, ed. David H. Close (New York: Routledge, 1993), 190-213.

Jones, Howard. *A New Kind of War: America's Global Strategy and the Truman Doctrine in Greece* (Oxford: Oxford University Press, 1989).

Karvounarakis, Theodosis. "In Defence of 'Free Peoples': The Truman Doctrine and the Impact on Greece During the Civil War Years, 1947-1949," in *Hellenic Foundation for European and Foreign Policy (ELIAMEP): Occasional Papers*, ed. Thanos Dokos (Athens: ELIAMEP, 2001).

Kennan, George. *American Diplomacy, 1900-1950* (Chicago: University of Chicago Press, 1950).

Kennedy, David M. *Freedom from Fear: The American People in Depression and War, 1929-1945*. Oxford History of the United States (Oxford: Oxford University Press, 2001).

Kennedy, David M. *The American People in World War II: Freedom from Fear, Part Two*. Oxford History of the United States (Oxford: Oxford University Press, 2003).

Kimball, W. F. ed. *Churchill and Roosevelt: The Complete Correspondence*. 3 vols. (New Jersey: Princeton University Press, 1984).

Kirby, Dianne. "Divinely Sanctioned: The Anglo-American Cold War Alliance and the Defence of Western Civilization and Christianity, 1945-48," *The Journal of Contemporary History* 35, no. 3, (2000): 395-412.

Kondis, Vasilis. "Greek Policies regarding the Balkans in the 1980s" Round Table Discussion, Sunday June 3, 2012, 12:00 to 14:00, at the conference: *War and Political Transformation: Scrambling for Power in the Balkans 1940s* (May 31 to June 3, 2012, University of Macedonia, Thessaloniki, Greece.)

Kuniholm, Bruce R. *The Origins of the Cold War in the Near East: Great Power Conflicts and Diplomacy in Iran, Turkey and Greece* (New Jersey: Princeton University Press, 1994).

Lagani, Eirini, *LES RAPPORTS DE LA GRECE AVEC SES VOISINS BALKANIQUES DE 1941 a 1949*. Doctoral Thesis (Paris: Sourbonne, 1985).

Lagani, Eirini. *"Nostos" and Cold War Political Considerations: The Case of the Greek Civil War Refugees* (Thessaloniki: University of Macedonia Press, 2005).

Lagani, Eirini. "The Education of Children of the Civil War in Yugoslavia as point of discord in the relations of the KKE and CPY after the Tito–COMINFORM split (1948-1956)," in *The Gun at the Ready: The Political Refugees of the Greek Civil War in Eastern Europe*, eds. Eftichia Voutira, Vasilis Dalkavoukis, Nikos Maranzidis and Maria Bontila (Thessaloniki: University of Macedonia Press, 2005), 125–46 (Title translated from Greek).

Lagani, Eirini. "US Forces in Greece in the 1950s," in *U.S. Military Forces in Europe: The Early Years, 1945–1970*, eds. Simon W. Duke and Wolfgang Krieger (Oxford: Westview Press, 1993), 309–30.

Lampe, John R. Russell O. Prickett, and Ljubisa S. Adamovic. *Yugoslav-American Economic Relations since World War II.* (Durham: Duke University Press Books, 1990).

Leffler, Melvyn P. and Odd Arne Westad, eds. *The Cambridge History of the Cold War*, Volume 1, Origins (Cambridge: Cambridge University Press, 2010).

Leffler, Melvyn P. and Odd Arne Westad, eds. *The Cambridge History of the Cold War*, Volume 2, Crises and Détente (Cambridge: Cambridge University Press, 2010).

Leffler, Melvyn P. and Odd Arne Westad, eds. *The Cambridge History of the Cold War*, Volume 2, Endings (Cambridge: Cambridge University Press, 2010).

Lopukhovsky, Lev. *The Viaz'ma Catastrophe, 1941: The Red Army's Disastrous Stand Against Operation Typhoon* (Warwick: Helion and Company; reprint edition February 29, 2016).

Manchester, William. *The Glory and the Dream: A Narrative History of America, 1932–1972* (New York: Little Brown, 1974)

Marantzidis, Nikos. "The Greek Civil War 1944–1949 and the International Communist System," *The Journal of Cold War Studies* 14, no. 3 (Summer 2012).

Maranizidis, Nikos and Kostas Tsivos. *The Greek Civil War and the International Communist System: The KKE within the Czech Archives 1946–1968* (Athens: Alexandria Publications, 2012). Title translated from Greek.

May, Ernest R., ed. *American Cold War Strategy: Interpreting NSC 68.* (London: Bedford Books of St. Martin's Press, 1993).

McCauley, Martin. *Origins of the Cold War: 1941–1949* (London: Routledge, 2016).

McNeill, William Hardy. *The Metamorphosis Of Greece Since WWII.* (University of Chicago, 1st edition, October 1978).

McNeill, William Hardy. *The Greek Dilemma: War and Aftermath* (Philadelphia and New York: J. B. Lippincott Company, 1947).

McNeill, William Hardy, Frank Smothers, Elizabeth Darbishire McNeill *Report on the Greeks* (Twentieth Century Fund, 1948)

Mearsheimer, John and Stephen Walt. *The Israel Lobby and US Foreign Policy* (New York: Farrar, Straus and Giroux, 2007).

Miller, James E. "Taking Off the Gloves: The United States and the Italian Elections of 1948," *Diplomatic History*, Vol. 7, No. 1 (WINTER 1983), pp. 35–55.

Miller, James E. *The United States and the Making of Modern Greece: History and Power, 1950–1974* (Chapel Hill: The University of North Carolina Press, 2003).

Morgan, Kenneth O. *Labour in Power, 1945–1951*. (Oxford: Clarendon Press, 1984).

Moss, Norman. *Picking up the Reins: America, Britain and the Post-War World* (London: Duckworth, 2008).

Mourelos, Ioannis. "La Grece et la strategie des Grandes Puissances dans les Balkans. Histoire d'un rendez-vous manque," *L'Annee '41. La Mondialisation du conflit* (Memorial de Caen, 1991).

Mourelos, Ioannis, Les origines de la guerre civile en Grece," *L'Annee '44. Les liberations* (Memorial de Caen, 1994).

Nachmani, Amikam. "Civil War and Foreign Intervention in Greece: 1946–49," *Journal of Contemporary History* 25, no. 4 (October 1990): 489–522.

Papastratis, Procopis. *British Policy Towards Greece During the Second World War, 1941–44*. (London: Cambridge University Press, 1984).

Paravantes, Spero Simeon Z. "A Tale of Two Referenda: The Greek Plebiscite of 1946 and the Referendum of 2015," *European Review of History* 26, no.2 (April 2019): 243–57.

Paravantes, Spero S.Z. "The issue of NATO 'out-of-area' operations: from West Africa to the borders of the Near East," www.cvce.eu/en/recherche/unit-content/-/unit/e7c423ed-a376-4a57-a415-f8519344e558/3a02a425-4d6a-419a-b61d-bef706c470d2/Resources#efcb0e9c-5b0a-47bd-8eb3-1b0bae19cf28_en&overlay.

Paravantes, Spero Simeon Z. "In for a penny: A Legal and Diplomatic History of Reparations and their impact on European (dis?) Integration," *International Journal of Legal History and Institutions* 3 (December 2019) ISSN 2515-9208.

Pechatnov, Vladimir O. "The Soviet Union and the World, 1944–1953," in *The Cambridge History of the Cold War, Volume 1, Origins*, eds. Leffler, Melvyn P. and Odd Arne Westad (Cambridge: Cambridge University Press, 2010).

Persico, Joseph E. *Roosevelt's Secret War: FDR and World War II Espionage* (New York: Random House, 2001).

Petrov, Vladimir. *Money and Conquest; Allied Occupation Currencies in World War II*. (Baltimore: Johns Hopkins Press, 1967).

Pettifer, James and Miranda Vickers. *Contesting the Waters: Lakes and Empires in Macedonian History*. (London, 2021)

Pettifer, James. "Woodhouse, Zervas and the Chams: Exploring the Second World War Heritage." Published at www.professorjamespettifer.com.

Pettifer, James. *The Greeks: The Land and People Since the War*. (London: Penguin Books, 1993).

Pichou, Maria. *The Notion of Aggression in International Law* (Thessaloniki: Sakkoulas Publications, 2012).

Reynolds, David. *Britannia Overruled: British Policy and World Power in the 20th Century* (London: Longman, 1991).

Richter, Heinz. *British Intervention in Greece, From Varkiza to Civil War: February 1945 to August 1946*. Marion Sarafis, Translator. (London: Merlin Press, 1986).

Rogers, Anthony. *Churchill's Folly: Leros and the Aegean — The Last Great British Defeat of World War II* (Athens: Iolkos, 2007).

Rosie, George. *The British in Vietnam. How the Twenty-Five Year War Began* (London: Panther Books, 1970).

Ryan, Henry Butterfield. *The Vision of Anglo-America: The U.S.-U.K. Alliance and The Emerging Cold War, 1943-1946* (Cambridge: Cambridge University Press, 1987).

Sargent, Daniel J. *A Superpower Transformed: The Remaking of American Foreign Relations in the 1970s* (Oxford: Oxford University Press, 2017).

Saville, John. "Ernest Bevin and the Cold War," *The Socialist Register* (1984): 68-100.

Scott-Smith, Giles, Matthieu Gillabert, Luc van Dongen, and Stéphanie Roulin. *Transnational Anti-communism and the Cold War: Agents, Activities, and Networks* (Houndmills: Palgrave Macmillan, 2014).

Scott-Smith, Giles: "The Politics of Apolitical Culture: The Congress for Cultural Freedom, the CIA and Post-War American Hegemony." (London and New York: Routledge/PSA Political Studies Series, 2002).

Sfikas, Thanasis D. *The British Labour Government and the Greek Civil War: The Imperialism of Non-Intervention* (Keel University: Ryburn Publishing, 1994).

Sfikas, Thanasis D. "Britain, the United States and the Soviet Union in the United Nations Commission of Investigation in Greece, January – May 1947," *Contemporary European History* 2 (1993): 243-63.

Smith, Ole L. "Communist Perceptions, Strategy and Tactics, 1945-1949," in *Greece at the Crossroads: The Civil War and Its Legacy*, eds. John O. Iatrides and Linda Wrigley (Pennsylvania: Penn State University Press, 1995).

Stafford, David. *Roosevelt and Churchill: Men of Secrets* (New York: The Overlook press, 2000).

Stavrakis, Peter J. *Moscow and Greek Communism: 1944-1949*. (London: Cornell University Press, 1989).

Stavrakis, Peter J. "Soviet Policy in Areas of Limited Control: The Case of Greece, 1944-1949," in *Greece at the Crossroads: The Civil War and Its Legacy*, eds. John O. Iatrides and Linda Wrigley (Pennsylvania: Penn State University Press, 1995): 227-57.

Stavrianos, Leften Stavros. *Greece, American Dilemma And Opportunity* (Chicago: Henry Regnery Company, 1952).

Stefanidis, Ioannis D. *From Civil War to Cold War: Greece and the Allied Factor* (Athens: Proskinio, 1999).

Sweet-Escott, Bickam "The Special Operations Executive in the Balkans," in *British Policy Between Wartime Resistance in Yugoslavia and Greece*, eds. Phyllis Auty and Reginald Clogg (London: MacMillan Press, 1975).

Thomadakis, Stavros, B. "Stabilization, Development, and Government Economic Authority in the 1940s," in *Greece at the Crossroads: The Civil War and its Legacy*, eds. John O. Iatrides and Linda Wrigley (University Park: The Pennsylvania State University Press, 1995).

Thomopoulos, Elaine. *The History of Greece*, Series: The Greenwood Histories of Modern Nations (Santa Barbara: ABC-CLIO Imprints, 2012).

Thorpe, Andrew. "In a Rather Emotional State? The Labour Party and British Intervention in Greece," *The English Historical Review* CXXI, no. 493 (September 2006): 1075–105.

Vali, Ferenc A. *The Turkish Straits and NATO* (Stanford: Hoover Institution Press, 1972).

Vaughan, Richard. *Post War Integration in Europe* (London: Palgrave Macmillan, 1976).

Vukomanovic, Svetozar (aka.General Tempo). *How and Why the People's Liberation Struggle of Greece met with Defeat* (London: The Merlin Press, 1985).

Warburg, James P. *Germany: Bridge or Battleground?* (New York: Harcourt, Brace and Company, 1946).

Weinberg, Gerhard L. *Visions of Victory: The Hopes of Eight World War II Leaders* (New York: Cambridge University Press, 2005).

Withers, George, Lucila Santos and Adam Isacson. "Preach What You Practice: The Separation of Military and Police Roles in the Americas," (Washington Office on Latin America, November 2010.) ISBN 978-0-9844873-4-9.

Wittner, Lawrence. *American Intervention in Greece* (New York: Columbia University Press, 1982).

Woodhouse, C. M. *Apple of Discord: A Survey of Recent Greek Politics in Their International Setting* (London: William Brendon and Sons, 1951).

Woodhouse, C. M. *Something Ventured* (London: Hart-Davis, 1976).

Woodhouse, C. M. "Summer 1943: The Critical Months," in *British Policy Towards Wartime Resistance in Yugoslavia and Greece*, eds. Phyllis Auty and Reginald Clogg (London: The MacMillan Press, 1975).

Woodhouse, C. M. *The Struggle for Greece: 1941–1949* (London: Hart-Davis, 1976).

Young, John W. *Britain and the World in the Twentieth Century*, Series: International Relations and the Great Powers (London: Arnold Publishers, 1997). "Slavoj Zizek & Stephen Kotkin New York Public Library." (April 3, 2015) 1hr 7 to 8 mins.: https://youtu.be/Z9voDV_ZsB8

Zubok, Vladislav and Constantine Pleshakov. *Inside the Kremlin's Cold War From Stalin to Khrushchev* (Harvard: Harvard University Press, 1997).

Index

Acheson, Dean 62-3, 76, 159, 169, 172-3, 184, 187-8
aid programs 5, 99, 104, 109, 113, 117, 123, 136-9, 143, 154, 163-4, 167-8, 178-81, 204, 208
Albania 75-7, 141, 165-71
Allied Mission for the Observation of Greek Elections (AMFOGE) 58-9
Alling, Paul 28
American business interests 27, 99, 207
American Economic Mission to Greece (1947) 90-2, 95
American Mission for Aid to Greece (AMAG) 123
amnesty policy 114, 162
Anglo-American relationship *see* foreign policy; "special relationship"
anti-communism 2, 8-11, 15, 19, 36, 53, 67, 71, 74, 84-5, 99, 106, 112-15, 208, 210
anti-fascism 11
Ardennes offensive (1944) 39
Attlee, Clement 4-5, 8-9, 12, 14, 37, 47-8, 52, 55, 65, 67, 73, 82-5, 91, 94-7, 127, 130, 135

balance of power 205
Beaverbrook, Lord 26
Ben-Gurion, David 134
Berlin blockade and airlift 131, 135, 158, 207
Bevin, Ernest 4, 8-9, 37, 40, 42, 48-9, 52-6, 61-9, 72-8, 81-7, 92-5, 109, 114, 119-24, 127-32, 135-41, 144, 148-51, 166, 169-70, 173, 193-6
black market 92
Britain
    aspiration to remain a world power 10-17, 31, 60, 83, 94, 107, 109, 124, 127, 151, 203, 206
    economic conditions in 93-5, 106 *see also* foreign policy

British Communist Party (BCP) 111-12, 130-1
British Empire 12, 15
British Economic Mission to Greece 114
British Isles, protection of 179
British Police Mission (BPM) 103
Brussels Pact (1948) 128-9
Brussels Treaty Organization (BTO) 118
Bulgaria 95, 136, 165-70, 179
Bullock, Alan 53
bureaucracy 4
Byrnes, James F. 47, 53-9, 73, 78, 81, 84-7

Cairo Conference, first (August 1943) 23-4
Cairo Conference, second (November 1943) 25-6
Cairo Conference, third (June 1944) 31
Casablanca Conference (January 1943) 25
Central Intelligence Agency (CIA) 9, 115, 130, 214
Chernichev, Nikolai P. 37
Chiang Kai-shek 25-6, 49, 175-6, 187
Chiefs of Staff
    British 65
    American 148, 172-5, 179
China 26, 175-6, 182
Churchill, Winston 4-5, 8-14, 19-47, 51-3, 66, 121, 173, 176, 206
Clinton, Bill 214
Cold War 7-10, 15, 60, 100, 119, 126-7, 147-8, 152, 201-4, 207-9, 214
"collectivist" view of Greece 208
Colombia 105
the Cominform 111, 137, 178, 180
Commonwealth preferences 8
Communist Party of Greece 10; *see also* KKE
Connolly, Tom 187
Constantine II, King of Greece 214
corruption 6, 92-3, 113, 141

Council of Foreign Ministers 57, 69, 72, 117, 159
Cox, Oscar 46
Crimea Conference 54; see also Yalta Conference
Cyprus 137, 175, 186-91, 195-7
Czechoslovakia 13, 119, 126, 129, 207

Dahl, Roald 9
Damaskinos, Archbishop 24, 40-1, 55-8, 64
decision-making processes 98
demobilization 60-1, 80, 90, 117, 178, 201
democracy, pursuit of 202-3, 206-7, 211, 214
Democratic Army of Greece 80-1; see also DSE
Diamedes, Alexander 163
diplomatic documents 3-7
Dodecanese Campaign (1943) 11, 23-4
Dodecanese Islands 74, 131
"domino theory" 98
Donovan, General 6, 140
Douglas, Lewis 102-3, 114-15, 130-1, 137, 145, 151
DSE (Democratic Army of Greece) 80-1, 91, 102, 107, 111-14, 122, 128, 133, 136-43, 146, 153-6, 162-8, 171, 204
Dulles, John Foster 4, 71

EAM (Greek National Liberation Front) 23-44, 48
Eden, Sir Anthony 4, 8, 20-1, 32, 43, 51-3
EDES (National Republican Greek League) 21-4
Edwards, William 145
Eisenhower, Dwight D. 201
ELAS (Greek People's Liberation Army) 21, 23, 27-9, 37-44, 48, 52, 68
energy crisis in Britain (1947) 94-5
Ethridge, Mark 100-1
euro currency 2
European Recovery Program (ERP) 117, 138; see also Marshall Plan
European unification 128-9
Export-Import Bank, US 75
export surpluses 99

Foreign Office 9, 20-4, 27, 53, 57, 60, 65, 67, 79, 100, 106, 111-12, 126, 161, 169, 205
foreign policy 3
American 98, 183-4, 189, 198-9, 201
American and British closely aligned 5, 10, 15-16, 107, 136, 145-52, 179, 187, 202-5, 210
British 83-5, 117, 120, 205
as distinct from military policy 98
"Four Policemen" plan 19-20
France 69, 107, 118, 184-5
Franks, Oliver 139, 169

gendarmerie in Greece 110, 140
George II, King of Greece 20-4, 28, 39-41, 57, 61, 78, 80, 100, 198, 205
Germany
dismantling and subsequent reconstruction of 106-7, 118, 184
division of 119
Girard, Rene 12
global financial crisis (2008) 2
Grady, Henry 145-8, 155-7, 162-3, 172-3, 178-83, 190-2
grand strategic objectives 10
Great Power politics 16
Greece
colonels' coup (1967) 209-10, 213-14
post-war reconstruction of 3, 191, 193, 202, 210, 212
social problems in 177-8
symbolic significance of 38, 42, 131, 171, 176, 205
Greek Civil War 1-3, 6-8, 15-16, 82, 86, 97, 101, 123, 131, 160, 167, 177-8, 202, 209
casualties of 204
Greek government in exile 21, 23, 34
Greek government of national unity 27-30, 34, 36
Greek politicians, shortcomings of 150
Griffiths, Jim 42
Gromyko, A.A. 158-61

Halifax, Lord 61
Hammond, Nicholas 20
Havana Convention (1922) 108
Henderson, L.W.H. 122

Hitler, Adolf 19, 106
Hull, Cordell 30-2, 37
Hungary 36

individuals, significance of 7
institutions
  building of 2-5, 16
  conflict with goals 211
insurrectionism 98
intelligence operations 5-6, 11, 14, 18, 20, 115, 128-9, 204
Inverchapel, Lord 79, 95, 127
isolationism 18-19, 201
Israeli declaration of independence (1948) 132, 134
Izvestiya (newspaper) 54

Jacobs, Joseph Earle 77
Japan 8, 36-7, 49, 198-9
Johnson, Herschel 76
Johnson, Lyndon 202

Kalyvas, Stathis 12
Kannellopoulos, Panagiotis 195
Karamanlis, Constantinos 177
Kardelj, Edvard 165
Katerini 146
Kennan, George 3, 8, 98-9
Kennedy, David 12
Kennedy, John F. 201
Kimball, John 11
KKE (Communist Party of Greece) 10, 23, 29, 34-51, 58-9, 62, 68-71, 74, 80, 91, 97, 102-3, 125, 133, 146, 153, 156-65, 172, 207-10
Knight, W.L.C. 145
Korea 105, 107, 186, 190-1, 201, 208
Kotkin, Stephen 12, 211
Kuniholm, Bruce 10

Labour Party, British 38, 42, 55, 67, 111-12, 127
language barriers 144-5
Lascelles, D.W. 74
League of Nations 19
Lebanon Conference (May 1944) 29-30
Leeper, Reginald 22-3, 28, 31, 43, 52, 56, 58-9, 63
lend-lease 19, 46
liberalization of markets 8

Litochoro 1, 202
Livesay General William 113

McCarthyism 182
Macedonia 104, 194, 196
McNeill, W.H. 9-10, 62, 159
MacVeagh, Lincoln 27-8, 31, 37-40, 44-5, 55-9, 62, 79-82, 90
Manchester, William 176
Mao Tse-tung 49
Marshall, George 4, 8-9, 92, 95, 101, 104-5, 108-11, 115, 117-18, 125, 131-4, 137-43
Marshall Plan 9, 99, 121, 129, 138
Mazower, Mark 12
military-industrial complex 201
Military Missions to Greece, American (AMM) and British (BMM) 93, 114-15, 139, 143, 156
Molotov, V.M. 87
monarchical government in Greece 11, 14, 21-4, 33, 55, 61, 70-1, 78, 181, 190, 198, 209, 211
Monnet, Jean 184
Morgenthau Plan 106
Morrison, Herbert 67
Mosadegh, Mohammad 9
Myers, E.C.W. 23

new world order 8, 13, 100
non-intervention, policy of 39-41, 52, 104, 201
North Atlantic Treaty 157-8, 173
North Atlantic Treaty Organization (NATO) 9, 115, 118-19, 135, 171, 196-7, 209
Norton, Clifford 68, 78, 81, 86, 95, 114, 123, 144, 148, 164, 172-80, 186, 189, 211-12
NSC-68 report (1950) 182-3, 186
nuclear weapons 135, 171-2, 182

occupation of Germany, plans for 33
Operation Overlord 24
Otto, King of Greece 17

Palestine 132-6, 152
  British mandate in 132
  partition plans for 132-3
Papadopoulos, Georgios 213-14

Papagos, General 155-7, 181, 190, 192, 197-8, 202
Papandreou, Andreas 214
Papandreou, George 28-30, 58, 82, 189, 213
paramilitary groups 165
Paul, King of Greece 190, 192, 197-8, 209, 213-14
Pax Americana 203
Peake, Sir Charles 178
Pearl Harbor (1941) 18-19
"Percentages" agreement (1944) 11, 30-1, 34-7, 205
Persico, Joseph 11
Peurifoy, John 197-8
Pipenelis, M. 149
Plaka Agreement (February 1944) 27
Plastiras, General 24, 41-4, 180, 183, 188-92, 202
plebiscite results 71, 76-7
Poland 95-6, 111
policing 209-10
political prisoners 114
Politis, Nicolaos 196
Polk, George 140-1
Popov, Grigorii 36, 50
populism 163
Porter, Paul 90-3, 181, 188
Potsdam Conference (1945) 47, 51
primary sources 13-14
public opinion 60, 71, 144, 157
"push back" 10

Rawlins, General 113
reconciliation in Greece 212
reconstruction, post-war 96, 180-1, 191, 193
Red Cross 14
refugees 177, 210
Regency Council in Greece 24
reparations 51, 130, 135, 201, 211
resistance movements in Greece 21-4, 29-34, 42
Roberts, Andrew 12
Romania 30-5, 95, 157
Roosevelt, Franklin D. (FDR) 4-14, 19-20, 25-36, 40-1, 47, 106, 176, 206-7, 214
Roosevelt, Kermit 9
Rusk, Dean 158-61, 167

Sargent, Daniel J. 3-4
Sargent, Sir Orme 56, 94
Schuman, Robert 184
Second World War 17, 20, 25, 39, 48, 90, 193, 204
　aftermath of 2-7, 12-13
　second front 26
Sfikas, Thanasis 209
sharing of information 6
Sophoulis, Themistoklis, 65-6, 163
Soviet Union 8, 12, 17, 19, 22-34, 45-6, 51-4, 57-77, 81, 83, 86, 89, 94, 97-8, 102-5, 112, 124-5, 133, 142, 146, 157-61, 168-9, 182, 193, 204-7
　objectives for Greece 207
Special Operations Executive (SOE) 6, 18-24, 29, 31, 35
"special relationship" between the United States and Britain 3-6, 13, 48, 130, 206-10
spheres of influence 30-5, 47, 52, 71, 104, 197, 205
Spyridon, Archbishop 190-1
Stafford, David 11
Stalin, Joseph 10, 12, 19, 25-37, 49-50, 62-3, 69, 97, 117, 122, 124, 129, 137, 153-4, 193, 204, 206
　attitude to world revolution 36
Stavrakis, Peter 11, 154
Stettinius, Edward 63-4
strike legislation 116
Svolos, Alexandros 30
Syria 110

Taylor, Vaughn 66-7
Tehran Conference (December 1943) 26
"Third World" 203
Tito, Marshal 27, 102, 117, 122, 133, 137, 153-6, 163-6, 180, 185, 193-6
tourism 193
trade 8
Trippe, Juan Terry 27
Truman, Harry 4-9, 12, 14, 46-9, 58, 90, 95-6, 127-34, 149-50, 156, 171, 181-3, 186-7, 197, 201-2, 207
Truman Doctrine 15, 78, 97-9, 105, 138, 182, 186-7
trust, need for 212
"truth" about specific events 1

Tsadlaris, Konstantinos 68, 73, 79, 132, 135, 137, 141, 143, 154, 163, 166-70, 175
Turkey 24-5, 32, 66, 78, 98, 147-8, 197

United Nations 8-9, 14, 62-4, 75, 84, 87, 89-91, 97-113, 133-4, 138-9, 143, 195-6
   Charter 75, 103, 107, 111
   General Assembly 89, 108-12, 139, 166-9, 174, 187
   Relief and Rehabilitation Administration 123
   Security Council 20, 62-4, 75, 87, 89, 91, 101, 104-12, 170, 187
   Special Committee on the Balkans (UNSCOB) 16, 89-91, 97-104, 107-12, 123, 161
   UNSCOB II 122, 125, 160, 164, 166
United States
   National Security Council (NSC) 119, 147, 180, 182
   Office of Strategic Services (OSS) 6, 31, 115
   role in the Greek coup (1967) 214

Vafiadis, Markos 97, 121, 128, 133, 156
Vandenberg Resolution 151
Van Fleet, Lieutenant General 188-90
Varkiza Accord 43-5, 51, 55-7, 68, 78, 97
Venizelos, Sophocles 163, 180-3, 189, 192, 195, 197
Ventiris, George 197

Western Union 9, 121, 158
Wilson, Woodrow 12
Woodhouse, C.M. 9, 20
World Bank 14
World Federation of Trade Unions 158

Yalta Conference (1945) 46-7, 54
Yugoslavia 32-6, 62-3, 74, 117, 122, 136, 143, 148-9, 153, 157, 163-4, 178, 185, 193-5

Zachariadis, Nikos 48, 63, 68, 156
Zionism 133

www.ingramcontent.com/pod-product-compliance
Lightning Source LLC
Chambersburg PA
CBHW072143290426
44111CB00012B/1956